GW01452579

VAJAZZLED & BEDAZZLED
Misadventures of Motorhome Virgins

by

John Meadows

John Meadows

Dedicated to

The Satnav Lady who kept us (mostly) on course.

We named her Bonnie Tyler… she kept telling us to 'Turn around, and every now and then it fell apart.'

CONTENTS

Phase Two: ENGLAND

Phase Three: WALES

Phase Four: EIRE and NORTHERN IRELAND

Introduction

Most readers will be familiar with titles such as Pride and Prejudice or Crime and Punishment... but Vajazzled and Bedazzled!? Where has *that* come from?

All languages evolve over time. Words go out of fashion while the Oxford English Dictionary includes new ones every year; Brexit, Internet, Facebook, and Satnav are just a few recent examples. The etymology of Vajazzled has clues in the word. I had never heard of it and had no idea what it meant. I found out in bizarre circumstances:

"Nudist or non-nudist?" asked the receptionist, matter-of-factly, as my wife Norma and I arrived at a beachfront caravan site.

"Er, non-nudist," we replied, perplexed. After all, we had a wardrobe full of clothes in the motorhome. We had inadvertently booked onto a site which also catered for naked clients. Now, anyone who has read my book, 'Sir Where's Toilet?' might remember that this has happened to me before. This begs the question, 'How many times does someone *inadvertently* stumble onto a nudist colony?' I have to admit that it has become a recurring event... every 50 years, last time in Greece. About as regular as Halley's Comet.

We went for a walk to explore our new surroundings. As we strolled along the beach, gradually, it dawned on us that swimming costumes were less ubiquitous. Emerging from the sea, a naked couple were bathed in afternoon sunlight. Put any thoughts of Daniel Craig, Ursula Andress, or Botticelli's Birth of Venus right out of your mind. These two looked as if they were about to be beached. Further on, there were games of badminton and volleyball. Games with lots of bounce.

"Don't look now, but I think the beach's most popular man is behind us," I whispered.

"What makes you say that?"

"He's on his way from the café carrying a cup of coffee in each hand...plus two doughnuts." Norma rolled her eyes.

"I'm beginning to feel overdressed in swimming shorts," I said.

"When it happened to you last time, you took off your cossie to blend in," she commented.

"Yes, but there's a *big* difference between being 20 in the 70s, and being 70 in the 20s."

We started to giggle at our predickament but behaved with dickoram. We looked for an exit, but most seemed to be exclusively for nudist-owned apartments. We should have realized because there wasn't a washing line in sight. We felt trapped on the beach. "I'm getting that Dunkirk feeling."

When I was an art student, life-drawing classes were a regular part of my training. I've seen more tits than a garden bird-table, but I was still shocked by the surreal image approaching along the beach. A group of nudist men and women were led by an attractive woman, but it's difficult to take in just peripheral vision when trying to avert one's gaze. The low sun reflected dancing beams of light from her nether regions. It took the term 'flashing' on to another level.

"She's had a vajazzle," said Norma.

"A what?"

"A vajazzle; when silver stars, shining jewellery and beads are embroidered into her pubic hair. They do it in beauty salons, sometimes with waxing in the shape of hearts or tramlines, like crop circles. It's called pubic topiary."

"Wow! What *will* they think of next? I'm bedazzled!"

As they got closer, I felt like a moth drawn to the lights; an Aurora Borealis, or more accurately, Aurora Australis, since it was down south.

"So, it's a random arrangement of shiny decorations, like on a Christmas tree?" I suggested, anxious to find out more.

"I suppose so, but without the glittery balls."

"I'm not sure that older ladies should have a vajazzle," I said, glancing serrupticously at others in the group.

"Why not?"

"I don't know. It's a bit of a grey area."

Then, one of the men in the group came into view. He had one as well.

"What's the male version called?" I asked.

"I don't know. I'm not sure if there is even a name for it."

"Well, can I suggest Bobby Dazzler? Or even better, Nobby Dazzler."

His decorations consisted of jewellery and small mirrors. Now, I ask you, why would anyone in his right mind want to have potentially lethal objects sewn around the base of his penis? One stumble, cracking a mirror, and he would end up with far worse than seven years' bad luck. It's like having the 'Sword of Damocles' hanging by a pubic thread. I don't know if Nobby Dazzler was insured, but I would love to read the claim form. I wonder if insurance companies even have a category for such an eventuality. Perhaps something like an Endowment Replacement Policy, New for Old.

The group went to a beach restaurant. Some Covid restrictions were still in place, and each person used the alcogel dispenser to disinfect their hands. They were as thorough as a team of surgeons about to perform an operation. They had followed government guidelines meticulously and had played their part in fighting the pandemic by maintaining a scrupulously high level of hygiene. A waiter then escorted them to a table, and they all sat down... bare-arsed on white plastic chairs.

Misadventures of motorhome virgins is a collection of anecdotes during life on the road around the UK and Ireland. In the same vein as my previous books, it is intended to be entertaining and informative with a sprinkling of trivia, history, art, geography, myths, and legends, all with a light-hearted touch. We will kiss the Blarney Stone and hear the myths and stories of the giant Finn McCool, Nessie, King Arthur, Dracula and Braveheart. We will visit castles, cathedrals, country estates, galleries, and battlefields and learn more about writers, artists, scientists, inventors and, of course, distilleries. We will encounter fascinating characters, such as a bow-tie-wearing performing duck, Dutch mechanics travelling in a converted vintage fire engine, and a Welsh UFO investigator.

Having travelled extensively, we felt it was high time we explored nearer home. After all, we had walked on the Great Wall of China but never even seen Hadrian's Wall, been on Route 66 and the fabled Asian Silk Road but never Scotland's North Coast 500, California's Big Sur but not Ireland's Wild Atlantic Way. We've seen the Pyramids but not Stonehenge, and walked the Inca Trail in Peru but not the Giants' Causeway in Northern Ireland. We felt that we were saving the best till last, so join us on our odyssey, and, to quote a line from Sinatra's 'Come Fly With Me,' 'Let's make all the stops along the way.'

My only previous experiences of caravan sites had been on family holidays in the 1950s and '60s to North Wales in places like Rhyl, Colwyn Bay and Llandudno. The only lighting in the caravan was by gas mantles, which were lit with a match. Younger readers, ask your grandparents (make that *great* grandparents.) Happy days when my sister Linda and I pedalled a Social Cycle, probably replaced now by e-scooters.

The time was right for us to fulfil our ambition and live in a motorhome. We sold our house in Wigan and off-loaded most of our worldly possessions via eBay, local newspapers, friends and relatives. I became on first-name terms with the volunteers at our local charity shop. Each day, something would leave the house, piece by piece. If our house-move was set to music, it would be Haydn's Symphony Number 45, which requires each member of the orchestra to leave the stage one by one as the music continues. It becomes an empty orchestra, which, coincidentally, is the literal translation of the Japanese word Karaoke. Even more coincidentally, when I sing karaoke in the pub people *do* tend to leave one by one.

Our final night was spent under a duvet on the creaking floorboards of an empty, echoing Victorian house.

On The Road With BBKing

We had found an ideal motorhome on the internet a few weeks earlier and put down a deposit at a dealership in Perth. We were met at Perth railway station and driven to the showroom dealership. People often give affectionate names to their vehicles, and as soon as we saw our motorhome on the forecourt, his new name shouted out to us. The registration plate was BBK and, from then on, he was named after the legendary blues guitarist BBKing.

"You don't realize just how long a 7-metre motorhome is until you stand next to it," 1 commented to the salesman, daunted by the prospect of driving it in busy traffic.

"The main thing to look out for is side-sweep," he replied, trying to reassure me. He pointed to the extra-long rear and said, "That's your bathroom, so careful you don't knock over our wheelie bins on your way out of the front gate."

The interior was very impressive, and the salesman explained how everything worked. After a few minutes, my brain started to overload and freeze, especially when he got to the part about chemical toilets. I forgot to ask him about gas mantles. At the showroom store we bought a few essentials such as an electric cable, toilet chemicals, and plastic champagne glasses for the celebratory bubbly, courtesy of the sales team. Our luggage consisted of just two small bags, travelling light, intending to buy-as-we-go.

I was handed the keys and climbed into the driver's seat. Anxiously, I kangarooed across the forecourt, worrying about my back end, in more ways than one. I swept, white-knuckled, on to the main road, which thundered with fast-flowing traffic. I noticed in my wing mirror that cars behind had slowed to a crawl, with some shrieking to an abrupt halt. Silly place to put wheelie bins.

When I asked Norma for satnav directions off her phone, she hesitantly took her hands down from over her face and gradually opened her screwed-up eyes.

"We turn right soon."

I flicked on the windscreen wipers, then the lights and, just in time, finally found the indicator signal to turn right.

"Are we taking the high road or the low road?" she asked.

"I'll let you know when we reach the bonnie, bonnie banks of Loch Lomond."

Phase One: SCOTLAND

Edinburgh was our first destination on our tour of Scotland. I had just about got used to handling the 6-gear BBK when we joined the M90 motorway, but I quickly got up to speed, physically and metaphorically. A big confidence boost was my first overtaking of a lorry, careful to allow plenty of space since they are slightly more resilient than a wheelie bin.

Go Forth and Multiply

The Queensferry Crossing took us over the Firth of Forth. Queensferry takes its name from Margaret, Queen of Scotland, who founded a ferry in the 12th Century, initially to take pilgrims to St. Andrew's. The coming of the railways meant that a bridge was necessary, and the Forth Bridge opened in 1890. There is a saying, 'It's like painting the Forth Bridge,' when describing a never-ending task. Having seen the bridge, with its three colossal cantilever steel structures and intricate architectural patterns, whoever coined that phrase was spot on. It was designed by Benjamin Baker and John Fowler and has become an iconic emblem of Scotland, taking 200 trains a day and is a UNESCO World Heritage Site.

Today, there are three bridges spanning not only the river but also three centuries. A suspension bridge opened in 1964, and in the early 21st Century, The Queensferry Crossing Bridge opened. A new style of suspension, it has cables radiating from massive columns, reminiscent of sails on a ship. The bridges are like three generations of a family, a marvellous sight to behold.

We arrived at Moreton Hall Caravan Park in Edinburgh, where the Hall has been converted into apartments, and the stable block is now a bar. After setting up, we enjoyed a drink in the cobbled yard. It had been a long day, and the temperature was dropping noticeably. The camping store had closed, so we took some bar snacks back to the motorhome. I vaguely remembered the instructions for operating the heating system, but unfortunately, there was a slight problem; my cable connector was incompatible with the pitch socket.

"I'll sort it tomorrow," I yawned.

For tea, we had crisps, cheese, biscuits, and what else but champagne, romantically illuminated by a streetlight through the window. We fell asleep fully clothed as we hadn't quite got round to buying pyjamas, let alone a duvet. We didn't sleep for long; the cold shuddered us into consciousness. A combination of bedtime champagne and cold temperature caused me to dash to the toilet block. When I returned, our beds had been made-up, as if by an attendant on a cruise. Nothing quite so glamorous. Norma had taken the curtains down to use as blankets.

"It's curtains for you tonight."

I slept well for the rest of the night despite the occasional plastic hook finding its way up my nose.

The following morning, I was woken by sounds of rumbling. My stomach, of course, and the sound of wheels along the paths. I looked out to see processions of campers pulling a variety of plastic contraptions, toilet cassettes, and what I later found out to be 'greywater' containers, like columns of worker-ants. After breakfast at the café, we went to the shop to acquaint ourselves with this mysterious world of caravanning.

"Excuse me, could you help me?" I asked the attendant.

"Of course, sir."

"We picked up a motorhome yesterday and need to stock-up on a few things."

"Ok, what have you got so far?"

"An electric cable that doesn't fit."

He waited a few seconds, expecting me to elaborate.

"That's it," I emphasised.

"I think we are going to need a bigger trolley," he said, sounding like Roy Schneider in Jaws.

We chose melamine plates and cups, microwave and oven ware, cutlery, and a hosepipe. Other customers soon picked-up on our mission and began offering suggestions based on their experiences, which seemed considerable. We felt as though we were being initiated into some secret society. We bought levelling blocks, a spirit level, fold-up chairs, collapsible clotheslines, and a TV aerial direction finder. I could go on, but I think you get the picture, especially with my new aerial detector. Never mind the fact that we didn't even have a television yet.

Auld Reeki

I've visited Edinburgh several times, but l can't remember ever seeing the sun. Indeed, the Scottish comedian Billy Connolly once joked that it takes a Scotsman two weeks in Spain just to turn white. Edinburgh's nickname, 'Auld Reeki', mean's Old Smokey, a reference to the coal-fire era, similar to London's 'The Smoke.' A black-and-white setting for a Film Noir has been etched on my mind, but not anymore. You may recall that in the classic movie 'The Wizard of Oz', the early monochrome footage transformed spectacularly into technicolour, to the amazed delight of Judy Garland. That was us arriving in Edinburgh by bus. Under a dome of cobalt blue sky, there was not a McCloud in sight. Princes Street was more like Las Ramblas in Barcelona, and gardens were thronged with tourists, school groups and picnic parties.

Like Rome, Edinburgh stands on seven hills, including three extinct volcanoes. Edinburgh Castle is built on the imaginatively named Castle Rock, which last erupted 350 million years ago. The most spectacular is Arthur's Seat at one end of the Royal Mile in Holyrood Park. It isn't clear how this name originated. It has been associated with the legend of King Arthur but was possibly named after a local hero.

The Royal Mile from the Castle to Holyrood Palace is so-called because it was the processional route for Kings and Queens of Scotland for 500 years, and an interesting walk today to explore this fascinating city. There are countless listed buildings, and the Medieval Old Town and the Neo-Classical new town today are both UNESCO World Heritage sites. This is a term we will be coming across many times on our travels, and it stands for United Nations Educational, Scientific and Cultural Organisation. Founded after World War II, it promotes peace and international cooperation to preserve heritage around the world. Also, we will be coming across the term 'listed building'. In simple terms, these are categorized into Grade I, which are of exceptional interest, and Grade II, which are important buildings of special interest. The second category makes up over 90% of all listed buildings. Edinburgh is renowned as one of the most haunted cities in the world, and the Castle is haunted by the ghost of a lone piper who disappears within its walls.

Since the 11th Century, Scottish Monarchs have lived at Edinburgh Castle, and Scotland and England have fought for control over the centuries.

The Stone of Scone

The Stone of Scone (pronounced Scoon), otherwise known as The Stone of Destiny, is a sandstone block of no intrinsic value, but it is priceless in terms of symbolism and historical significance. It has been part of coronation thrones for over 1,000 years, but its origin is lost in time. One legend is that the Old Testament Prophet Jacob rested his head on it when he had a dream in Bethel about a stairway to heaven. Perhaps it should be called the Led Zeppelin Stone. Over the centuries, it found its way to Scone Abbey in Perthshire. It has been used for many coronations, including that of Macbeth, the 11th Century King immortalized by Shakespeare. The stone was removed to England by Edward 1st in 1296, who had it fitted into a wooden throne. Eventually, The Stone of Scone was returned to Edinburgh Castle in 1996 and was loaned back to London for the Coronation of Charles III, who was crowned on the same ancient Throne in 2023.

At the risk of bursting the balloon of myth, or zeppelin in this case, carbon dating and research have proved that the stone was actually quarried in Scotland and is nowhere near as old as Jacob's Ladder. It was Kenneth MacAlpine, the first King of Scotland, who took the stone to Scone. Perhaps that's the answer... It's a MacAlpine breeze block.

King Edward of England became known as 'The Hammer of the Scots' during the Scottish Wars of Independence. He also had the nickname Longshanks due to his exceptional height. He was 6 feet 2 inches at the time when the average height in the 13th Century was about 5ft 5 inches. Evidence of this is shown by the suits of armour in Castles and Museums. Yes, the knights were shorter in those days. My theory is that when Edward was a Prince on a Crusade to the Holy Land, he must have been captured and stretched on a torture rack.

Scotland is renowned for its scientists, inventors and writers, and Edinburgh's railway station is said to be the only one in the world named after a work of literature, Waverley, by Sir Walter Scott. JK Rowling wrote her first Harry Potter book at the Elephant Castle Café, overlooking Greyfriars Cemetery. This cemetery has become famous for the true story of Greyfriars Bobby, a faithful Skye Terrier who refused to leave his master's grave. The dog's statue has become quite a tourist attraction.

Edinburgh hosts the world's biggest arts festival, the Fringe. First staged in 1947, there are 55,000 performances across 300 venues over 25 days. Many recognize The Perrier Award as the 'Oscar' of the arts festival world.

Strolling down the Royal Mile, there are alleyways and courtyards, each with a story to tell. We ventured into Dunbar's Close, which led to a beautiful secret garden. Tartan-themed gift shops, restaurants and bars were everywhere along the Royal Mile. The Witchery Restaurant was billed as the most haunted, while the most notable is The Deacon Brodie Tavern. William Brodie was a 'Jekyll and Hyde' character. Why?... because he was the *actual* person who was the inspiration for the novel by Robert Louis Stevenson. By day, Brodie was a wealthy, much-respected craftsman and citizen who was elected Deacon Councillor of Edinburgh. But, by night, he was a notorious gambler, thief and burglar who was hanged in 1788. His story has been embellished over the years, and his legend has passed into folklore.

The World's End Pub has an interesting history. In Medieval times, Edinburgers lived their entire lives within the city walls, less than half a square mile. This was because there was a toll to enter, which pre-dates London's congestion charge by centuries. Residents were born, lived and died there, which puts the Covid 19 lockdown into some kind of perspective. Consequently, house building went upward centuries before New York, Hong Kong and Dubai. Inevitably, buildings collapsed, but that's another storey. The World's End Pub marks the limit of the wall, to the inhabitants, literally the world's end.

We joined the Blair Street Underground Vaults walking tour. These are a series of caverns once occupied in the 18th century by jewellers, offices and taverns. Gradually, they were abandoned, and squatters and criminals moved in. Lots of artefacts, such as barrels and glassware, are left and the mood lighting created a ghostly ambience. We couldn't resist the Edinburgh Fudge shop, which gave us the idea to try food and drink famous for particular places. This could be a theme for our tour around Britain and Ireland.

Being a retired art teacher, I always love to spend time in galleries. The National Gallery of Scotland is outstanding, located in a Graeco-Roman style Neo-Classical building. This is a term which will crop up many times during our travels, as it is the most ubiquitous and enduring of architectural styles. In simple terms, it is based on the architecture of ancient Greece and Rome, the Parthenon in Athens being the most famous example. The basic styles are Doric, with a simple capital at the top of each column, Ionic with scrolls, and Corinthian, bell-shaped decorated with acanthus leaves. Indeed, Edinburgh has so many imposing Classic buildings that it has often been dubbed 'The Athens of the North'.

Unlike larger galleries such as London's National Gallery or the Louvre in Paris, the Scottish Gallery is an ideal size that enables visitors to view many of the paintings in a couple of hours. The usual suspects like Raphael, Titian, El Greco, Rembrandt, Constable, and Monet are on show. I was particularly interested in the Scottish Collection. I was intrigued by the 'Skating Minister' by Henry Raeburn, a quaint, eccentric painting with great charm.

Raeburn was one of Scotland's foremost portrait painters of the 18th Century, Sir Walter Scott being a notable commission. However, his most famous painting is The Skating Minister, an enigmatic study of the Reverend Robert Walker gliding elegantly on a frozen lake. He is dressed in black and wearing a black, brimmed hat. It has a mysterious aura, and perhaps this is why it is one of the best-known Scottish paintings. The famous 'Monarch of the Glen' was majestic, a magnificent stag in a Highland setting by Edwin Landseer, who was hugely popular in Victorian times.

Van Gogh is an artist whose work can only be fully appreciated first-hand. Reproductions can't convey the vibrancy, texture, and colour of the original. One painting in particular, The Head of a Peasant Woman, has an interesting, recent post-script. In July 2022, in Scotland's National Gallery, a previously unknown self-portrait of Vincent was discovered by X-ray on the reverse side of one of his paintings. The Gallery's senior conservator, Lesley Stevenson, was carrying out routine work when she was shocked to find Van Gogh staring back at her. The peasant woman was from Nuenen in Holland, where Van Gogh lived from 1883 to 1885. It's well known that he only ever sold one painting in his lifetime, and that was to his brother

Theo. Impecunious Vincent often painted on the back of his paintings to save money. The Head of a Peasant Woman changed ownership several times, and in 1923 it was owned by Evelyn St Croix Fleming, the father of Ian Fleming, creator of James Bond. Can I suggest that Vincent's time in Nuenen should be known as Van Gogh's BOGOF period: buy one, get one free.

Scotland is full of macs, and I'm not talking about the inclement weather. The prefix Mac, common in Scottish surnames, began as a patronymic tradition, meaning son or daughter, similar to the Viking suffix, son. The origins of this are complex, beyond the realms of this book, and a similar tradition exists in Ireland. We will find out more when we cross the Irish Sea. Incidentally, it was the Irish that gave Scotland its name, a tribe of Gaelic raiders that the Romans translated as Scotti.

Scottish Borders

Leaving Edinburgh, we followed the coast of the Firth of Forth, passing Gosford Bay, Aberlady Bay and Gullane Bay and endless golf courses to North Berwick. We drove through Dunbar towards Pease Bay and turned inland towards the Scottish Border country. It was a little disorientating to go through Preston and Swinton, and for a moment, we felt as though we had entered some Scottish timewarp portal and had been transported to Lancashire.

The town of Coldstream is on the banks of the River Tweed, which marks much of the border between Scotland and England. Coldstream is synonymous with the oldest continuous regiment in the British Army. How did a Scottish town give its name to a Regiment based in London? During the English Civil War, Oliver Cromwell permitted one of his generals, George Monck, to form a new regiment in the New Model Army. Monck founded the Regiment of Foot Soldiers in 1650, played a crucial part in the Battle of Dunbar, besieged the castles of Dunnottar and Stirling, and stormed Dundee. When Cromwell died, General Monck had a change of heart and decided to support the restoration of the exiled Charles II and marched south to defend the King. His Regiment was named after the place where it had crossed the bridge over the Tweed into England: Coldstream. Apparently, the distinctive bearskin was introduced to make the soldiers appear bigger and more fearsome in battle. A Coldstream Guards monument in Henderson Park is a rugged rock with a plaque.

A leisurely drive west took us through some beautiful countryside and villages to a lunch break in Kelso, at the confluence of the river Teviot and Tweed. We parked near the 12th Century ruined Abbey, where King David of Scotland had brought Benedictine Monks from Chartres in France to revive the Catholic religion. The monks wrote The Kelso Liver, which documents history from the 12th to the 16th Century. Like many we will see on our travels, the abbey fell into ruin following the dissolution of the monasteries by Henry VIII.

As we continued through the Scottish Borders, the scenery was idyllic. Hawick lies on the confluence of the River Slitrigg and Teviot, and settlement here dates back to the 7th Century. The river provided power, particularly for the textile industry, and today, it is still a centre for wool, clothes, and carpets. The 12th Century Mott (fortress) is a testament to a turbulent history in cross-border battles. In 1513, most of the men of Hawick were killed at the Battle of Flodden, and a year later, the town's only defence was its teenage boys. There is a touching statue to commemorate their bravery.

One Small Step...

From Hawick, the drive along the A7 was spectacularly scenic through Teviot Dale, with rugged views on either side of Tudhope Hill, Broad Head and Arkleton Hill. We stopped for a break at Langholm, on the River Eske, an important textile centre where The Edinburgh Woollen Mill was founded in 1946. Gilnockie Tower, the seat of the Armstrong Clan, boasts a world-famous descendant: none other than Neil Armstrong, the first man on the moon in 1969, 'a giant leap for mankind'. There is a commemorative plaque and photographs of Neil Armstrong visiting the town.

We drove through Gretna, famous for its runaway marriages. This began in 1754 when a new law was introduced in England which prohibited marriage for under 21-year-olds without parental consent. In Scotland at the time, anyone over 15 could get married, and a church wedding wasn't compulsory. A blacksmith would strike an anvil to seal the marriage, and even today, people come from all over the world to get married at Gretna Green.

Burns Country

Dumfries is a bustling, working town with solid stone buildings, pebbledash and whitewash. It doesn't have the same aesthetic quality as some towns that we have seen, but it does boast one particular distinction. It is the final resting place of poet Robert Burns, one of Scotland's most famous sons. He bought Ellisland Farm near Dumfries in 1788 and built his house, which is now a museum. There were rooms recreating the 18th Century, with some original furniture. A personal touch is where Robert Burns had etched his name with his diamond ring on a window pane.

Burns had little schooling, but he wished to broaden his horizons and escape a life of perpetual debt. He joined a bachelor club and debated controversial topics. He developed an eloquence which would help later in his career when reciting his works.

He was an ambivalent character whose life was full of contradictions. He actually worked for a while as an overseer of slaves on a plantation in Jamaica, a slave driver who was inspired by agriculture, country people, and even a mouse.

Robert Burns was a scathing satirist who wrote about corruption and hypocrisy. Yet, in order to make money, he re-invented himself and moved to Edinburgh and became a Mason. Edinburgh was an intellectual centre, and Burns used his social contacts to further his career. He found a publisher, and he became a popular performer in his recitals. He commissioned a portrait of himself, which eventually found its way on to the Scottish banknotes, which, in my experience around the world, including England, are about as negotiable as a 9-bob note.

His mausoleum is at St. Michael's Church in Dumfries, which was the setting for his most famous poem, Tam O' Shanter. It tells the story of a drunken farmer who witnessed witches dancing with Satan. They chased him from the church to a bridge, but witches cannot cross running water. They managed to snatch the tail off his horse Meg.

Incidentally, today, he is often referred to as 'Rabbie' Burns, but he *never* signed his name that way; it was always Rob or Robert. He was quite a ladies' man and a prolific, energetic lover. All his women must have thought that he *really was* poetry in motion. He fathered twelve children by four different mothers, perhaps this is why he died in poverty at the age of 37. The best-laid plans of mice and men…

Garlieston

The Caravan Club site at Garlieston is a superb location, where rows of stone terraced cottages, painted in a range of soft pastel colours, overlook a bowling green and boats in the harbour. Our pitch was on the waterfront, and a spectacular floral display of purple and white petunias in hanging baskets at the reception gave us a colourful welcome. The local pub, the Harbour Inn, served an excellent roast dinner. A real bonus was that we were able to visit relatives who live in Newton Stewart. Our nephew Brian had invited us to a barbeque, and he picked us up at the site. We hadn't seen his wife, Gillian and daughters, Katie and Emily, for a while, so it was a great reunion.

"I know it's a silly question, Uncle John, but would you like a whisky?" asked Brian, opening a cupboard to reveal a collection of bottles from what seemed like every distillery in Scotland, not to mention gin.

"Dad's a bit of a whisky connoisseur?" said Katie.

"That's because when your dad was a baby, Uncle John used to secretly dip his dummy in whisky," confided Norma conspiratorially to her niece.

Back at the caravan site the following day, we had a hair-of-the-dog at the Harbour Inn.

Our next destination was the most southerly point of Scotland: the Mull of Galloway. We followed the coast around the peninsula with Luce Bay to the west. The A747 took us along the edge of the rugged coastline, through Port William, Glenluce and round the bay to our caravan site near Sandhead. We spent a couple of days enjoying the continuing balmy weather on the beach. We drove to the village of Drummore and went into 'Scotland's most southerly store', as a sign proudly proclaimed. The road to the lighthouse at the Mull of Galloway was single-track, and the gleaming white lighthouse had many information boards. From the cliff tops, we could see the Isle of Man and the Lake District. The cliffs were rugged and spectacular, plunging vertically into the sea. The folding strata of the rock formations had subtle changes of colour, like an abstract painting. It was very tempting to take that extra step to snap the ultimate photo, almost mesmerising as the thunderous, crashing waves below seemed to draw you in. Underfoot, well-worn patches indicated the optimum view, evidence that one or two intrepid souls had ventured perilously close to the edge.

"Don't even think about it," warned Norma, sternly.

She pointed to a warning sign which solemnly stated, 'Caution, 3 Cliff Walkers Have Been Killed Here.'

"That's an amazing coincidence," I commented.

"What is?"

"That all three of them should have the same name."

She just rolled her eyes. Never mind, some fall on stony ground... especially along this path.

Turn Around...

Now was the time when our Bonnie Tyler Satnav *really could* tell us to 'Turn around'. We took the A715 north along Luce Bay to Stranraer on Loch Ryan and the A77 along the shore to Ballantrae. I'd only heard of this place through the novel 'The Master of Ballantrae' by the famous Scottish writer Robert Louis Stevenson. I've mentioned this before in a previous book. The Master of Ballantrae was written on an island. Any guesses? Mull? Islay? Skye? Believe it or not, it was Tahiti, where Stevenson arrived in 1888, about as far removed from Scotland as possible, geographically, culturally, or meteorologically.

We continued north along the Firth of Forth through Girvan and Turnberry, a popular golfing area, towards our next port of call in Ayr. Since we had learned much about Robert Burns, we decided to stop at the village of Alloway on the River Doon. This was where the Scottish Bard was born in a thatched cottage, which is now a museum. The Burns Gardens is beautifully laid out, a fine setting for the Burns Monument.

Ayr

Our following motorhome site was Ayr Craigie Gardens, situated by the River Ayr next to the University of West Scotland campus. It was a pleasant walk along the river footpath into the town centre. Ayr can trace its history to the 12th Century when a castle was built by the river. A town gradually built up and prospered on fishing, ship building and weaving, and was a busy port exporting hides and importing salt and wine.

The River Ayr cuts through the centre of the town and is spanned by several bridges, the most famous being the Old Bridge, a pedestrian stone bridge. The architecture is solid and typically Scottish. We walked through Burns Statue Square and Wellington Square and passed several imposing civic buildings. On Main Street is the Tam O' Shanter Inn, where Robert Burns is reputed to have frequented. On our way to the sea, we crossed an area of open lawn called Lower Green. The sandy beach was as golden and fine underfoot as some Caribbean beaches we have been on. Large individual houses look out over the Firth to the island of Arran on the horizon.

The town is dominated by the Wallace Tower, dedicated to the freedom fighter. We will be coming across William Wallace many times, and there are many monuments dedicated to him.

I Was Never His Subject

Contrary to what Mel Gibson would have us believe, William Wallace was *never* called Braveheart. This was a name given posthumously to Robert the Bruce, when his 'brave heart' was placed in a casket and carried into battle.

Wallace was a prominent leader during the wars of Scottish Independence, but little is known about his early life. He was born in the 1270s to middle-class landowners, and his first steps on the road to fame, legend and myth followed the death of the Scottish King Alexander III in 1286. This resulted in a crisis of succession, with several claiming to be the rightful King, and eventually John Balliol succeeded to the throne. King Edward 1st of England (The Hammer of the Scots) took advantage of the instability and invaded and won the Battle of Dunbar to take Scotland. Wallace rebelled and led a group to kill the English High Sheriff at Lanark. Wallace raised an army and famously defeated the English in 1297 at the Battle of Stirling Bridge, even though the Scots were heavily outnumbered. However, the following year, he was defeated by Edward at the Battle of Falkirk, although he survived and went on the run as an outlaw. He was captured in 1305, taken to London and tried for treason. The only words he spoke were,

'I could not be a traitor to Edward, for I was *never* his subject.' He was hung, drawn and quartered, and his head was displayed on London Bridge.

Wallace must have had military training to lead armies and a family seal, which illustrates a longbow. The name of his wife only appeared in later chronicles, and she was called Marion. Hold on a second... An outlaw and archer? Who kills the sheriff? Whose wife is called Marion? Where have I heard this before? Stories and ballads of Robin Hood (Robyn Hode) were popular at the time, and perhaps chroniclers wanted to turn Wallace into a Scottish version of Robin Hood. Why let the facts get in the way of a good story? I'm surprised Mel Gibson didn't give him a Deep Fat Friar McTuck or a Wee John.

Glasgow

Quote: *"Glasgow defies description. Many have tried to describe its spirit and failed miserably. What do you say about a town that dances, sings, plays and jokes differently from everybody else?"*
                                          Glaswegian comedian Billy Connolly.

A statue with a plastic traffic cone permanently on his head encapsulates the quote.

We went by train from Ayr to Glasgow, which was our first visit, and I had a pre-conceived notion of a dour, grimy place. How wrong could I be? As with Edinburgh, the glorious sunshine brought out the best of an impressive, vibrant city with a pleasant, friendly ambience. Glasgow in Scottish Gaelic translates to 'Lovely Green Place,' an appropriate name since there are ninety parks and gardens, notably the Botanical Gardens with its magnificent 19th Century wrought iron glass dome.

George Square, named after King George III, is home to a collection of statues of historical figures such as Sir Walter Scott and Robert Burns. A statue I wanted to see was the Duke of Wellington in front of the Gallery of Modern Art. There he is, mounted on his horse, Copenhagen, while wearing a plastic traffic cone on his head. I asked attendants in the gallery if they knew the origins of the traffic cone, but answers were vague. One guide told me it is a testament to the Glaswegian sense of humour, a symbol of Glasgow. Pretentious? Moi? A symbol of Glasgow? Who donated it?... the Tar Macadam Clan? In plain English, it was a lark that has caught on. The Lonely Planet Guide has even featured it in its list of 'the ten most bizarre monuments on Earth.' Whoever wrote that should get out more.

The Gallery of Modern Art is located in a magnificent Neo-Classical building. The interior has been converted to a light, modern space showing colourful works of art and famous pieces include: Andy Warhol's Campbell's Soup, an embroidery by Grayson Perry and Salvador Dali's Crucifixion, which portrays the scene from above.

The 12th Century Glasgow Cathedral, St. Mungo's, overlooks the city from a hill behind the Necropolis, City of the Dead. This has become an unusual tourist attraction with its Victorian sculptures, Celtic crosses, exotic monuments and buildings, some by Charles Rennie Mackintosh, one of Glasgow's most famous sons. His masterpiece was the Glasgow School of Art, which sadly has been damaged by fire.

However, much of Mackintosh's work can be seen throughout the city and also in the Kelvingrove Art Gallery and Museum. This is a fantastic place to visit, with one side dedicated to natural history, animals, armoury and even a World War II Spitfire. There is a spectacular pipe organ, and the tiled floor and cavernous building create superb acoustics like in a Cathedral. The other side is an art gallery displaying a vast collection of paintings and sculptures.

Particularly impressive are 19th Century paintings of the Scottish Romanticism genre of Highland landscapes and Scottish history, such as a dramatic painting of Robert the Bruce in battle. There are some excellent examples of Charles Rennie Mackintosh's unique style of Art Nouveau, particularly a recreation of Catherine Cranston's famous Glasgow Tea Rooms, with set tables and distinctive high-backed chairs.

In common with many artists over the centuries, Charles Rennie Mackintosh was unappreciated during his lifetime, and he became better known in Austria than in his native Glasgow. In 1900, he was invited to Vienna to exhibit his work. He influenced a group of artists known as the Cessessionists, in particular their leader Gustav Klimt, whose distinctive style is popular today.

Back in Glasgow, Mackintosh found some commissions, but his life went into a downward spiral as he drank and had a nervous breakdown. The outbreak of war prevented him from returning to Austria, so he and his wife moved to a small seaside town in Suffolk called Walberswick in 1915. A bizarre series of events took over his life. He sketched and made notes along the shore, and, being wartime, locals became suspicious of his activities. The police visited him at home and found letters from his friends in Austria and Germany. He was accused of being a spy and was ordered to leave. He ended up in poverty in a bed-sit in London, where he died in 1923 of cancer. Today, his work has global significance, and he has become a favourite son of Glasgow.

Once at the forefront of the Industrial Revolution and shipbuilding industry, after the war, the city became rundown, but investment and rejuvenation have returned it to a modern city. The juxtaposition of solid, traditional Victorian and Edwardian buildings alongside modern designs works well. It is the home of the Scottish Opera, Scottish Ballet and National Theatre. Buchanan Street was buzzing with shoppers, like Sauchiehall Street and Argyle Street in the West End.

Glasgow has a thriving music scene in the pubs and on the street. One young boy was proudly supervised by his parents as he expertly played the bagpipes. Dressed in a kilt and traditional regalia, he attracted a good-sized audience.

Springfield Quay was built in the 1840s and transformed from industrial grime to a Cultural Centre with galleries, museums and cafés. Some buildings reminded me of the Sydney Opera House, especially with a blue sky as a backdrop. The Riverside Museum has ships, vintage cars, horse-drawn carriages, trams and locomotives.

Glasgow council commissions artists to paint murals on buildings. Most are in a super realistic style but with perhaps some hidden meaning for viewers to make their interpretations. There is a vast painting of a black taxicab rising from the ground by balloons. My favourite was a photo-realistic painting of an old man with a bird perched on his hand. It is thought to be of St. Mungo, who performed the miracle of bringing a dead bird back to life. I have seen street art worldwide, including New York, Los Angeles, San Francisco, Sydney and Rio, to name a few. In my opinion, Glasgow is up there with the best.

Gateway to the Highlands

In Scotland, mountains are separated into Munros or Corbetts depending on height. Sir HT Munro outlined his definition in the Scottish Mountaineering Mountains Journal in 1891, and John Corbett added to it in 1930. Munros are peaks over 3000ft, and The Corbetts are defined as Scottish between 2,500-3000ft.

Travelling north from Ayr, we hugged the coast, known as the 'Golf Coast', through Troon, Irvine, West Kilbride and Largs. From Greenock, we followed the Firth of Clyde, crossed the river via the Erskine Bridge and headed for Loch Lomond.

At 36 kilometres long and 8 wide, Loch Lomond is classified as a ribbon lake, filling a deep gorge carved by glacial erosion during the last Ice Age. Known as the 'Gateway to the Highlands', this beautiful Loch is surrounded by mountains, the highest being Ben Lomond at 974 metres. The road skirts the western bank, and we made several stops for refreshments and photo opportunities. For me, the only downside is that Loch Lomond Whisky sponsors Wigan Rugby League Club. Being a Saints fan, I found it hard to swallow.

We continued along the length of the Loch and via Glen Falloch through the spectacular Loch Lomond and Trossachs National Park. At Crianlarich, we turned west towards the coast and our next caravan site at Ledaig on Ardmucknish Bay. The beautiful site is on the beach, but a stretch of water with Ardmuck in its title is hardly inviting. Despite its name, it was crystal clear. We enjoyed stupendous sunsets across the Firth of Lorne towards the Isle of Mull. The cool palettes of mauves, lilacs and magenta gradually gave way to warmer pinks, oranges and crimson, memorable Turneresque images.

Oban

The bus stop for Oban was at the site entrance, and the coastal route took us through beautiful villages and yachting marinas of North Connel, Dunbeg and Ganavan Bay. On the way, we had a magnificent view of Dustaffnage Castle, standing on a promontory in the bay.

Ever since the arrival of the railway in 1880, Oban has been popular with tourists, but it is still a working town and maintains a fishing fleet. Scattered around the harbour are clusters of nets, pots, ropes and all the paraphernalia of the fishing industry, looking as decorative as still-life artistic arrangements. A lone piper at the harbour wall underscored the Scottish atmosphere.

The Scottish ambience of the town is emphasized by some of the shops framing the harbour: Chalmers Highland Tweed, the Iona Shop, The Tartan House of Scotland, and The Highland Soap Co. We couldn't pass the Oban Chocolate Company without ticking off another for our foodie list.

The town is overlooked by McCaig's Folly, on top of Battery Hill and the defining monument on the skyline. It looks as though the Colosseum has been air-lifted from Rome and dropped in Oban. Indeed, The Colosseum was the actual inspiration for the structure when John McCaig commissioned it in 1897. The circular, arched building encloses a public park as a quiet retreat offering spectacular views over the town and out to sea and the Islands. The luminescent sunsets viewed from high on the hill are even more dramatic than our campsite up the coast.

Isle of Mull

We boarded a ferry to the Isle of Mull, and as we sailed out of the harbour, the view looking back to Oban was terrific. The crossing on the Caledonian McBrayne took us across the Firth of Lorne, and as we approached the Isle of Mull, the dominant feature was Duart Castle standing protectively on Duart Point, guarding entry to the Sound of Mull. Disembarking the ferry terminal at the small village of Craignure, we walked to the castle.

Duart Castle is the ancestral home of the MacLean Clan and has stood since the 14th was restored in 191. Rather than stone shaped into building blocks, the castle walls comprise massive rocks of all shapes and sizes, a sort of vertical crazy-paving, with round, turreted towers. We toured the Great Hall, where the usual family portraits and displays of elegant silver tableware were displayed. The state bedrooms were sumptuous, the traditional kitchen was re-created, and the castle dungeons had chains and manacles. There was an exhibition of weaponry and a reference to wrecks of the Spanish Armada. We had a coffee in the castle café and a slice of Duart Cake, which had a flavour of orange and poppy seeds. Delicious and another foodie box to tick. We caught a glimpse of deer in the woodland. Craignure comprises a row of houses, a grocery store, a gift shop, and, most importantly, a pub where we sat in the front garden and watched the ferry arrive.

The world-famous Oban Whiskey Distillery is in the town centre, nestled at the foot of the cliffs beneath McCaig's Folly. It is the smallest distillery in Scotland because there is no room for expansion. I asked our guide if they had ever considered re-locating within Oban to expand. He said they were proud to keep the title of the *smallest* whisky distillery, which helps the brand to market its uniqueness. The tour explained all the different stages of production and emphasized that local ingredients were used, including water from a nearby loch, which gives Oban its distinctive flavour. The whisky tasting in the bar was excellent; I still have my complimentary glass with the engraving 'Oban Distillery'. I use it regularly.

Our next motorhome site from Oban was at Morvich on Loch Duich, about 4 hours away. A beautiful coastal drive took us north along the banks of Loch Linnhe, and at Loch Leven, we took a detour inland to Glen Coe.

Glen Coe

The glen is U-shaped, desolate and magnificently rugged, one of the most beautiful areas of the Highlands. It is most well-known for the massacre of 1692, when the Redcoats, mainly Campbells, murdered 38 members of the MacDonald Clan while they slept. The visitors' centre is modern and well-designed, with boardwalks linking various buildings. There are photographs, scale models of the mountain ranges, films, early mountaineering equipment and a history of the mountain rescue service. An interesting installation is a re-creation of a turf house, well insulated to keep out the harsh weather.

We re-traced our steps to continue along Loch Linnhe to Fort William, a popular destination for hikers and climbers. The town is overlooked by Ben Nevis, the highest mountain in the UK at 1343 metres, and it is also a starting point to walk The Great Glen Way, following the Caledonian Canal and Lochs to Inverness. Another attraction for Harry Potter fans is the Jacobite Steam Train, or the Hogwarts Express, which goes over the Glenfinnan Viaduct.

Fort William has outdoor pursuit's stores and the usual gift shops, galleries and pubs. The town takes its name from King William III (Willian of Orange), who built a fort there in 1698. Cameron Square is named after the local Clan Cameron, and a bizarre bronze statue is of Henry Alexander sitting in a Model-T Ford motorcar. Why? Because he *drove* the car to the summit of Ben Nevis in 1911!

We continued north via Spean Bridge and along the banks of Loch Lochy and Loch Oich to Invergarry, where we turned west towards the coast. So far, from Oban to Invergarry, we had followed the Great Glen, a geological fault line which splits Scotland in half. This was created by the tectonic plate movement millions of years ago, forming a ribbon of Lochs, the largest and most famous being Loch Ness.

Thomas Telford

It's worth pausing at this point to acknowledge the astounding achievement of Scottish Civil Engineer Thomas Telford, who built the Caledonian Canal through the glen. He linked all the lochs with a series of canals to enable shipping to move from one side of Scotland to the other, thereby avoiding the long and treacherous voyage around the north coast. The Caledonian Canal was started in 1803 and stretches 60 miles. Neptune's Staircase comprises eight locks and is quite a tourist attraction. The British Government invested a great deal of money into the building of the canal. At a time known as 'the Highland clearances', landlords were evicting tenant farmers and workers from their land to make way for lucrative sheep farming to cash in on the booming wool trade. Many emigrated or became close to starvation, but the new canal project provided jobs for navvies. An early Government job-creation scheme on a grand scale.

Telford was born in 1757 on a remote sheep farm in the Scottish Borders. With little formal education, he trained initially as a stonemason and went on to design canals, bridges, aqueducts and roads; 'The man who built Britain' and paved the way for the likes of Brunel and Stephenson. From a lowly sheep farm to burial in Westminster Abbey is a testament to his work. His most famous project, his signature achievement, is the Menai Bridge, and, dare I say it, we will cross that bridge when we get to it.

Driving through the highlands, the logging industry seems to be thriving and it was fascinating to see the rotation from felling trees to re-planting and all the stages in between. I wanted to find out more, so I decided to log on. All very interesting, except when we were stuck behind massive lorries, unable to overtake on this trunk road.

Morvich

We left Invergarry just a few miles south of Loch Ness, and we appreciated the surrounding countryside, particularly Lochs Garry, Loyne and Cluanie, and their lovely loch-side villages. Sheep and cattle were everywhere. There are several types of Scottish cattle, including Aberdeen Angus, Galloway and Ayrshire. Highland cattle, typical of this area, are a hardy breed with long horns and a shaggy coat to withstand the harsh climate. This breed is popular with artists and framed multi-coloured, pop-art paintings are in most galleries and craft shops, looking as if they had wandered into the middle of a paint-ball fight. We arrived at the campsite at Morvich, close to Loch Duich, tired but invigorated by another day of spectacular Scottish scenery. After setting up, we walked down to the lochside for a meal at the restaurant, which was called… The Jac-O-Bite. Depending on your point of view, this name is either inspiring or excruciating. Of course, it refers to the Jacobite Uprising, and Bonnie Prince Charlie being smuggled by Flora MacDonald 'over the sea to Skye'. (More of which when we visit the site of the Battle of Culloden).

Over the Sea to Skye

The Intercity bus from Inverness to Portree on Skye glided into view. The two-hour journey skirted lochs, the most impressive view being of Eilean Donan Castle on Loch Duich. Crossing the Skye Bridge gave us sensational views in all directions. The bus route skirted the coast and was like a guided tour. Skye, one of the Inner Hebrides, is a rugged island of natural rock formations, towering mountains and dramatic cliffs. The Cuillin Hills provided magnificent views before the road took us trough Glen Varragill to Portree, the main town.

In Portree at Macnab's Inn, Flora MacDonald and Bonnie Prince Charlie had their final meeting in 1746 before he set sail for refuge in France.

Amongst the row of historic, stone-built houses in pastel shades, pubs and craft shops skirting the harbour was a fish and chip shop, a perfect lunch and a fabulous view.

Back at Morvich the following morning, we decided to go on a long hike along the Crowe River, which sounds like something from a John Wayne western. We followed the footpath along a U-shaped glacial valley to view a waterfall. The panoramic photo opportunities were sensational, but by the time we returned home to BBKing, we had been out for about 7 hours. We were bedraggled (not bedazzled) as we trudged along like Laurel and Hardy in 'Beau Chumps'. A mirage of a cool beer and a G&T got us through the final few miles.

Kinlochewe

Leaving Morvich, I drove north to Kinlochewe. We followed the east coast of Loch Carron and through Glen Carron, passed smaller lochs Dughaill, Sgamhain and turned west at Achnasheen along the north shore of Loch Chroisg and through Glen Gocherty.

We were becoming spoiled for choice when deciding the best Highland view, but the jaw-dropping panorama before us took some beating. The perfect U-shaped glacial valley revealed Loch Maree in the distance. A small car park by the roadside provided the perfect view, and an information board pointed out the physical features below. From that spot, Queen Victoria had often stopped to take in the natural beauty.

As we continued down the Glen to Kinlochewe, the town seemed full of cyclists and bikers, all doing the North Coast 500, a 500-mile circular route from Inverness. We checked in at the caravan site, yet another beautiful location, and later went to the Kinlochewe Hotel for an evening meal and a few drinks. I congratulated the landlord on our excellent shoulder of lamb, and he beamed with pride as he told us they had recently been awarded the 'West Highland Pub of the Year' title. The general dress- code seemed to be lycra and leather, reflecting the clientele.

"The Lycra and Leather would be a good name for this pub," I suggested to Norma.

"I don't think so; it could be misinterpreted on the website."

North Coast 500

There was a convivial atmosphere, and the 500 seemed to be the common focus. The world's most famous route is America's Route 66 with its shield logo. The NC 500 has copied this idea, and the Scottish version of the badge can be seen everywhere in shops, pubs, garages and on T-shirts. It has become very popular with all modes of transport: motorhomes, caravans, cars, hikers, bikers and cyclists. Give something a name and a sense of achievement, and it will attract people; for example, the English Coast to Coast Walk, The Pennine Way, The Jurassic Coast and Ireland's Wild Atlantic Way.

At the bar, we chatted with some University students on a geology field trip, who seemed more interested in whisky samples than rock samples.

In conversation with the landlord, he told me that he and his wife had previously lived in Texas, where his wife had taught in a high school. It was obvious from their accents that they were neither Scottish nor American, so I asked where they were from.

"Oh, it's a town not far from Liverpool you might have heard of, known mainly for glass and rugby league… St Helens."

"Heard of it? It's our home town."

They introduced themselves as Dave and Karen and told us they had met in the 6th form at Cowley School. I had been a pupil at the same school before their time, and returned as a teacher just after they had left. We spent the rest of the evening reminiscing.

The following morning, we decided on another hike and followed the trail towards Ben Eighe, punctuated by several stops at photo vantage points. The tourist information centre had a scale model of the mountain ranges, photographic displays and information about the history and geology of Ben Eighe and Loch Maree.

That evening, we returned to the pub, and I took a gift for the owners, a copy of my book, 'Sir, Where's Toilet?' about school trips abroad, including anecdotal stories concerning some of the teachers they remembered. They were so delighted that we ended up on free drinks, not a bad swap.

The astounding beauty of the western coast of Scotland is encapsulated in the drive from Kinlochewe to Ullapool, enhanced even more by yet another glorious sunny day. We followed the south west shore of Loch Maree and followed the coast through Gairloch, Poolewe, passed Loch Ewe and Guinard Bay. The road snaked around Carn Bhiorain and Carn Breac Beag and north to Ullapool. There were countless wow-factor views.

We pulled over quite sharply when we saw a sign advertising a sheepdog demonstration at a farm. I walked up to the farmhouse to find out more. The farmer's wife told me that he brings the sheep down from the hills at a certain time. It wasn't a demonstration like one would see at a country fair, more an opportunity to observe life on a working farm. The flock approached from a distance and we could hear the farmer shouting and whistling instructions to his border collie, which stalked, crouched and zig-zagged to keep the sheep in close formation. Most fascinating, and amusing, were two puppies copying their mother, learning on the job. They earned a round of applause from the few people watching.

The Ardmair Point caravan site was directly in front of the pebble beach of Loch Broon, where it opens to the sea. We walked along the pebble beach, enjoying the breathtaking views and met a fisherman pulling ashore his prawn nets. We chatted for a while, and he gave us a bucket of prawns straight from the sea. So that was tea sorted.

Ullapool, a charming harbour town, is just a 20-minute bus journey along the coast. Ullapool to Stornoway is one of the main ferry links to the western Isles, and the views from the picturesque harbour out to sea and the mountains islands were sensational. The well-known

Seafood Shack was on the harbour, and we had the famous seafood platter for lunch.

Next on our itinerary was our most remote destination: Altnaharra, in the middle of the Highlands. We detoured from the coastal route to experience a different aspect of this beautiful area. As we travelled inland, we felt more and more remote. Mainly single-track, a ribbon of tarmac snakes its way through the Highlands, punctuated by 'Passing Places' indicated by white triangles mounted on high poles. Presumably, this is so that they can be seen from a distance and stand above snow. So, who decided on white?

This stretch of road must be the most courteous I have ever driven along: Giving way to on-coming traffic or faster vehicles looming large from the rear resulted in smiles and waves from car drivers, Harley Davidson Chapters and the occasional white-van-man. As we approached a remote pub, we noticed that motorbikes were parked on either side of the road, like a gathering of the clans. There must have been 50 riders, all enjoying a drink. I had let them all pass earlier, and as we went by, I gave them a wave and a toot, which was reciprocated with a roar of appreciation. I had to let them overtake me again about half an hour later.

The surrounding landscape was like moorland, reminiscent of the Pennines. We knew that the site at Altnaharra was miles from any shops, pubs or restaurants, so we stocked-up at the town of Lairg at the southern end of Loch Shin.

Duel

After a while, I noticed the glint of a motorhome in the distance approaching us. As we got closer, we both pulled over simultaneously, about 50 metres apart. We flashed our headlights at each other, and both paused momentarily. I took the initiative and pulled out. After about 20 metres, he pulled out also, with no passing place between us. I felt as though I was in the Steven Spielberg film, 'Duel', in which Dennis Weaver was terrorised by a mysterious truck driver. I stopped, but my adversary continued towards me. I reversed back into the passing place, a wise decision because as the motorhome got closer, I could see that the driver was a huge, Hagrid lookalike with a glistening metal display of facial adornments. He stopped alongside us. He had forearms like Popeye, covered in multicoloured tattoos. Lettering in gothic script ran the length of his arm. I spotted a glaring spelling mistake. As a retired teacher, my first instinct was to point it out, but I resisted the temptation. His wife fitted the same description but without the beard. I had decided to keep the window closed, but he gestured for me to lower it. I tentatively complied with his instruction and looked at him, wondering what his attitude would be. We were like two boxers at the face-off. To my great surprise, not to say relief, he smiled broadly and said,

"I'm sorry, I was letting you go first, but this motorhome is on hire. I'm not used to it and pressed the accelerator by mistake."

We chatted amiably for a while until a car appeared. As we pulled away, I told him, "When you get to the coast, don't get your pedals mixed up. It's a long way down to the rocks." They laughed and waved.

If that was a scene from 'Duel', my next encounter was more like 'Driving Miss Daisy'. I gave way to an immaculate Morris Minor, driven by a little grey-haired octogenarian lady, a Miss Marple lookalike. She smiled gracefully as she tootled by, and I didn't know whether to gasp or laugh when I noticed the sticker on her car: 'I ♥ Tongue'. Now, call me old-fashioned, but in the circumstances, that is too much information. As I laughed in mock horror, Norma, with raised eyebrows, pointed on the map to a town on the north coast: Tongue.

Sheep Do Not Have Any Road Sense

Altnaharra derives from a Scottish Gaelic word meaning a stream at a boundary wall. It is a hamlet, and the campsite was located on the banks of Loch Naver, surrounded by hills, forests and sheep. A sign on the road stated, 'Sheep Do Not Have Any Road Sense.' They wondered freely along the rocky outcrops throughout the site, and each morning, the warden had the unenviable task of collecting droppings in a bucket. Many caravaners like to display 'humorous' stickers: 'Home is where I park it', and so on. Perhaps The most popular is 'Don't Bother Knockin' if the Caravan is Rockin'. During our first night, BB King *really did* start to rock. We woke up startled, wondering if it was an earthquake. I stepped outside to find a couple of sheep on their knees stretching underneath the motorhome, chomping away at the grass as if there wasn't enough around.

The beautiful remoteness of our location meant that we couldn't get TV or WiFi reception, not even Roamin' in the Gloamin'. (Sorry). We climbed the hillside overlooking the site to see the ruins of a Mesolithic village. We continued the steep climb to the top of Meall a'Bhrollaich and enjoyed a picnic with a fabulous view of Loch Naver below us.

My beer supply in the fridge was running dangerously low, a sure indicator that it was time to get back to the road. After a quiet, leisurely drive north along the beautiful Loch Loyal, we reached the north coast of Tongue. We didn't see Miss Marple. We continued east through Strathy, Melvich, to Thurso, where we stopped briefly for petrol and groceries. The historic town stands at the mouth of the River Thurso, which flows into Pentland Firth. The town was named Thorsa by the Vikings, meaning Thor's River, and it became a major fishing and trading post.

We continued along the coast through Castletown to our caravan site at Dunnet Bay.

The site was right on the beach, close to Dunnet Head, which, contrary to popular perception, is the Scottish mainland's most northerly point rather than the more famous John O'Groats. It was a beautiful location, and the icing on the cake was a gin distillery right next door. We went for a stroll towards the Head and came across Mary Anne's Cottage, which is preserved to show the life of a crofter in days gone by.

Gin and Dubonnet

Our first excursion was a short bus ride to the Castle of Mey, the former home of Queen Elizabeth, the Queen Mother. As we walked up the long driveway, we realised that the Union Jack on the roof was the first we had seen throughout Scotland. The Scottish flag of St Andrew, the Saltire, was everywhere, perhaps a statement of patriotism or independence.

The castle dates from the 16th Century, and the Queen Mother bought it in 1952 after the death of her husband, King George VI. Decay and dilapidation had started to take its toll (in the castle, that is, *not* the Queen Mother). It has been restored to its former glory, and the rooms are preserved with personal effects, paintings, table settings, furniture and carpets. We were escorted on a very interesting guided tour by a lady who was once the local Post Mistress. She knew the Queen Mother personally and enlivened our visit with anecdotal stories. She confirmed that Queen Elizabeth's favourite tipple was gin and Dubonnet, and, since she lived to be over 100, l felt like quoting the famous line from the movie 'When Harry met Sally'… 'l'll have what she's having?' Our guide told us that on the occasion of the Queen Mother's 100th birthday, she must have cycled up the half-mile driveway about 20 times. (The postmistress, that is, *not* the Queen Mother).

The following morning, we caught the bus to John O'Groats, named after a 16th Century Dutch immigrant, Jan de Groot, who operated the ferry to Orkney. We posed for the obligatory photo in front of the famous signpost, which was installed in 1964 as a visitor attraction run by a Cornish photography company to match its counterpart at Land's End, 874 miles away.

There is a small campsite a hundred yards from the signpost, a gift shop, restaurants and a compact, picturesque harbour. We bought tickets for the ferry to Orkney and also a guided tour. After a 50-minute crossing on the Pentland Venture, we were met by a guide to take us on a coach tour. We stopped in Kirkwall, the main town of Orkney and visited the impressive 12th Century Cathedral of St Magnus.

Standing Stones and Sagas

Orkney is a rugged, mysterious group of islands which are gradually unearthing more of its secrets. The Orkneyinga Saga, written in Iceland in the 13th Century, tells us it was once the most southerly of Norse territory. We visited a pub with stories written on its walls of monsters, villains and heroes. Plenty to read while enjoying a pint. When the Vikings arrived in the 8th Century, they found evidence of earlier ancient people.

The landscape is like a sculpture park of standing stones, pre-dating Stonehenge in England. Archaeologists have suggested that Orkney could have been the birth of the era of Stone Age building, of which there are hundreds of examples throughout Britain and Ireland. Stone Age and subsequent prehistoric epochs will be mentioned often during our travels. In very simple terms, they are as follows: The Stone Age was a period when, would you believe, stones were used for everything, including cutting and making fires. The earliest evidence of stone tools is 2.6 million years ago. This era lasted till around 3,300 BC when the Bronze Age began, followed by the Neolithic (New Stone Era) when technology improved tools. Then Iron Age began around 1200 BC, and the rest, as they say, is pre-history.

Orkney has not had forests due to the climate, and consequently, stone was the only alternative. A burial mound called Maes Howe has multi-stone-built chambers and is aligned so that the setting sun at the winter solstice sends a shaft of light along the narrow entrance corridor. Pure Indiana Jones.

The Stones of Stenness and the famous Ring of Brodgar date back 5,000 years and command a spectacular setting on a peninsula surrounded by water. The route between them appears to have been a processional way, with ceremonies possibly related to the seasons using the circles as observatories. The stones were brought from various local sites, and each could have been donated and named after individual settlements, an early form of sponsorship. I hope not because one of the towns has the unfortunate name of Twatt. Somehow, I don't think an erection called the Twatt standing stone quite works.

The Neolithic settlement of Skara Brae is thought to pre-date the pyramids of Egypt. It has been buried under sand at the coast for thousands of years and was only uncovered by a severe storm in 1850. It is a stone-built warren of eight interlinked houses. The narrow tunnels linking them were winding to protect against fierce winds, and the undulating hobbit-like turfed roofs provided insulation against the unforgiving climate. They were lit by oil lamps, and they actually had indoor plumbing and inside toilets, a mere 5,000 years before the western world! The furniture is all made of slabs of stone: chairs, tables, kitchens, beds and even a dressing table. Personally, I think the Vikings must have got a glimpse of all this flat-pack furniture and returned to Sweden to start IKEA.

Scapa Flow is quite an attraction due to rusting, half-sunken ships. It isn't a bay, but a natural sheltered harbour surrounded by several islands, and it has an interesting war-time history. At the end of the First World War, German ships were scuttled and sank in Scapa Flow. It was a deliberate act, not by the British, but by the Germans themselves. While peace talks continued in Paris, the defeated German fleet was instructed to sail to Scapa Flow and drop anchor. They were basically prisoners of war held on their own ships, and boredom and even mutiny was in the air. The head of the German Navy, Admiral Von Reuter, sent orders that the fleet should be sabotaged and the sailors abandon ship. Over the years, some were raised and salvaged, while locals stripped what they could for scrap-metal. The artificial reefs became popular with divers, and it attracted some tourism. In fact, it created work and, in some ways, helped Orkney through the depression years.

During the Second World War, the British Fleet was based at Scapa Flow and one entrance was protected by the sunken German ships. However, it had been symbolic to the Germans since 1918, and in 1939, a U-Boat commanded by Prien found a way through the wrecks and torpedoed some of the fleet. Winston Churchill ordered defences to be improved and built extra causeways, The Churchill Barriers. U-Boat Commander Prien continued to cause further mayhem elsewhere before a depth charge finally got him. Churchill actually praised his bravery.

Back at John O'Groats, we caught the bus home to BBKing. Since we stepped off right outside the Gin Distillery Pub, we were drawn in for a drink. It would have been rude not to.

The following morning, the drive south along the east coast required intense concentration due to the volume and *speed* of traffic. The ubiquitous white-van-man seemed intent on committing suicide over the cliffs, while juggernauts gave the impression that the Scottish 500 is a massive hindrance. More than once, I had one right up my backside as if I had stepped back into 'Duel'.

By chance, we came upon a trout farm and pulled over for a break. We were surprised at the number of cars, and photographers with long-lens cameras mounted on tripods. I didn't realise that trout were so interesting. Then the focus of attention came into view. A magnificent Osprey (a.k.a. Sea Eagle) swept majestically overhead, showed off some acrobatic swirls, as if to entertain the crowd, then swooped to catch a trout with its lethal talons. As it flew away, I swear it performed triumphant wing tilts, like a Spitfire pilot. Many of the photos will probably appear in glossy country magazines. I asked the owner why he didn't have nets to protect the expensive trout. He said that the donations by visitors more than make up the difference, and the Osprey comes every day at the same time.

Wick

We stopped in Wick for a break and a supermarket shop. Wick is another town with a very strong Viking heritage, Vik in Old Norse meaning Bay. The town has a unique claim to fame, recognized in the Guinness Book of Records:

Trivia Alert…Ebenezer Place, at 6ft 9in, is the shortest street in the world.

The great Scottish engineer Thomas Telford enhanced the prosperity of Wick by extending the harbour, and he is remembered in the names of buildings and a street. Here's an interesting story we picked up in Wick. In the 1920s, local fishermen consumed copious volumes of whisky, resulting in drunkenness and trouble. The council introduced prohibition in 1922 and closed 40 pubs and the distillery. Illegal drinking dens sprang up called shebeens. Doctors prescribed alcohol for all kinds of ailments, and restaurants served alcohol in tea pots. More tea vicar?

Brora

We continued through some pretty coastal towns, including Ubster, Berriedale and Helmsdale, to our next caravan site at Brora. The name sounds more like a Pacific Island, and the turquoise blue sea and clear sky reinforced this comparison. The campsite was at the edge of a links golf course, with access to the beautiful beach. As we walked into the quiet village and the compact fishing harbour, the '500' signs were common. The main feature was a war memorial castellated clock tower at the side of the bridge over the River Brora. A major local attraction is Dunrobin Castle, which sounds like the name a retired burglar would give to his house. It is the family seat of Clan Sutherland and was designed by Charles Barry in the 19th century in the Scottish Baronial style. We were getting 'castle fatigue', so we didn't go in, but we walked around the formal gardens and watched a falconry display.

Inverness

We continued our drive south towards Inverness on the busy A9, which took us across bridge over Dornach Firth and Cromarty Firth. As we came off the bridge over the Moray Firth, we had an aerial view of the Inverness Caledonia Thistle football club. We arrived at the Culloden Moor Caravan site, set up our pitch, and relaxed for the rest of the day.

The bus stop for Inverness was conveniently situated in front of the site. Inverness simply means 'mouth of the River Ness', and it is the most northerly city in the UK. It has rich architectural detail with neo-classical Greek columns alongside Victorian Baroque-revival buildings. There are lots of lively pubs, and I was particularly impressed with the Hootananny Bar, which showcased live Scottish music.

We walked up to the castle, which was built in red sandstone in 1836, and there is a statue of Flora MacDonald, who, as we know from the Jac-o-Bite restaurant, helped Charles Edward Stuart (the Bonnie Prince himself) escapes after the Battle of Culloden.

Battle of Culloden

From the caravan park, it was just a 30-minute walk to Culloden Moor, where we joined a guided tour of the battlefield.

There had been several Jacobite uprisings over previous years, culminating in The Battle of Culloden in 1746. The Jacobite Army, led by Bonnie Prince Charlie, the son of the exiled King James II, met the British Redcoats led by the Duke of Cumberland, son of the Hanoverian King George II.

Trivia Alert... Our guide told us that the most common question she is asked is why were they called Jacobites. The simple answer is that Jacobus is Latin for James, and the Jacobite Rebellion was an attempt to restore James II to the throne.

To put this into a very brief historical context, James II had converted to Catholicism, and Protestants invited Dutchman Prince William of Orange and his wife Mary (the daughter of James II) to invade, which became known as the Glorious Revolution of 1688. James escaped to Ireland, but eventually, William defeated him at the Battle of the Boyne in 1690. William and Mary were crowned joint monarchs; the only time this has happened in British history since it is usually a monarch and consort.

Amazingly, the Battle of Culloden lasted barely one hour as the Jacobites were bogged down and bombarded by the Redcoats' canons. I was surprised to learn that the battle wasn't quite so simple as England versus Scotland. One-third of the Government troops were Scottish, and there were English on the Jacobite side. Famously, Charles Edward Stewart escaped to the Highlands and was helped by supporters along the way. As mentioned earlier, disguised as a maid, he was taken by Flora MacDonald 'Over the sea to Skye', from where he escaped to France.

At Culloden Moor, there are mass graves marked by the names of the clans rather than individuals. Astonishingly, it has not been designated as an *official* war grave. One marker was for Clan Fraser, which put me in mind of the television time-traveller series Outlander. The fictitious Jamie Fraser was warned by his wife not to go to Culloden because, being from the future, she already knew the outcome. He survived the massacre, of course, probably because another series had been commissioned.

The visitors' centre is light and modern with a well-designed and informative exhibition and an excellent restaurant.

Nessie

No tour of Scotland would be complete without a visit to its most famous resident, Nessie. Leaving Inverness, we took the A82 along the north shore of Loch Ness to Urquhart Castle. If prehistoric monsters were to have survived the mass extinction of 65 million years ago, there would be no better place to hide than Loch Ness. It is 22 miles long, 1 mile wide and 754 feet deep, with very dark water caused by the high content of peat.

The spectacular mountains provide a stunning backdrop, while the ruins of Urquhart Castle create a mysterious, timeless atmosphere. We parked the motorhome at a Lakeside Hotel, and in the hotel grounds was a model of Nessie, which looked more like Fred Flintstone's pet Dino the Dinosaur. Personally, I think something must have got lost in translation when ordering the model. The manager probably asked for a Pleistocene monster, but whoever took the order must have thought he said plasticine. So, instead of a Pleistocene monster, they ended up with a plasticine monstrosity. No-one seemed too bothered, considering the number of people having photographs taken in front of it.

I refer to monsters in the plural because there needs to be a breeding colony to have survived millions of years, and Adrien Shine of the Loch Ness Project has analysed evidence from a scientific point of view. He estimates that 30 to 40 creatures would be needed to maintain a population and avoid extinction, but there is only enough food available to sustain about 10. The very dark water prevents sunlight from penetrating deep enough for microscopic algae and plankton to thrive as food for fish, which becomes food for Nessie's family. I have seen photographs of Adrien Shine, and he looks born to this lifestyle. His luxuriant long grey hair and flowing grey beard frame a face etched with character and intelligence. He looks like the model for a marble sculpture by Michelangelo of an Old Testament Prophet.

There have been reported sightings of the monster for over an incredible 1,400 years since St Columba, a monk from Ireland, first saw a sea serpent in the year 565AD. In the 1970s, the American Academy of Science Expedition published murky underwater photographs of a flipper, body, neck and head. This was dismissed by 'experts', but over 1000 eyewitnesses over the years can't *all* be wrong. They *must* have seen something. On the other hand, prehistoric long-extinct creatures don't just reappear out of the blue, or the brown in this case. Or do they? In 1938, off the coast of South Africa, a silicanthe fish, believed to have been extinct for 80 million years, was caught live and kicking. I bet that was the first time a fisherman has said to his mate, 'We're gonna need a bigger boat.'

Many eyewitnesses can be explained away and discounted, but some accounts seem plausible. For example, David Monroe, an intelligent, articulate man, gave a highly credible account of his close encounter. Oh, by the way, did I mention his profession? He just happened to be the owner of a hotel on the banks of Loch Ness.

Other explanations have included wakes from boats, flocks of birds on the water, massive fish, and seismic activity creating underwater wave activity, which surfaces dramatically. Another candidate is the giant fish, the Baltic Sturgeon. What could be more appropriate than having a Loch Ness monster with the same name as a former Scotland First Minister, Nicola? Her predecessor was Alex Salmon, so by the time you read this, the next one could be Captain Haddock. Just a thought.

The most famous image of Nessie is the 'Surgeon's Photograph.' It was taken in 1934 and became a world-wide sensation. It was taken by the eminent Doctor Wilson, whose word could not be questioned. Over the next 50 years, this became one of the most famous photographs of all time until it was revealed to be a hoax. It was perpetrated by a big-game hunter called Marmaduke Weatherell, who launched a 2-foot model made by his son. He took photographs of it and persuaded Dr. Wilson to claim that they were his to add authenticity, such was the social standing of a doctor in the 1930s.

Weatherell's son revealed the true story 50 years later, and the plot thickens. A year before the photo, Marmaduke had been hired by the Daily Mail Newspaper to search for proof of the Loch Ness monster. Within an unbelievably short period of time, he found a footprint and made a plaster cast of it, which was sent to the Natural History Museum in London for analysis by world-renowned experts.

However, the report announced that it was, wait for it, a hippopotamus! Now, 1 will concede that hippos are excellent swimmers; they are, after all, called the water horse, but 1 can't imagine them roaming in Scotland and going for a dip in Loch Ness. Weatherell had used a souvenir from his days of big game hunting in Africa to create a footprint. It was a silver ashtray with a hippo's foot base. How any supposedly sane and intelligent person thought he could con archaeologists and historians at the British Museum with a hippopotamus ash tray is not just bizarre; it's surreal. He was disgraced and ridiculed, but Marmaduke was now out for revenge and went on to create one of the greatest hoaxes in history.

In the 1930s, monster stories were all the rage in books and movies. When the Fay Wray movie King Kong was released, it was a massive (monster) hit. There was a scene in which Kong fought a dinosaur, and the special effects, for the 1930s, were frightening. A couple on a motoring holiday stopped abruptly and watched in terror as the Loch Ness Monster crossed the road up ahead. When asked to draw what he had seen, the driver produced an image *remarkably* similar to what he had seen at the cinema. In reality, it was probably a Hippo Mac Potamus.

In 2023, an Irish Nessie hunter with the improbable name of Eoin O' Faodhagain claimed he had webcam footage of the monster and made the profound announcement, 'Nessie might not be alone.' Has he not been paying attention? Mr O' Faodhagain's webcam footage was taken near Fort Augustus on the southern shore.

Quote: *'The calm conditions and clear evening colours of the surrounding landscape were picturesque, the only thing missing was the Loch Ness Monster, and up she popped.'* How very obliging of her. By the way, the webcam used by Eoin is owned by a company called V.I.L.N., which stands for, get this, Visit Inverness Loch Ness.

So, the myth and legend of the Loch Ness monster has endured all these centuries. Begun by St. Columba, it's a mystery that even Lieutenant Columbo would struggle to solve.

Huntly

We drove back along Loch Ness, hoping that Nessie would pop up and wave goodbye, and from Inverness, we continued east via Nairn,

Elgin and Keith towards our next site at Huntly Castle Park, a short walk from the village of Huntly. We spent an interesting couple of hours exploring the 14th Century castle, which was the ancestral home of the Chief of the Clan Gordon, the Earl of Huntly. It is a relatively small, homely castle, and we were most fascinated by the many intricately carved stone fireplaces.

Stonehaven

We continued south along the coast to Stonehaven. The Queen Elizabeth Caravan Park is on the sea front, adjacent to an Art Deco outdoor swimming pool, a popular holiday centre. The harbour is as impressive as any we have seen. It was very pleasant to sit on the harbour wall opposite the Ship Inn, enjoying a drink in the sunshine taking in harbour life.

From the harbour, we climbed the steep steps up the hillside towards Dunnottar Castle, which in Scottish Gaelic means 'fort on the shelving slope.' Something of an understatement since it is located on a sensational, rocky cliff-top outcrop, with crashing waves adding to the dramatic atmosphere. It was one of the most impregnable castles in Britain. During the English Civil War, The Honours of Scotland (the Scottish Crown Jewels) were taken there to keep them from falling into the hands of Oliver Cromwell.

Stonehaven has a unique claim to fame: it is the home of the Scottish gastronomic delicacy… the deep-fried, battered Mars Bar. The sign over the Carron Fish Bar must have been photographed more times than Dunnottar Castle.

The Granite City

We took the bus into Aberdeen, which lives up to its name of the Granite City. Union Street is dominated by an imposing town hall with its impressive clock tower. The solid grey buildings are a juxtaposition of architectural styles: Scottish cone-shaped turrets, Victorian Baroque revival and Graeco-Roman fluted columns. All provide a dramatic backdrop to a thriving city with up-market shops.

We had lunch at the Wild Boar, a 17th Century pub which I'm sure claimed to be the oldest in Scotland.

Up your Kilt

As we sat at the bus stop a wedding reception close by was in full swing with a band playing and confetti all over the pavement. Guests holding drinks began to spill out in more ways than one since some looked the worse for wear. Although slightly dishevelled, the principal group of, presumably, the groom, best man and ushers looked very impressive in their formal Scottish outfits, tartan jackets with sprigs of heather, neckwear of frills, sporran, tartan socks and kilts. The bridesmaids wore beautiful peach satin dresses.

We became aware that everything wasn't quite what it seemed. Voices got louder, and a commotion started. Some pushing and shoving occurred, but it didn't look as though it was going to escalate into a brawl because, amongst some harsh words and crying, we could also hear laughter.

One of the guests sauntered unsteadily in our direction. With a swing of his kilt and an off-centre sporran, he punctuated his stagger with an occasional swig of whisky. Instinctively, we kept our heads down to avoid a 'What are you looking at?' confrontation. He sat next to us and started to giggle between hiccups. He nudged me and asked, "Would ye like a wee dram?"

"No thanks. You look as though you're all having a good time," I said, hoping he would enlighten us.

"Man, you wouldn't believe it," he said, smiling broadly.

"Believe what?"

He leaned forward and asked Norma, "Have you ever wondered if a Scotsman wears anything under his kilt?"

"Can't say I have," she answered calmly, hoping we weren't about to witness a drunken flashing.

"Well, the bride, my sister, has just found out the hard way?"

"Hard way?" I asked, hoping it was just an unfortunate turn of phrase.

"Yes. She was still in her white wedding dress in the dining room, joking around. She asked the Best Man if he wore underwear and pretended to lift up his kilt. He sat on her knee and gyrated with a 'wey hey hey' as everyone laughed. When he stood up, she found the answer to her question. Without putting too fine a point on it, he had left a skid mark on her dress. It wasn't so much satin as sat on. Some laughed. Some gasped. She screamed. The groom angrily pushed the Best Man, who happened to be his brother, but eventually, most people laughed… Except my sister. At least she was on her way to her room to get changed for the evening reception".

I laughed at the story, but Norma put her hand to her face in horror.

"Anyway, I'd better get back. Nice talking to you. Cheers," he said, raising his glass ceremoniously as if proposing a toast.

"Cheers," I responded, raising my imaginary glass, "Bottoms-up."

Cow Pie On the Menu

From Stonehaven, we took the A92 south along the rocky coastal formations from Dunnottar Castle, passed Trelong Bay and Bervie Bay, through Montrose and Arbroath to our campsite near Dundee, our final destination in Scotland. Located on the north bank of the Firth of Tay, Scotland's longest river, Dundee is a typical Scottish city of solid, grand Victorian buildings embellished with Classical columns. As with many other cities, the ornate architecture is symbolic of the wealth and grandeur due to the Industrial Revolution. A major landmark is the 15th Century Tower of St. Mary, known as The Steeple Church. Along its perimeter wall there is a row of penguin sculptures, the mascots of the city. Others are around the town. This is because sailors from Dundee were aboard The Discovery on an expedition to Antarctica in 1901 and made the first sightings of Emperor Penguins.

Throughout Dundee, there are over 500 pieces of public art, including fountains, statues and sculptures. There is Queen Victoria and Robert Burns, but one of the most popular is, wait for it... Desperate Dan. Why? The Dandy Comic was published in Dundee in 1937. There is also a sculpture of a Polar Bear attacking a man. I assumed this was a reference to Arctic adventures, but it was an incident which actually happened in Dundee. A Polar Bear was brought as a novelty on exhibition, but it escaped and ran amok. It went into a shop (possibly a china shop) but calmed down as it became fascinated by its own reflection. Its handlers captured it, but it sounds to me more like a job for Desperate Dan.

We went into Henry's Coffee House on Seagate and I looked for cow pie on the menu. We settled for Dundee Cake to add to our foodie list.

We left Dundee via the Tay Bridge and followed the A92 south around Dunfermline and over the Firth of Forth via the Queensferry Crossing. We had completed the full circle of Scotland and the first phase of our odyssey. We bypassed Edinburgh and followed the coastal route towards England and looked back on our fantastic experiences around Scotland.

Quote: *'With the possible exception of Classical Greece, no small country in the world has contributed more than Scotland to the development and well-being of mankind.'* Winston Churchill.

In the fields of engineering, science, medicine and literature, what Scotland has achieved is incredible. It's well known the John Logi Baird invented the television (what did he watch?) and Alexander Graham Bell invented the telephone (who did he call?) Originally, he used the naval term 'Ahoy' to answer, but his friend Thomas Edison, who invented the lightbulb, suggested a made-up word 'Hello' instead. Was this the very first 'lightbulb' moment? Civil Engineer Thomas Telford built the Caledonian Canal through the Great Glen. James Watt developed the steam engine and his name is immortalised as a unit of power. Alexander Fleming discovered penicillin (antibiotics). In a good year, John Dunlop invented pneumatic tyres. These are just a few of the better-known examples, but the list seems endless: The mackintosh, fingerprinting, insulin, typhoid vaccine, hypodermic syringe, refrigerator, general anaesthetic, the SAS, Chicken Tikka Masala and of course, whisky. I'll stop there otherwise it will end up sounding like Billy Joel's 'We Didn't Start the Fire'.

You might have noticed that some quintessentially Scottish items are conspicuous by their absence, namely haggis, kilts, bagpipes, and tartan. That's because *none* are Scottish. Haggis dates back to ancient Rome; kilts were invented in Ireland (the word kilt is of Viking origin), tartans date from Bronze Age Europe, and bagpipes are from ancient central Asia. How about this one: in 1893, the electric toaster was invented by Alan McMaster. Now, here's the thing: sliced bread wasn't invented till 1928. Now I know what was the best thing *before* sliced bread.

A common misapprehension is that the flushing toilet was invented by Thomas Crapper, but he was actually a manufacturer. The flushing, re-filling porcelain toilet with an S-bend was invented by Alexander Cumming in Edinburgh in 1775. Crapper's name lives on as, for example, 'crapping in the bathroom' when it should really be Cumming. On second thoughts, perhaps not.

Let's move on from toilets and consider Scotland's rich literary heritage. We saw Sir Walter Scott's statue and monument in Edinburgh, and he is regarded as the father of the Romantic novel: Rob Roy, Ivanhoe. JM Barrie created Peter Pan in 1904 and royalties still support Great Ormond Street Children's Hospital in London. Robert Louis Stevenson created Dr Jekyll and Mr Hyde and Treasure Island; Arthur Conan Doyle wrote the Sherlock Holmes series and Lost World. Robbie Burns wrote Auld Lang's Syne and Tam o' Shanter, and we mustn't leave out JK Rowling's Harry Potter books. It has been said that she is responsible for re-engaging children with the joy of reading, a significant achievement.

The general impression while travelling was that the people of Scotland have a strong national pride, and the flag of St Andrew was everywhere. We discovered the heroic exploits of William Wallace in his battles against the English. And yet, despite all that, the people of Scotland had the chance in 2014 to vote for independence and voted against it. William Wallace must have been spinning in his grave, or should that be graves, plural since he was hung, drawn and quartered.

Some of our Scottish friends voted for independence, and early exit-polls suggested victory. They began to celebrate exuberantly in the pub only to be disappointed. A clear case of premature Jockulation.

Phase Two: ENGLAND

Berwick-Upon-Tweed

England's most northerly town, Berwick-upon-Tweed, must be on wheels because it has alternated between England and Scotland about 15 times over centuries due to continuous wars. As we arrived at the farm campsite we thought we had driven into a rusting junk yard. I was about to blame the satnav until we saw a sign advertising an 'antique' farm. A masterstroke of marketing. Put dilapidated machinery in a field, and the public will pay for the privilege of viewing them, including me. I had an artistic hour photographing tractors, ploughs, harvesters, and unidentifiable medieval-looking implements.

Confusingly, Berwick is the only English football team to play in Scottish leagues, but we got certain proof that the town had not been transferred to Scotland overnight because our OAP passes were accepted on the bus. The journey of about 5 miles into town was through beautiful green countryside.

Berwick-upon-Tweed, in common with many places in the northeast, is a hidden gem. A charming, picturesque town with many Georgian buildings enclosed by Elizabethan town walls. The beautiful setting at the mouth of the river is enhanced and overlooked by a 13th Century castle. We went for a sunny stroll along the river under the spectacular stone, multi-arched Bridge designed by Robert Stephenson and opened in 1847.

Like many towns that adopt famous celebrities, Berwick-upon-Tweed has numerous references to the artist LS Lowry. He is mainly associated with his native industrialised north west, but he also loved Berwick-upon-Tweed, where he regularly went on holiday. Lawrence Stephen Lowry is, of course, associated with his trademark figures, which became the inspiration for the UK number 1 hit record 'Matchstick Men and Matchstick Cats and Dogs,' by Brian and Michael. He worked as a rent collector in the Salford area, often stopping to make drawings in his sketchpad. There were probably a few twitching curtains as anxious tenants wondered what he was up to! In Berwick-upon-Tweed, there is a Lowry Trail which follows in his footsteps. Information boards help the viewer to compare the painting with the actual view. One of Lowry's eccentricities was that he would wear a suit and tie when painting, totally splattered in paint. He looked as though he had just met Jackson Pollock, or perhaps he had been out to lunch fighting off thieving seagulls at a seafront fish and chip shop.

An interesting anecdote is that Lowry's epiphany moment, the birth of his unique style, was in front of the Acme Company's Spinning Mill in Pendlebury, Lancashire. He watched, quote: 'Hundreds of little pinched figures, heads bent down, pouring out after a shift.' Acme? The only time I've seen that name is in cartoons. I must revisit the painting to see if there is a matchstick Coyote chasing a matchstick Road Runner… beep, beep.

Miracles, Manuscripts ... Mayhem

A short drive down the coastal A1 took us to Holy Island, where Lindisfarne Castle sits on an extinct volcanic crag. We drove along a causeway at low tide and it was important for us to take careful note of the crossing times, especially when driving a motorhome containing all our worldly goods. Many have foolishly taken a chance, and we saw photographs of vehicles almost totally submerged many a flooded carburettor. The Island is only about 4 square miles in area and has a permanent population of 200.

We arrived at a car park near to Lindisfarne village. There is a statue of St. Aidan, the Irish Monk who founded the Priory in 634AD to spread Christianity. The Vikings invaded in 793AD and killed monks and stole treasures. The monks finally decided to leave, and they took with them the coffin of St. Cuthbert, an earlier Bishop. When he was exhumed, the coffin was opened to reveal a body that had not decayed. This was interpreted as a miracle and a sign of Saintliness and, consequently, a place of Pilgrimage. Today, the 11th Century St. Mary's Church stands on the site of the original wooden priory. A dramatic sculpture inside depicts six hooded monks carrying the coffin of St. Cuthbert. It is roughly hewn from solid oak beams, a modern piece with a medieval feel. The church also houses a copy of the famous Lindisfarne Gospel illuminated manuscript.

Lindisfarne Castle is a short walk away and provided us with panoramic photo opportunities, including a view of Banburgh Castle across the sea, like a giant sandcastle on the beach. Back in the village are stone cottages, shops, gift shops and cafés. We visited St. Aidan's Winery for Mead, a medieval drink made from wine and honey, known as 'The Nectar of the Gods'. To continue our theme of sampling locally produced food and drink, we couldn't resist The Holy Island Gin Distillery, whose history goes way, way back to the year... 2016. It was time to get back to BBKing before high tide I can't remember a visit where I've looked at my watch quite so often.

Viking Legacy

The invasion of Lindisfarne marks the beginning of the Viking era, when the north became known as Danelaw and the Vikings left a legacy in names and language. There are about 1,000 words in the English language which are derived from the Vikings, but don't worry, I'm not going to list them. A notable example is in the northeast, where children are referred to as bairns. Anyone with a surname ending in 'son', meaning son of, as in, for example, Johnson or Harrison, will have Scandinavian heritage in their DNA and possibly a face like a Norse. Towns ending in borough, such as Scarborough, refer to a fortress, while those ending in Thorpe, for example, Scunthorpe refer to a farm. The Vikings even gave us days of the week: Thursday (Thor's day) and Wednesday (Odin's day). Many street names, particularly in the north east, have the suffix gate, which in Old Norse means street. A modern twist to this is that, since the Watergate political scandal in Washington in the 1970s, 'gate' has been cobbled on to the end of anything with a whiff of controversy. The latest, at the time of writing, is Partygate, referring to goings-on in Downing Street during the Covid lockdown.

Fortress Northumbria

Just a few miles down the coast is Bamburgh Castle, which looks exactly like a castle should be: a giant square keep, as if moulded from a child's bucket, standing on a rocky outcrop looking out over the North Sea. There are many castles along this coastline, and the historic timeline seems to follow the same pattern: Original location of a 5th Century Celtic Fort, control alternated between Anglo Saxons and Britons, inevitable destruction by the Vikings (994AD in this case) and rebuilt by the Normans. At the entrance is a scale model of the castle, which illustrates an overview of the Keep and outer walls. The King's Hall has a magnificent wooden ceiling, while state rooms are furnished with antiques, artefacts, and tapestries. We climbed the stone staircase to the armoury to view an exhibition of weapons: suits of armour, pikes, muskets and a 17th Century Flemish crossbow. The kitchen was easily large enough to service a castle of this size, with tiles, parquet floor and a range. We finished in the dungeon, which was well-presented with atmospheric mood lighting, mannequins chained up in chains and a chamber of horrors. It was like a film set, which is appropriate since Banburgh Castle has been used as a location for many movies and television series. The time-travel series Outlander, the movies Macbeth, Indiana Jones and Robin Hood. The village of Bamburgh has quaint cottages and shops. The Castle overlooks a golf course and a manicured cricket pitch, providing the most dramatic backdrop.

Harry Hotspur

To continue the theme of movie locations, our next stop was Alnwick Castle, just south of Bamburgh. Alnwick has been used over 40 times for filming television series and films, including Star Trek, Robin Hood Prince of Thieves, Black Adder, Elizabeth starring Kate Blanchett, and Downton Abbey. Inside its walls, Joan of Arc was burned at the stake in the Hollow Crown, and a Quidditch Match at Harry Potter's school of Hogwarts took place there. Indeed, would you believe it, we were greeted with witches giving out brooms and invited to join the 'how-to-mount-a-broom' class.

Alnwick is the second largest inhabited castle in England, after Windsor. Building started in 1086 by the Normans and was acquired by the Percy family in 1309 to control the border skirmishers with Scotland. Inside the castle grounds, there is an impressive equestrian statue of the most famous member of the family, Henry Percy. Due to his lightening quick raids against them, the Scots nicknamed him Harry Hotspur, and his fame has been kept alive in Shakespeare plays. Also, his nickname has been adopted by Tottenham Hotspur football club because Henry's descendants had close connections with the Tottenham area, owning land around the marshes. When the club was founded in 1882, they played matches there before moving to White Hart Lane. To avoid castle overkill, I don't need to describe such a well-recorded building, and the interior has all the trappings of furniture, tapestry, state rooms and so on.

The market town of Alnwick benefits greatly from tourism, and not surprisingly, there stands a metal sculpture of Hotspur in full armour brandishing a sword ready for combat.

Newcastle

We were looking forward to visiting the Newcastle area because we were staying with our friends Keith and Sue, which meant the luxury of a proper bed! We timed it to coincide with Sue's birthday barbeque. Keith was a mechanic with his own garage, so he could arrange a service, habitation service and an MOT certificate for the motorhome while chauffeuring us around as our guide.

They live in the small seaside village of Cullercoats north of the River Tyne, nestled between Whitley Bay and Tynemouth. The three practically fuse into one and the renovated promenade evokes memories of the heyday of the 1920s.

St. Mary's Lighthouse to the north is a popular tourist attraction. We strolled along the sea front of open lawns and elegant housing to Whitley Bay. A prominent landmark is the gleaming dome of the Spanish City, a white building reminiscent of an Eastern Citadel or a hill-top Spanish village. It opened in 1910 and included a concert hall, shops and arcades. Gradually, it fell into disrepair and the onset of cheap foreign holidays in the 1960s, ironically to Spain, made matters worse. It had been renovated and the whole area has regenerated with a vibrant holiday atmosphere. The town was originally called Whitley after a local Lord who owned the land. However, it was often confused with Whitby, and mail and parcel deliveries often went astray. The final straw was when one particular delivery arrived at Whitby instead of Whitley. It was a dead body. So that's someone who *really was* late for his own funeral. Bay was added to give the town a new identity.

As we approached Cullercoats, the two-mile beach met a rocky outcrop and cliffs, creating a natural sea pool ideal for swimming. We continued to the promenade and arrived at the gorgeous village of Tynemouth, which, more than once, has been voted the best seaside village in Britain. If an artist or architect tried to dream up an ideal, aesthetic fantasy village, Tynemouth would be the result. A Victorian clock tower looks down Front Street of Victorian and Georgian architecture with countless pubs, cafés and shops. It leads to a ruined 7th Century Benedict Priory and Castle standing on a promontory overlooking King Edward's Bay and the North Sea. Three of the early Kings of Northumbria had their courts and are buried there, commemorated by the three crowns on Tynemouth's coat of arms. As we have seen travelling down the coast, the Vikings inevitably plundered the Priory.

We ended a fabulous day with a pub crawl and a great meal at a Tynemouth restaurant. Cullercoats does have a claim to fame. The children's television series 'Supergran' was filmed there! Back home, Keith put on a DVD of an episode of Supergran. Her car had broken down and a mechanic arrived in his pick-up truck. You've guessed it; it was a very young Keith. We roared with laughter.

"One of the TV production team came into the garage and asked if anyone would like to appear in Supergran. We thought he'd escaped from an institution," explained Keith proudly.

The following morning, the four of us set off to explore Newcastle, the city of Geordies. Why are the people of Newcastle known as Geordies? The term originates from the Jacobite Rebellion. Newcastle favoured King George II, hence the name Geordie.

The name given to the city is more straightforward. William the Conqueror built a new castle in the 11th Century over the site of a former Roman fort. The castle has the usual features of Norman architecture: a square keep, round arches with zig-zag style carving, surrounding moats and drawbridges. Later, it proved a strong defence against Scottish raids, and for 200 years from the 16th Century it was a prison. A fate worse than death, looking at the pits that housed prisoners.

The signature emblem of Newcastle is the famous Tyne Bridge. It was opened in 1928 by King George V and it's well known that it is the forerunner of the 1932 Sydney Harbour Bridge, nicknamed 'the Coathanger' by the Aussies. I didn't know that the Tyne Bridge design was from the Hell Gate Bridge in New York. Seven bridges span the Tyne, including the High-Level Bridge of 1829, the Swing Bridge and the pedestrian Millennium Bridge, which tilts to let vessels through. Just to show it's not just the Australians who can give nicknames to everything, this bridge is called 'The Blinking Eye.'

We walked across the Millennium Bridge to the former Baltic Flour Mill, now known as the Centre for Contemporary Arts. The building was originally used for storing grain and is now a modern, light, open space for exhibitions, including paintings, sculptures, and installations. One popular attraction is the guillemots nesting high-up along a ledge beneath the Baltic Flour Mill sign. Visitors can step on to a small outside platform on the 6th floor to look at these birds, oblivious to the gawping presence of humans. The birds probably think we are a peculiar species inhabiting this 'cliff face' alongside them.

Adjacent to the arts centre is the Gateshead Sage Music Centre. Glistening in the sunshine, it is a silver and glass rounded structure, like a folded-up Sydney Opera House, complementing its own 'Coathanger.'

The area is now known as the Baltic Quarter, and it is amazing how a run-down dockside area has been transformed into a cultural centre and tourist attraction. Back over the Millennium Bridge, the quayside has a lively collection of hotels, restaurants, bars and shops. Along the quayside are stylish yachts and pleasure boats where once commercial ships would load and unload cargo. Newcastle has a huge student population and the city buzzes with that unique University City ambience.

The city centre comprises solid, imposing Georgian buildings with all the usual embellishments of Greek columns, niches and porticos, the Theatre Royal of 1837 being an excellent example. Grey Street is a major thoroughfare, while on Blackett Street is the column of Grey's Monument dedicated to Lord Earl Grey, the Prime Minister who passed legislation to abolish slavery and child employment, but is best known today for tea.

Just Another Brick in The Wall

The following morning we said our goodbyes to our friends. We drove back to Newcastle and visited Segedunun, a Roman fort which protected the east end of Hadrian's Wall. It is a World Heritage Site and the museum displayed objects found during excavations along the wall, including evidence of everyday life plus weapons, tools and even a skull. We visited the museum of Antiquities and then on to Hadrian's Wall. It was begun in 122AD at Wallsend on the Tyne and stretches 74 miles to the Solway Firth on the Irish Sea.

We drove inland to a parking place and set off to explore along the wall. There are some informative displays explaining various ruins along the way. The wall was built as protection against invasion by northern tribes, the Picts in particular. Unlike the Great Wall of China, where some slave labour was used, Hadrian's Wall was actually built by soldiers who had received training in such trades as stone masonry, building and surveying. From inscriptions on tablets, we know some of their names and which legions were employed. The first archaeological digs along the wall only began in Victorian times, and, amazingly, only 1% has been excavated. Many more secrets are waiting to be unearthed.

Hadrian decreed that 17 forts and 37-mile castles should be along the wall. These accommodated soldiers, and small settlements grew up around them with bath houses and shops.

We met a group of young people who were carrying out an excavation. They were York University students who had been permitted to examine this particular section.

The area was roped, and neat trenches had begun. A student came over excitedly and said to her tutor, 'I've just found this.' It was a piece of blue glass, probably a perfume bottle. We were strangely delighted to have been present when something from 2000 years ago was uncovered for the first time.

The wall was built along an existing road, which made it easier transferring stone from quarries and deliver supplies. Not all Romans were from Rome. Legions comprised many nationalities from the Empire: North Africa, French, Spanish, Germanic and Hungarian. A multicultural, multi-lingual mix reflected in the artefacts discovered.

Wherever possible, the wall follows the ridges of steep-sided escarpments to provide extra defence. The Emperor had given instructions that arched gateways should be included every mile.

"Come and look at this one," suggested some students.

An archway wide enough for carts opened right onto a sheer drop. The lay of the land levelled off a couple of hundred yards on either side.

"Why didn't they put it over there?" I asked.

"Because this is exactly one mile from the last one, and would *you* disobey the Emperor of Rome?"

"Definitely not," I answered, "Especially if his name was Caligula!"

One of the most important sites along the wall is called Vindolanda, where many writings have been discovered. We were told that they are called Vindolanda Tablets.

"Vindolanda Tablets? Sounds like something you would take after an Indian curry," l said, thinking l was being devastatingly witty.

The rolling eyes and knowing smiles suggested they had heard that line before.

Angel of the North

Driving south, the famous sculpture The Angel of the North came into view. One of the best-known landmarks in Britain, it stands on a hilltop close to busy roads in Gateshead. We pulled over for a closer look. Designed by sculptor Anthony Gormley, it was manufactured at Hartlepool Steel Fabrications. Unveiled in 1998, it stands 66 feet tall and 177 feet wide. It has attracted a lot of criticism. The Gateshead Post newspaper featured a photo of it, comparing it to a very similar Nazi sculpture of the 1930s. It was deemed to be a dangerous driving distraction and a lightning conductor, and furthermore, it was feared that the 400-ton structure could topple in strong winds. Digital technology analysed wind flow so that it could withstand gales of 100mph. I hope so; otherwise, they will have to re-name it The Hang-Glider of the North; after all, it does have a wingspan of a Jumbo Jet.

Gormley has explained that from an early age, he has had an affinity with Guardian Angels, but he has described it as 'An ugly brute'. It has been compared to the Statue of Liberty in New York and

Christ the Redeemer in Rio; I have stood beneath both and felt they have meaning and personality. One of his most famous installations in Britain is called 'Another Place; the lonely figures looking out to sea on Crosby Beach in Liverpool. We will take a closer look when we arrive there on our tour.

Most of his statues, including the Angel of the North, are modelled from plaster casts of the artist's body. Anthony Gormley seems to have spent as much time swathed in bandages as Tutankhamun.

A phenomenon of recent years is that the nearby shrubbery and trees carry emotional messages of condolences or love pinned to the branches. Perhaps this is because of the Angel title, or it could be interpreted as a crucifix.

Durham

A short drive down the A1 (M) took us to our next stopover in Durham.

When we visited Holy Island, we learnt that the monks of Lindisfarne Priory had fled to escape the violent raids by the Vikings. They took with them the remains of St. Cuthbert, and Durham is where they ended up. The story goes that the monks saw an apparition of St. Cuthbert, which they interpreted as his wish to be laid to rest (again) there. He probably uttered those immortal words that every traveller has heard, 'Are we there yet?'

St. Cuthbert must have had a good knowledge of defence strategy because the site chosen is on a U-bend of the River Wear, which acts as a natural moat. The peninsula created is known as the Bailey, which is the outer area around a Castle. Now a World Heritage Site, Durham Cathedral and Durham Castle are adjacent on higher ground called Palace Green and Castle Green. The original monks were well aware that the 'Pilgrim business' was highly lucrative, and so it proved. They became extremely wealthy as pilgrims were encouraged to give generous donations. The magnificent Cathedral stands on the site of the original shrine to St. Cuthbert and is one of the great Norman buildings in Britain, an icon of the city with its central tower and two matching towers overlooking the Wear. Harry Potter must have loved the north east of England because the Cathedral's cloisters featured in the first two films. The Bishop's Throne called the Cathedra (from which the word Cathedral is derived), is on a high elevation. We were told that the first Bishop sent an envoy to Rome to check the height of the Pope's throne so that his could be even higher.

When the Cathedral was being built, the only known way to build an arch was the round arch. There are examples of typical Norman arches, with simple chevron and geometric carved decoration, supported by massive round columns. It was discovered that a pointed arch could be made higher, and crossing pointed arches became the standard structure of cathedral ceilings. All subsequent architecture followed this pattern, originating at Durham Cathedral. The interior is magnificent and awe-inspiring, and the organ of 1876 is split on either side of the choir to provide superb acoustics. An early example of stereo sound?

Trivia Alert... Here's something which might be of particular interest to American readers. Have you ever wondered why the American Flag comprises stars and stripes? We know that the red and white stripes represent the original states, and the white stars represent the present number. But why stars? Why stripes? They could be anything. Why not ships to illustrate the Pilgrim Fathers on the Mayflower? Or wavy blue lines to represent the Atlantic crossing? The permutations are endless. Here's the explanation. In the 15th Century, a man named John Washington was an important member of the church in Durham and the Benedictine Monastery in the area. Some of his family descendants moved to America, and eventually, one of the lines to be born was none other than George Washington himself. The Washington family crest is displayed in Durham Cathedral: Three White Stars over red horizontal stripes.

Today, believe it or not, the castle is actually owned by Durham University, and students live, eat, sleep and study inside a Medieval Castle. It put my own experience into perspective. When I went to Leeds University in 1970, they put me in a council flat in Hunslet. Great fun, though.

The city of Durham is relatively compact. Framwellgate is the oldest bridge, dating back to the 12th Century. It crosses the River Wear onto Silver Street, which gets its name from the silversmith shops or possibly a small mint. This took us up to the Market Place, which holds a weekly market dating back centuries. Durham thrived and prospered during the Industrial Revolution, and in 1920 approximately 170,000 miners worked in County Durham. The Miners' Gala has been held since 1870 and continues to this day. The Shakespeare Pub is another which claims to be the most haunted. One pub is the smallest gin bar in the world. It can hold 16 at a push literally, and what is it called? What else but... The Tin of Sardines.

Memory Lane

Another short run today to stay near The Beamish Museum, a superb re-creation of village streets from different eras. An omnibus with a spiral staircase takes visitors on a journey through time. The main village street seemed strangely familiar since it has been used as a film and TV location, one of the most notable being Downton Abbey. There was, of course, a pub, The Sun Inn where we had lunch and a beer.

"Is a pint still the original price?" I inquired, tongue-in-cheek.

"Of course, Sir, provided you can pay with Edwardian pennies and threepenny bits!"

I suspect it wasn't the first time the landlord had been asked that question.

Every building in the street had been constructed with meticulous attention to historical detail, and some were brought brick by brick from several locations in the Northeast. There is a photographer's studio, a tea room, a garage and a wrought iron bandstand in the park. In the shops, actors wore period costumes while serving in the confectioners and Herron's bakery. The giant toffee jars took us back to our childhood, but in the hardware store, l couldn't get the Two Ronnie's 'Four Candles' sketch out of my brain.

The railway station has a signal box, a traditional booking office, 1920s-style holiday posters and a map of the area as a tiled wall. A 1913 pit village has miners' cottages, a mine, coal machinery, a school, a church, a farm and an 1820s steam train. The latest attraction, which was under construction, is a 1950s street. As with the 1900s version, they are all replicas of actual buildings. It was fascinating to listen to a talk by one of the staff describing the research involved. Indeed, a Hairdressing Salon has been transported from Middlesborough, and we were told that former clients have visited and been amazed at the authenticity. Someone once coined the clever phrase, 'Nostalgia isn't what it used to be.' At Beamish, it hits the right note.

Continuing South, our next stopover was at Whitby at the edge of the North York Moors National Park. Driving past Hartlepool, I had a vague recollection of a story which I told to Norma.

During the Napoleonic Wars, a French Navy ship capsized off the coast near Hartlepool. The only survivor was the ship's mascot, a monkey amusingly dressed in a French sailor's uniform. The exhausted creature scrambled ashore and was captured by locals. The naive, simple souls, bless 'em, actually thought that he was an enemy sailor, jabbering away in what they thought was French. So what did they do? They arrested their prisoner of war and put him on trial. He was found guilty, sentenced to death, and the poor thing was executed by hanging.

Two hundred years later, supporters of West Hartlepool Football Club are taunted by rival fans with the chant, 'Who hanged the monkey?' You couldn't make it up.

We continued along the major roads, passing Stockton-on-Tees and Middlesbrough and followed the North Yorkshire and Cleveland Heritage coast to Whitby.

Dracula and Fish 'n' Chips

Whitby is famous for several things: Whitby Jet, kippers, Captain Cook, Dracula, the 199 steps leading up to the ruined Abbey, the Synod of Whitby, and, of course, fish and chips. It is quirky and quaint, with narrow cobbled streets and 18th Century fishermen's cottages on either side of the mouth of the River Esk. The ruined Whitby Abbey is an atmospheric backdrop as it overlooks the terracotta roofs of a beautiful town. Viking invaders destroyed an earlier monastery on the site, while the 13th century Abbey was left to decay following the dissolution of the monasteries by Henry VIII in 1538. The historically significant Synod of Whitby was held in the 7th century, which was a meeting which decided that England would follow Roman rather than Celtic religion.

The 13th Century St Mary's church stands adjacent, its graveyard providing inspiration for Abraham 'Bram' Stoker's Dracula. From 1890, Stoker enjoyed visiting Whitby on holiday, and Whitby adopted him. Victorian Gothic horror was popular then, and Stoker's novel Dracula interweaves facts with fiction. A Russian shipwreck had washed up on the beach at Whitby. It was called the Dimitry, and in the novel, it became the Demeter, which had sailed from Transylvania with Dracula on board. He turned himself into a big black dog and ran up the steps to the graveyard. There is a gravestone there with the name Mary Swales, which Stoker used as one of Count Dracula's early victims. Bram Stoker based his novel on Vlad Dracula, a 15th Century ruler of the Draculesti Dynasty in the Eastern European provinces of Wallachia and Transylvania. He acquired the intimidating name of The Impaler, and personally, I think the true story is far more terrifying than anything the fictitious Dracula got up to. Vlad's modus operandi was to impale victims on long poles inserted through the anus to exit through the mouth. During an invasion by the Ottoman Turks, which Dracula spoke of in the novel, soldiers came across a 'forest' of 20,000 impaled bodies. The shock and horror of seeing this vision from hell broke their spirit, and they retreated. Perhaps this was the origin of the Turkish kebab. From there, the legend of Dracula was born: crosses, fangs, wooden stakes, Bela Lugosi and Christopher Lee.

In the 1990s, the Goth community started an annual convention in Whitby, including exhibitions, fairs and parades. It wasn't taking place when we were there, but we saw plenty of photographs, the most dramatic being amongst the gravestones and in front of the Abbey.

"I don't' think we would have fitted in, do you?" I said to Norma.

"No, we'd have stood out like Brad and Janet in the Rocky Horror Show."

Back down in the town, we continued to explore the maze of alleyways called Ghauts, a name only used in Whitby, thought to be of Viking heritage. Incidentally, the name Whitby was given by the Vikings, meaning White Village, replacing the original Anglo-Saxon name of Streonshalh.

We visited a museum dedicated to Captain James Cook. He was probably the World's greatest navigator and cartographer, who charted a third of the world to a remarkable level of accuracy and probably discovered more places than anyone. He was a Yorkshireman who came to Whitby in 1746 as a naval apprentice to maritime traders called The Walker Brothers. Here's an amazing link: Two centuries later, in the 1960s, the Walker Brothers had a UK chart hit with a song called (spookily) 'My Ship Is Coming In.' I suspect that they were time-travelling vampires! Cook learned his trade operating Whitby Cats, flat-bottomed boats to transport coal and timber. There is a statue of him in the town and a replica of his ship, The Endeavour. His career came to a tragic end when he was killed by warriors in Hawaii.

Whitby's early existence and prosperity were based on the textile industry, and human urine was an important additive in manufacturing. Tons of it was imported from public toilets in London and Newcastle.

Trivia Alert... It was a source of income for poor people to sell their own urine, and this is the origin of the term 'piss poor'. The extremely poor didn't even have a 'pot to piss in'.

Fortune's Kipper Shop has had a smokehouse since 1872. The smell was too good to resist, so we bought a box. Many shops specialise in Whitby Jet, a local black gemstone that can be polished and made into jewellery. Queen Victoria helped to popularise it following the death of her husband, Prince Albert, in 1861 since the black accessories matched the colour of the clothes she wore for the rest of her life.

I can't think of a town with as many fish and chip shops as Whitby. We decided on fish and chips, then noticed an all-day breakfast served on a *plate-sized* Yorkshire pudding. It was too good to resist, and it also ticked a box on our foodie-themed journey: Yorkshire pudding in Yorkshire. Delicious, but we couldn't eat for the rest of the day, not even kippers, and Vlad the Impaler has put me off kebabs for life.

Are You Going To Scarborough Fair?

Just 20 miles down the North Sea Coast we arrived in Scarborough, one of Britain's most popular and oldest seaside resorts. It was founded in 1626 when a spring of water infused with calcium sulphate was discovered. This attracted visitors to take the health-giving waters, and the holiday resort grew from there. A Victorian Health Spa is still popular on the site of the original spring.

Scarborough Castle stands on a headland of rock which separates North Bay and South Bay, which have two very different characters. We hiked up to the castle to give us an overview of the town and the coast. Ringed by cliffs and sea, it's not surprising that there has been a fortification on the site for 3,000 years, with evidence of the Iron Age, Roman and Viking settlements. The current buildings date back to the 12th Century and command a spectacular view, including both bays. South Bay is more a traditional holiday resort, whereas North Bay is more natural, with a cliff-top road and fewer seafront buildings.

On South Bay, walking along the beautiful beach of fine sand along the curving bay and picturesque harbour, it's easy to understand the town's popularity. The famous Grand Hotel overlooks the Bay, and its Victorian façade has the grandeur of a Baronial Castle.

The Victorian Tramway opened in 1887 and is still going strong. In the ticket foyer, a large painting depicts Victorian society promenading in their 'Sunday best'. The tramway is actually a funicular railway which transports us up the cliff to the old town.

The cavernous market hall echoes with the hustle and bustle of shoppers. Sandside is the main road and promenade, and Westborough and the Brunswick Shopping Centre have the usual array of chain stores. Walking down towards the harbour, we came across Leeds Fisheries chippy, notable for featuring in the Michael Caine movie 'Little Voice'. Scarborough Railway Station is an architectural splendour with a most extravagant clock tower. It looks more like a miniature Victorian northern town hall.

Back along the seafront there are lobster pots, nets, ropes and fishing boats framing the harbour of yachts and pleasure boats. There is even a blue police box like Dr. Who's TARDIS. A lighthouse at the mouth of the harbour completes the picture and standing in front of it is an elegant Diving Belle statue delicately balanced, poised to dive into the sea.

At St. Mary's Church, the grave of writer Anne Bronte rests. She loved Scarborough and visited many times, particularly during her time employed as a governess with the Robinson family in York. Born in 1820, Anne was the youngest of six Bronte children. Her Irish father, Referend Patrick Bronte, was from County Down and was appointed curate in Howarth. His original surname was Brundy, which was an Anglicised version from his Irish Gaelic name. While at Cambridge University, the ambitious Patrick changed the name to Bronte to sound more distinguished.

Trivia Alert... He chose the name as a tribute to Lord Nelson, The Duke of Bronte.

The three surviving Bronte sisters, Charlotte, Emily and Anne, adopted male pseudonyms to become 'brothers' Currer, Ellis and Acton Bell in an attempt to be accepted by publishers. They kept the same initials. Anne wrote the acclaimed novels Agnes Grey (1847) and the Tenant of Wildfell Hall (1848) but was overshadowed by the phenomenal success of Emily's Wuthering Heights and Charlotte's Jane Eyre. When Anne was gravely ill, Charlotte took her to Scarborough for the sea air. Sadly, Anne died there and this is why she is the only member of the family not buried in the Bronte family vault at Haworth Church.

Wipe-Out

The social club at the caravan site advertised a weekly fun quiz, so we thought we'd give it a go. The quizmaster arranged for us to join another team. There was Gary and Alison from Lancashire and Emma from Leeds. Moira Fairbrace sounds pure Yorkshire, but her accent told us straight away that she was from Sarf London, an Essex girl, innit.

The quizmaster asked for team names: Pointless, Scrambled Eggheads, and Universally Challenged were some put forward. For some reason, our team was called Brass in Pocket. The format of the quiz comprised specific categories and the usual Trivial Pursuit range of questions. The final round of general knowledge had a sting in the tail. It was called the wipe-out round, in which any wrong answer resulted in zero points for the whole of that round.

Moira volunteered to write down the answers and we gelled quite well as a quiz team. Gary excelled at music while Moira seemed to be very clued-up in the Crime and Punishment round, in particular gang rivalry in London. I thought she must have a degree in Criminology or perhaps first-hand knowledge. I didn't like to ask.

There were sixteen teams taking part and we felt confident that we were doing well. Then came the dreaded wipe-out round.

"If you know the answer, write it down. If you don't, leave it out," we were reminded.

"We mustn't wipe-out," whispered Gary, "let's see how we get on and then decide how many answers to keep." We appointed him as

'Devil's Advocate' to make the final decision. There were some tricky questions and some which we felt were too obvious, tempting us into a trap. One question was about British Politics in the 1960s, and I knew the answer.

"Which member of Prime Minister Harold Wilson's Cabinet was the first-ever female Secretary of State?"

I leaned forward and whispered to Moira, "Barbara Castle, she was Transport Secretary." I got blank looks from our team. Gary didn't seem convinced enough to take a risk. I assured them that I was 95% confident. After deliberation, the team decided to go with it, and we submitted just six answers.

Moira filled in the answer sheet and handed it in to be marked. There was much laughter and banter between us until the quizmaster came over the loudspeakers with the answers. He repeated each question and gave the answers to the accompaniment of various cheers and groans. We were doing quite well.

"Now for the wipe-out answers. Eight teams have wiped-out," he added gleefully.

My heart sank. Had I let down my new best friends? I was nervous as the answers were given. Then came the Harold Wilson question. My teammates gave me a woeful expression.

"Who was Harold Wilson's female Secretary of State? The answer is ... Barbara Castle."

The cheers from our team couldn't have been louder if we'd just scored the winning goal at the cup final. We had even left out an answer that turned out to be correct.

The final scores were announced in reverse order, and we were confident of victory. It came down to the last two.

"In second place ... it's Brass in Pocket, and in first place, it's Pointless." We were stunned.

We had been given six points less than we had counted, which would have been a winning score. We called him over for a steward's inquiry.

"You wiped out," he informed us.

"No, we didn't. Our six answers were *all* correct."

"You got the political question wrong."

"No, we put Barbara Castle."

Without a word, he held up our answer sheet and pointed to our answer. It said... Barbara Cartland!

Much laughter ensued from other teams as we looked incredulously at Moira. Her bemused expression was priceless.

There is a denouement to this tale: We all arranged to meet in the bar the following evening. Gary and Alison whispered to us that they had been to Scarborough earlier to buy a present for Moira. At an opportune moment, Gary gave Moira a gift-wrapped present. She opened it to more howls of laughter. It was 'The Castle of Fear' by... you've guessed it, Barbara Cartland.

Eboracum

From Scarborough, we detoured inland from our usual coastal route to a caravan site near York. Approaching York by bus, the Minster looms to dominate this beautiful city on the river Ouse. Why does such a magnificent Cathedral have a rather modest title of Minster? All cathedrals usually start out as ministers or a Ministry Teaching Church, and at York, the name seems to have stuck. That's hardly surprising considering that it's official title is The Metropolitical Cathedral and Church of St Peters in York.

The cathedral was begun in 1220, taking over 200 years to complete. It incorporates evolving styles of architecture from Norman through the stages of Gothic, culminating in the magnificent stained glass of the west window, which depicts stories from the Old Testament. The South Rose Window commemorates the union of the Houses of York and Lancaster following the victory by Henry Tudor over Richard III at the Battle of Bosworth in 1485.

The interior is magnificent from ceiling to floor and has many interesting features: The Kings Screen is a row of sculptures of Kings from William the Conqueror onwards. An astronomical clock is dedicated to airmen of the First World War. A crypt has remnants of Roman walls and columns. There was a fire in 1984, and here's a point to ponder: A vicar, David Jenkins, was a controversial figure who declared that he didn't believe the Bible stories should be taken literally. Campaigns were launched to prevent him from becoming a Bishop, but The Archbishop of York, John Habgood, nevertheless consecrated Jenkins as Bishop of Durham. Three days later, York Minster was struck by lightning, causing a devastating fire. A thunderbolt from heaven?

The original boundary wall enclosed an area called the Liberty, which Archbishops over the centuries have regarded as almost private kingdoms. The vicars, nuns and monks were allowed to visit local taverns. They were in the habit (pun intended) of getting outrageously drunk, causing mayhem on the way. They made a stag party to Benidorm seem like a vicar's tea party, as it were. They were never caught as they had a bolt hole in the Liberty. The local authorities started to enter to regain some order.

Trivia Alert... This is the origin of the saying 'Taking a Liberty.'

The Roman name for York was Eboracum, a name which lives on in the Ebor Handicap, one of the English horseracing classics. There is a statue of Constantine the Great dating from 300 AD, and he was actually proclaimed Emperor while he was in York. A Roman column was found and rebuilt in 1969, and the well-preserved Roman city walls are a popular walk for visitors.

The rich history of York is most associated with the Viking period. As we discovered in Orkney and the North East of England, the Vikings began to raid coastal settlements, targeting rich and vulnerable holy sites. In 865 AD, a coalition of Scandinavian countries organised themselves into what became known as The Great Heathen Army and was led by three sons of Ragnar Lothbrock, the legendary Viking; a full-scale invasion and York was taken. Viking legacy is all around, particularly in street names which add the suffix 'gate.' In Coppergate is the Jorvik Centre, an award-winning museum that re-creates the Viking world. We saw displays of weapons, jewellery, coinage, clothes, and helmets (not a horn in sight). The weapon of choice of a Viking warrior was the axe. They were originally farmworkers and peasants who were familiar with axes, and they redesigned them more for chopping heads and bodies than wood.

We were transported through the museum in an automatic buggy, ghost-train style, and village life went on around us, including movement and sound from some eerily-looking robotic villagers. The most famous Viking in Jorvik was the terrifyingly named Eric Bloodaxe, who sounds like he should be a singer in a heavy metal band.

We know of Eric's life only from surviving snippets of Chronicles: As you might have guessed from his name, he was a cruel, ruthless character who killed his brothers and ruled the whole of Norway. He was exiled for brutality. Too brutal for the Vikings!? He arrived in York and led a series of battles against Aeldred, King of Wessex. Eventually, Eric Bloodaxe and his army were defeated at the battle of Stainmore, and Aeldred became King of a united England.

Trivia Alert... There is a link between the Vikings and modern-day technology. Most will have heard of Bluetooth, a registered Wi-Fi system. The name goes back over a thousand years to King Harald 'Bluetooth' Gormsson, who united Denmark and Norway in the year 958 AD. His bluish bad tooth earned him his nickname, and his insignia is the Bluetooth symbol today.

In 1996, the bosses of Intel Ericson and Nokia met to plan the standardisation of the new technology, and the name Bluetooth was suggested as a temporary working-title, a tenuous link, but the name stuck. Personally, for a Hi-Tec brand logo, I would have opted for Bloodaxe… it's more cutting-edge.

Apparently, the Bluetooth system creates a wireless link between various gadgets. As a kid in the 1950s, I remember that everyone had a big square bakelite wireless and listened to the Home Service, Light Programme and Radio Luxemburg. Tuning was by a dial, which made strange whistling sounds like the theme from Doctor Who. Now, here's the thing: the wireless was plugged into the wall… via a wire. I never quite worked that one out.

Recently, there have been rumours of several social network systems combining. If You-Tube, Twitter and Facebook came together, perhaps they could call it YouTwitFace. Just a thought.

York rivals Edinburgh as the most haunted city in Europe, with over 500 sightings. For example, there is the Dungeon and the Golden Fleece pub with its resident ghost 'One Eyed Jack.' The cobbled, narrow streets of the Shambles is a bustling tourist area with shops, galleries and coffee houses.

Trivia Alert... The area used to be full of butchers, abattoirs, hanging meats, stalls, and offal. This is how the Shambles got its name, originating from the Anglo-Saxon word fleshammels, which means flesh shelves, butchers' shelves.

Stand and Deliver

Dick Turpin, the notorious 18th Century highwayman, is buried in York. He was born in Essex in 1705, and far from being a romantic, heroic character, he was a thief, burglar and murderer operating around Epping Forest. He was a butcher by trade and became involved with poachers by butchering their ill-gotten meats. The 'gentleman of the road persona' was created in the 19th Century in a book by William Ainsworth, which used Turpin's name and created stories about his fictitious ride to York on his horse, Black Bess. He did actually travel to York, but to escape arrest for stealing horses. He posed as a horse trader and took the name of John Palmer. Once again, he was arrested and sentenced to death without the officials first realizing who he was. His gravestone reads John Palmer, aka Richard Turpin.

Bonfire of the Vanities

Another infamous character has connections with York. Guy Fawkes was born near to the Minster in 1570 and was a pupil at St. Peter's school. He was employed as a Footman for a Lord and later moved for a time to Belgium, where he changed his name to Guido. Contrary to popular perception, he was not the leader of the Gunpowder plot. That was a man called Robert Catesby, a nobleman in Westminster. Catholics planned to blow up Protestant King James I, who would be in Parliament on November 5th, 1605. They were betrayed, arrested and hung, drawn and quartered. I've always thought it strange that all England makes bonfires every November 5th to burn an effigy of a political terrorist over 300 years ago. I found out that Parliament passed the Thanksgiving Act in 1606, stating that every year, we give thanks and pray. That was the start of Guy Fawkes night.

Trivia Alert... While on the subject, King James 1st, when he became King of England as well as Scotland in 1603 he, decreed that all public buildings, including Public Houses, should display the heraldic arms of Scotland, The Red Lion. This is why it is the most common pub name in Britain, with over 600.

The National Railway Museum is another of York's numerous attractions and well worth a visit. Stephenson's Rocket in 1829 started the nostalgic era of steam, while the famous Mallard still holds the 120-miles-per-hour record. We were able to view Royal carriages, and there is even a Bullet Train from Japan.

York is famous for chocolate, such as Terry and Rowntree, and to keep up our 'foodie' theme, I got on the bus eating a Yorkie Bar.

Leaving York, we passed close to Stamford Bridge. This was where a Viking invasion was repelled in the fateful year of 1066. The battle had serious ramifications and played a significant role in changing English history. More of which later when we visit the site of the Battle of Hastings.

Saltaire

From York, we continued to Shipley, just outside Bradford, to visit The World Heritage Site of Saltaire, which also includes the David Hockney exhibition. Saltaire is a village built for his workers by Sir Titus Salt, a 19th Century mill owner who became wealthy and powerful through the wool trade. Saltaire takes its name from Salt and the River Aire. Unlike the majority of Victorian Industrialists, Titus regarded his workers as valuable assets rather than mere commodities. The 'dark satanic mills' is an apt description of conditions suffered by inhabitants of industrial cities like Leeds, Manchester, or Birmingham. Bradford was worst of all, with 112 factories and mills, overcrowding, pollution and appalling sanitation, culminating in outbreaks of cholera and typhoid in 1848. A newspaper of the time reported: 'To gain a first-hand taste of what the damnation of Purgatory must be like, visit Bradford'. Titus attempted to persuade other mill owners to improve conditions, but it seems that most of them were a cross between Bradley Hardaker, from the television comedy series 'Brass', and Ebenezer Scrooge, with a touch of Marie Antoinette thrown in for good measure.

Titus opened Saltsmill in 1853 next to the River Aire. The wool wasn't from Yorkshire sheep but from the Peruvian Alpaca. By trial and error, he developed the techniques to comb, spin and weave this longer length of fibre into a fine worsted. He presented a roll to Prince Albert, who had a garment made for Queen Victoria. She wore it in public, and this priceless advertising worked wonders for Salt's business. This reminded me of Alec Issigonis, the designer of the revolutionary Mini Car, who had presented one to celebrity couple Richard Burton and Elizabeth Taylor and also to Princess Margaret and Anthony Armstrong-Jones.

The village had a park, hospital, school, library, church and gymnasium. Perhaps you have noticed that there is a notable absentee from the list of amenities… there was no pub. Titus disapproved of drinking and the effect that alcohol had on workers. Don't let that put you off visiting, there are pubs nowadays. One of them is ingeniously called 'Don't Tell Titus'.

Four sculptures of Lions guard the village centre. They are named War, Peace, Vigilance and Determination. They were originally intended for Trafalgar Square but were too small, so Titus gave them a home.

Saltsmill is now the 1853 Gallery, part of which is the David Hockney permanent exhibition. Hockney was born in Bradford and first came to prominence in the 1960s with his California 'Swimming Pool' series. Influenced by Picasso, Hockney has always been an innovative artist, willing to experiment with various techniques, media, and subject matter. I was particularly impressed by his iPad paintings of trees, landscapes and flowers created electronically and then enlarged. The vibrancy and freedom of colour reminded me of 20th Century Fauvism. An excellent day out rounded off with a pint… but don't tell Titus.

Hull

We headed back towards the coast for a stay in Hull. The city gets its name from a Celtic word for 'deep' and Norse for 'muddy', and there has been a settlement there on the banks of the Humber estuary going back to the Iron Age. The Rivel Hull, a tributary of the Humber, flows through the city. Inevitably, the Vikings settled there in the 9th Century and used the wide Humber estuary as a major gateway inland.

In the 13th Century, Edward 1st created his Kings-Town-Upon-The River-Hull.

Independence-of-thought and rebelliousness are traits in the city's DNA. Hull played a crucial role in determining the course of English history. In 1642, King Charles 1st was refused entry to the city, the first signs of rebellion which sparked events leading to the English Civil War, and Hull became a hotbed for anti-Royalists.

A unique feature of the city are the cream-coloured public telephone boxes, which can also be regarded as a metaphor of Hull's character. In the early 20th Century, phone boxes throughout the country were painted in a variety of colours. In 1936, to mark the Silver Jubilee of George V, the Post Office decided to paint them all red to match the post boxes. However, telephone boxes in the Hull area were owned by the Hull Corporation Phone Department. In keeping with its contrary nature, they wanted to be different and decided on cream instead of red. It evoked the spirit of 1642.

In common with many other British maritime cities, Hull has reinvented and invigorated itself through regeneration and modernisation to re-focus and reboot its raison d'être. It follows a similar template we saw in Newcastle. Old waterfront warehouses are now clubs and bars, and Humber Street buzzes with nightlife. The city grew rich during the 19th Century Industrial Revolution, and today it has many grand Victorian buildings. Hull's most famous son is William Wilberforce, the Member of Parliament responsible for the abolition of slavery in the 19th Century, and his statue stands on top of a column overlooking the old docks.

The marina can accommodate over 200 boats, ranging from small fishing vessels to luxury cabin cruisers. The Spurn Light Ship was once a floating lighthouse at the mouth of the Humber and is now moored as a museum. Princes Quay has new shops and restaurants, and it's evident that Hull has benefited from being the UK City of Culture in 2017 when it attracted 5 million visitors.

The original Hull Dock offices of 1872 is an elegant, traditional building with a unique feature. The massive tentacles of a gigantic blue octopus protrude from its windows, enveloping the building… Somebody's idea of culture. That's Hull for you.

The iconic emblem of the city is the mighty Humber Bridge, opened by Queen Elizabeth II in 1981. It was designed and built by Sir Ralph Freeman, the world's pre-eminent engineer on suspension bridges, with the Severn Bridge and Forth Road Bridge to his credit. The two concrete towers are a colossal 155 metres high, just short of Blackpool Tower. The sections that make up the road are a miracle of aerodynamics. They are actually hollow and are based on aircraft technology; the higher the wind speed, the more stable it becomes. As we drove over, the incredible height is quite disconcerting, especially when being overtaken by a juggernaut. The bridge was designed to withstand anything nature could throw at it, including presumably a giant octopus.

There is an intriguing back-story to the construction of the Humber Bridge; it could almost be described as a political bribe. For decades, there had been campaigns demanding a bridge. The death of a Hull Labour MP, Henry Solomons, was the catalyst that set the wheels in motion. If the Labour Party were to lose the subsequent by-election, they would be left in a precarious position of having a Parliamentary majority of just one.

The election was crucial, so Prime Minister Harold Wilson sent senior ministers to support the Labour Candidate. The Transport Secretary gave a momentous speech and promised unequivocally, 'You *will* have your Humber Bridge'. It worked, and Labour won. The Transport Secretary was our old friend Barbara Castle. Or was it Barbara Cartland? I always get those two mixed up.

Lincoln

Following our crossing of the Humber, we reached terra firma and headed south to our next stopover in Lincoln, yet another beautiful and historic city.

Whereas Hull was a touchstone during the Civil War of the 17th Century, Lincoln was at the forefront of an earlier and lesser-known Civil War 500 years earlier. Known as 'The Anarchy', it was a medieval battle royal, literally, over succession to the throne on the death of King Henry Ist in 1135. In Medieval times, the line of succession of a monarch was far from clear-cut. His nephew, Stephen, a grandson of William the Conqueror, seized the throne and was crowned soon after. Another claimant to the Crown was King Henry's daughter Matilda, who gathered support, which led to civil war.

At the first Battle of Lincoln in 1141, Stephen was captured, and Matilda was declared 'Lady of England' until her Coronation could be arranged. On the eve of the ceremony, Stephen's forces raided Westminster Abbey, and Matilda fled to Normandy and she was forced to release Stephen from imprisonment. He was re-crowned on Christmas Day. She was never formally declared as Monarch;

otherwise, she would have become England's first Queen. She got the last laugh; her son followed Stephen as King Henry II.

Lincoln was a focal point because of its strategic defensive value, standing out from the surrounding flat landscape. My burning leg muscles were personal testimony to the steepness of the walk up to the Cathedral and Castle. The cobbled street taking us to the 'summit' is called Steep Hill Street, as if we hadn't noticed.

The Fudge Pantry, Brown's Restaurant and Pie Shop look like a Dickensian film set. A Norman house from 1170 is now occupied by Imperial Tea and Coffee. There are small galleries, and handily placed is the Mayor's Chair, a resting place based on a 17th Century carved seat. The prize for the most aptly named business must go to Basecamp Antiques.

Silver Street and Mint Street suggest silversmiths and coinage, and indeed, a well-known local woman was executed in the 13th Century for clipping gold coins to make counterfeit currency. We were particularly fascinated by an old-fashioned sweet shop which had a window display typical of each decade. A sweet Memory Lane as passers-by of all ages reminisced about their childhood favourites.

The Magna Carta Pub is well-named since one of only four surviving copies of the Magna Carta (Great Charter) is displayed in Lincoln Castle. This is because the Bishop of Lincoln was present in 1215 when it was signed by King John at Runnymede. The IIth Century Castle was built on the orders of William 1st on a site which had earlier been occupied by a Roman fortress. The north of England was still under Viking Danelaw when the Normans invaded in 1066, and rebellions were common. The Conqueror built a series of castles as fortifications to subdue the constant skirmishes. A Georgian former prison is within the castle walls, and Lucy Tower is a Norman keep standing on a motte. Cob Hall in the castle has a dungeon and was a place of public execution to entertain the mob below.

Lincoln Cathedral was begun in 1072 and took over 250 years to complete. The tower once had a sky-scraping 520-foot spire, making it the tallest building in the world until the spire toppled during a violent storm in 1548.

Because it took centuries to build, Lincoln Cathedral incorporates evolving architectural styles from Norman through Early English Gothic and Decorated Gothic. The west façade has huge round towers richly decorated with chevrons, composite columns, carved manuscripts, faces and animals. Flying buttresses along the side transfer the massive weight to the ground. The interior takes your breath away with its ceiling of rib-vaulting, two huge stained glass rose windows called the Dean's Eye and the Bishop's Eye. Embellishment is everywhere, and the polished Purbeck marble enhances the light.

Engineering has been an important aspect of Lincoln's prosperity, and with the arrival of the railways in 1846, it became a regional hub. A local firm, William Foster & Co, is credited with creating the world's first tank during World War One. The tank made its debut at the Battle of the Somme.

The symbol of the city is the Lincoln Imp, and dotted around are small, grotesque little sculptures of it. The origin dates back to Norman times, and the story goes that two of these mysterious creatures were sent to Earth by Satan to create havoc. In Lincoln Cathedral, they smashed valuable furniture and an angel is said to have come to life telling them to stop. One of the imps threw rocks at her, so she turned him to stone. His face is one of the many carvings in the Cathedral. The other imp escaped, and it is believed that the wind echoing around the Cathedral is him. Lincoln City Football Club is called … The Imps.

Robin Hood

We drove south and stopped briefly in Nottingham, a place synonymous with a certain outlaw. Robin Hood must be the most famous person to have *never* lived. Or did he? University academics have researched tangible evidence to separate fact from fiction, but it's like opening Pandora's Box as numerous possibilities emerge. Most of us will know the standard story of a nobleman, Robin of Loxley, returning from the crusades to find his land had been confiscated by Prince John. He becomes a sworn enemy of the Sheriff of Nottingham and becomes an outlaw in Sherwood Forest with his Merry Men and Maid Marion, robbing the rich and giving to the poor.

The stories of Robin Hood first appeared in the 14th Century in ballads based on tales handed down by word of mouth. The earliest stories were set in Barnsdale in Yorkshire, not Sherwood or Nottingham, and Robin was a yeoman, not a nobleman. This would seem plausible since a yeoman would easily survive living permanently in the forest. Little John, Will Scarlet and Much the Miller's son are mentioned from the beginning. Friar Tuck comes in later, while Maid Marion isn't introduced until 1599 in a play. Sherwood Forest isn't mentioned at all until 1700.

Modern stories are set in the reign of Richard the Lionheart (1189-1199), but evidence from the ballad suggests much later. A man called Robert Hood of Wakefield lived at the time of Edward II, while over in Lancashire, a Robin Hood was part of a royal revolt. Furthermore, there are lots of other ballads about rogues, vagabonds and thieves during these cruel, lawless times, and the forests were full of violent, desperate outlaws. One can only imagine what they must have looked like filthy, battle-scarred, gnarled and bedraggled, like: lions on the Serengeti. I doubt if any of them looked like Errol Flynn. Like most myths and legends, there is a seed of truth somewhere. Ballads over the years have amalgamated, and stories have been embellished over the centuries to what we accept today.

Trivia Alert... Pub quiz question: Where is Robin Hood Airport? Nottingham, of course. Wrong. It's Doncaster.

Melton Mowbray

Our next major area to explore was East Anglia, but on the way, we felt compelled to visit Melton Mowbray for one reason: to buy a pie, of course. We couldn't seriously continue our place-named foodie-themed tour without including the world-famous Melton Mowbray pork pie. It would be like compiling a list of greatest-ever artists and missing out Rembrandt. The pies were for sale everywhere, but we chose Ye Old Pork Pie Shoppe, dating from 1853.

Melton is derived from the old English word Medeltone, meaning Middletown surrounded by small hamlets, and Mowbray was the Norman family name of early lords of the manor. Melton Mowbray market dates back over 1000 years, and it takes over the town. History is reflected everywhere, and we came across a blue plaque dedicated to the 7th Earl of Cardigan, who led the famous Charge of the Light Brigade in 1854 during the Crimean War. The impressive Georgian-style house with its front portico supported by classical columns was modestly described as his hunting lodge.

In the 19th Century, the town became popular as a centre for fox hunting, famously described by Oscar Wilde as 'The unspeakable in pursuit of the inedible', and the landed gentry were allocated lodges. In fact, this became the origin of the pie since the stable lads used to make pasties for the day. Unfortunately, the pastry wasn't quite robust enough and became a flaky mess. Through trial and error, a recipe for a more substantial pastry was created, and Mary Dickinson used this to produce the first pork pie in 1853.

Trivia Alert… In 1837, drunken fox hunters, led by Irish Lord, the 3rd Marquis of Waterford, staggered from the pubs onto the streets of Melton Mowbray. The Marquis found a bucket of red paint and started daubing walls. He was ordered to stop by a town official, who ended up being painted as well. The Marquis was arrested and fined for the crime of 'painting the town red.' This is the origin of the phrase.

Wind in the Willows

The magnificent Ely Cathedral stands proud, with its Octagon Tower dominating the surrounding flat landscape. Actually, seascape would be a more apt description because, at the time, Ely was an island, and the Cathedral is known as 'The Ship of Fens.' The area was drained in the 7th Century to provide lush, fertile land, access and routes for through-traffic.

The Cathedral was built in the 11th Century and displays all the hallmarks of the Norman architectural style: round arches, chevron decoration and massive round pillars. Yet another awe-inspiring Cathedral on our travels, and one which uniquely has a museum dedicated to stained glass.

The settlement, and now the City of Ely, was founded by a community of monks and nuns in 673 AD and takes its name from eels, the slippery fish which were abundant in the surrounding water. Located on the Great River Ouse, the beautiful waterfront is lined with pubs and cafes, while St. Mary's Green is surrounded by quaint, historic buildings.

Cromwell

The most notable is a timber-framed house, once the home of Oliver Cromwell, a significant figure in history. Life-size models of Cromwell and his wife, Elizabeth, greet visitors at the door.

'Paint me warts 'n' all' was his famous instruction to artist Peter Lely. The mannequin at the door must have been a younger 'pre-wart' and pre-war Oliver.

He was born in Huntingdon in 1599 into a well-respected family and a Member of Parliament. He was deeply religious and, as a Puritan, was against ceremony and pomp, not mentioned in the Bible. Events leading up to the English Civil War (or the War of Three Kingdoms as the Irish preferred to call it) are well documented. King Charles 1st dissolved Parliament to become a dictator, his God-given right. Unfortunately, he lost his head. An imposing statue of Cromwell (warts 'n' all') stands today outside the Houses of Parliament.

Trivia Alert... Following the Restoration, when the Monarchy was restored under Charles II, Cromwell's body was exhumed... and executed! How can that be possible?

Hereward the Wake

Hereward, the Wake, which in Anglo-Saxon means the watchful, is synonymous with the Isle of Ely in the Fens. Hereward was born in the 11th Century to minor nobility. His father was the earl of Mercia, and historians have suggested that his mother was actually Lady Godiva. As a boy, Hereward was never far away from trouble, and his exasperated father asked King Edward the Confessor to banish him for a while. He returned after the Norman Conquest to find that his home had been destroyed, his family killed, and his brother's head mounted on a spike at the front gate. He slaughtered a group of drunken Norman knights in a pub and placed their severed heads on stakes. He became a freedom fighter and arranged for King Sweyn of Denmark to come over to help secure the treasures of Peterborough Cathedral to prevent the Normans from getting their hands on it. The

Danes generously offered to take the treasure to Denmark, and, surprise, surprise, it was never seen again.

Hereward gathered a small army and continued to fight the Normans with guerrilla tactics. His sanctuary was the wetlands of the Fens on the Island of Ely, accessible only to those who knew the geographical layout. William the Conqueror was determined to defeat Hereward. He built a wooden causeway, but this collapsed under the weight of his troops. Hundreds of Normans weighed down by chain mail, helmets, swords and shields, drowned in ignominious defeat. Eventually, William bribed local monks who guided the Normans across the wetlands to Ely. The Conqueror had been surprised and disturbed by the earlier defeats, so he adopted a revolutionary tactic before the battle with Hereward. He engaged the services of a witch, who, from a wooden tower, screamed curses, profanities and obscenities at the Anglo-Saxons, using language that would make a blue comedian blush. The witch would finish each hysterical tirade by (I kid you not) baring her backside and launching a rip-roaring blitzkrieg of flatulence at the enemy. It seemed to work. It was as devastating as First World War mustard gas. The Normans massacred the Anglo-Saxons. But Hereward disappeared… gone with the wind.

The Battle of Ely was the final resistance to the Norman Conquest, and legend has it that Hereward became an outlaw. It has been suggested the he became the inspiration for the stories of Robin Hood. Hereward, the Wake seems to be slipping into obscurity. To counter this, The Hereward Society was launched in 2017 to promote greater recognition and, dare l say it, tourism.

Sandringham House

The caravan site was in woodland near Sandringham House. Surrounded by 20,000 acres in Norfolk, the original house was acquired by Queen Victoria in 1862, basically to get her wayward son Edward, Prince of Wales, out of London. He was a gambler, a drinker, an insatiable womaniser who loved parties and unlimited quantities of food. A house had occupied the site for centuries but was demolished for a new build. Edward involved himself in the project. He insisted on a bowling alley and billiards room, and later, he introduced 'Sandringham Time' by altering the clocks to give more time for partying and shooting, so much for getting him out of London. As the saying goes, 'You can take the man out of London, but you can't take London out of the man'. He married Princess Alexandra of Denmark, and they had a happy marriage despite his lifestyle. Sounds to me more like Graceland than Sandringham.

A bronze statue of a racehorse called Persimmon stands on the gravel driveway. The horse was given to Edward in 1894, and it went on to win the 1896 Derby. Persimmon had a dramatic impact on the Royal Stud (no, 1 don't mean Edward), siring many Classic winners. Incidentally, a jockey's weighing machine was kept at the house so that guests could be weighed on arrival and departure to measure how much weight they had gained. There was competition amongst the great houses as to who could provide the most lavish hospitality, and the proof of the pudding was on the scales.

We joined a guided tour. The Salon is the largest room, the setting for lavish dinner parties or balls with music from the Minstrels' Gallery. The drawing room has portraits, statues and sumptuous Victorian decoration, the dining room has a Spanish influence with Goya paintings, and the ballroom has swords and shields on every wall.

Guests included the aristocracy, nobility, overseas Royalty and politicians, and many actors and entertainers. Performances took place in the ballroom, and there was a photo gallery of famous Victorian and Edwardian celebrities; Henry Irving was perhaps the most famous. The ballroom is occasionally turned into a cinema, often showing the latest movies before being premiered at the Odeon, Leicester Square.

"Does the Queen come to watch a movie?" I asked.

"Yes, she loves movies."

"So, where is the Royal Box?" I joked.

"She sits anywhere she can squeeze in."

Sandringham is where the Royal Family traditionally spend Christmas, and in 1932 the first Christmas Day broadcast was made by King George V. 'The King's Speech' starring Colin Firth told how George VI overcame a crippling stammer to bravely get through his ordeal.

Some of the original stables have been converted into a café and a museum displaying historic photographs and artefacts. There is an electric mini racing car which was presented to Prince Charles as a boy. Also, there is a miniature Aston Martin with the registration JB

007, a present for Prince Andrew following the Queen's visit to the Aston Martin factory.

"Does anyone know what the Duke of Edinburgh liked to drive when he was in London?" asked our guide.

"Yes," I answered quickly, as if it was a pub quiz. "It was a Black Taxi Cab."

"Correct, sir, and that's it over there."

A Japanese tourist in our group looked puzzled, and the guide explained that the most anonymous vehicle in London is the ubiquitous Black Cab. Prince Philip could hide in plain sight. Our guide told us a story that Prince Philip himself had told:

He was waiting at a red light when a member of the public jumped into the back. Philip had forgotten to lock the passenger door.

"Sorry, Sir, I'm not for hire," said the Prince, trying not to sound too posh.

The lights changed, and The Duke of Edinburgh didn't have time to argue. He followed directions and even entered into an over-the-shoulder conversation.

"And do you know, he gave me a good tip," said Philip.

Our guide told us that the Prince related that story over dinner at Buckingham Palace with the Queen, who was a talented mimic, helping him with a Cockney accent.

Edward VII was the first member of the Royal Family to own a motorcar, a Daimler. He loved cars and technology in general. He was the first to introduce electricity and install a telephone at Sandringham. Queen Elizabeth II followed this trend, having been a motor mechanic during the Second World War. Also, she stipulated that all Gas Engineers should be Corgi Registered.

From Sandringham, we followed the coast of The Wash and the North Sea via Hunstanton and through beautiful villages with distinctive names like Holmes Next to The Sea and Wells Next to The Sea. We stopped for a break at the popular resort of Cromer before continuing to our next site near Great Yarmouth at the edge of the Norfolk Broads.

Great Yarmouth

The caravan site was actually on the racecourse, within walking distance of the town. Great Yarmouth is a popular holiday resort, but it does have a long history, as shown by the foundations of a Roman fortification, castle ruins and a town wall built of typical East Anglican flint, as we saw in the coastal villages and the 11th Century Great Yarmouth Minster. The town is a bright, lively resort full of glitzy arcades, the inevitable fish and chip shops, an excellent beach and donkey rides. As with most seaside resorts, it peaked in days gone by, but looking to the future, a new Marina Centre is under construction, and an interesting photo exhibition along the perimeter wall of the building site showed masses of holidaymakers all over town, in particular visitors arriving by train from the north when all factories closed down for two weeks. Standing proud on the seafront is The Empire, an elegant building dating from 1911 with decorative architectural embellishments fronted by Egyptian-style columns. It once housed amusements and will soon re-open. It proudly displays a poster, 'The Empire Strikes Back.' A note of optimism for the town's future. At the end of Britannia Pier is Long John's Showbar, designed to look like a ship with beer-barrel tables and regular summer shows. There is an extensive Pleasure Beach Amusement Park, and, like Blackpool, the seafront promenade is called The Golden Mile.

Trivia Alert... Great Yarmouth was the first place bombed during the First World War, and during the Second World War, it was heavily bombed as the Luftwaffe left a final parting shot leaving England.

The Broads

Great Yarmouth is a perfect base for exploring the Norfolk Broads. We went by bus to the village of Wroxham to book a guided tour on a pleasure cruiser. I've heard of a town called Alice and even a town called Malice, and Wroxham should be a town called Roy. The name seems to be everywhere. It is a family name dating back to 1899, investing in various businesses ever since.

The Broads are a series of 125 miles of navigable waterways of small rivers, canals and the wide River Yare. I had a pre-conceived notion of empty marshes, reeds and grasslands. How wrong could I be? I was amazed at the luxury houses lining the rivers as we cruised by leisurely. It was like sailing through a model village. Stunning and a great couple of hours. Back in Wroxham, we had coffee and cake in a quaint cafe, probably called Roy's Rolls (pinched from Coronation Street), before taking the bus back to the racecourse and BBKing.

Gainsborough

We continued along the coast via Lowestoft and Ipswich and on to Sudbury, where Thomas Gainsborough was born in 1727. A statue of Gainsborough stands at the top of the Market Hill, looking down Gainsborough Street to his childhood home, now a museum and gallery. We parked BBKing for a few hours as we explored this beautiful town. Gainsborough, famous for his landscapes and sumptuously attired portraits, seemed destined for this career from an early age. An anecdote, probably apocryphal, suggests that he had an early gift for capturing a likeness. As a boy, he sat near an orchard painting the landscape when he saw a thief stealing pears. He quickly sketched the offender, and the thief was apprehended on the strength of the painting. The first identikit conviction, perhaps.

The primary industry of Sudbury was weaving, and Thomas's father was a trader in fine materials: silks, satins, brocades, and lace. Thomas grew up surrounded by these fabrics, and understanding the subtleties of light, reflection, colour, and texture became almost second nature. At the family home, there was even a mulberry bush to feed the silkworms so that Thomas's father could even manufacture his own silk, the ancient Chinese art of Sericulture.

Thomas Gainsborough's first love was the landscapes in which he had grown up, but as a subject matter, the landscape was regarded as unimportant unless it included a historical, classical, or mythological theme. He tried to overcome this particular problem in one of his most famous paintings, Mr & Mrs Andrews. The couple are well to the left of the scene, which is basically a landscape painting of their property. They were delighted as it demonstrated their wealth.

Gainsborough needed a more lucrative market to improve his income, so he moved to Bath in 1759. The town was populated by actors, musicians, and gentry who clamoured for flattering portraits. Gainsborough was commissioned by the most famous actress of her time, Sarah Siddons, which helped to establish his reputation.

His genius for painting luxurious fabrics was evident, and he almost instinctively created a luminosity that seemed to rustle with authenticity. Look at any Gainsborough gown; close up, it looks like a disorganised mess of colour and texture. Step away, and it magically transforms into natural silk or satin. Indeed, Gainsborough often used brushes the length of a broom to help him identify shape and form. Apparently, he didn't particularly enjoy what he called 'the face business', but he found it difficult to give up. He was the best at painting an excellent likeness dressed in sumptuous, expensive clothing. He tried to squeeze in a landscape background whenever possible. He moved to London and painted portraits of King George III and Queen Charlotte, and he became a founding member of the Royal Academy in 1769. It is ironic that Thomas Gainsborough's most famous painting is The Blue Boy. Who is he? Considering previous commissions, anyone could be forgiven for assuming that he is a Prince or a Lord, but is thought to be the son of a friend who was asked to model an outfit for Gainsborough to practise his silky techniques. The Blue Boy is now famous-for-being-famous, like the Mona Lisa. We will go to see the painting in the National Gallery when we get to London.

Constable Country

Only about 20 miles away was home to another great English painter, John Constable.

We booked a motorhome site on a working farm in the heart of Constable Country. The barn was full of machinery, some of which looked as though it dated back to the time of John Constable. We knocked on the farmhouse door and were greeted by the owner. Unfortunately, I asked a cringe-worthy question.

"Do you know the Haywain?"

"Yes, 1 think I've heard of it," he replied, deadpan.

After a brief pause for dramatic effect, he opened the door to his living room.

"You mean that one?" he asked, pointing to a reproduction over his fireplace.

Norma raised her eyebrows with an 'ask a silly question' expression.

He told us that Willy Lot's Cottage was only 400 metres away, following a footpath through the fields.

Standing on the spot where John Constable created his most famous painting, The Haywain, *really was* like walking into the painting. Obviously, landscapes change over time, but this was still recognizable from 200 years earlier. In fact, Willy Lot's cottage is probably in much better nick now than it was in the 1820s.

An anecdotal story we came across was that John Constable was returning to East Bergolt by horse-drawn passenger coach when he remarked to a fellow traveller, 'It really is beautiful countryside around here.' The passenger replied, 'Yes, this is Constable Country.'

Relatively few historical characters are remembered for having an era named after them: Elizabethan, Victorian, Napoleonic, Dickensian, Shakespearean, to name but a few. John Constable joins this illustrious group due to Constable country... or does he? The beautiful area around Flatford, Dedham Vale and East Bergolt, where he grew up, was known as Constable Country during his lifetime. It was originally referred to John's father, a local businessman and landowner who owned mills, windmills, barns and a fleet of barges to transport flour to London. The family lived in a mansion in the centre of East Bergolt. It really *was* Constable Country; he owned most of it. Even if this is the origin of the term Constable Country, I think we can assume that John Constable is now acknowledged as the inspiration.

Many of Constable's most famous paintings depict scenes within a mile radius, and it is a pleasant walk to take in Flatford Mill, Dedham, and Flatford Lock. Early in his career, Constable didn't receive many commissions because his particular genre of landscape painting was way down the pecking order of art subjects. In fact, some of Constable's paintings could almost be described as Cloudscapes because he studied cloud formations meticulously and became a meteorological expert through his art.

John Constable was a direct contemporary of another great English painter, JMW Turner, but whereas Turner has always been thought of as a revolutionary, experimental artist and an influence on modern art, Constable has been thought of as traditional, whose paintings appear on tea towels, jigsaw puzzles, coffee mugs and the like. He was appreciated more in France than at home, and the Haywain won a gold medal at the Salon des Beaux Artes in Paris. It wasn't until the French Impressionists of the 1870s that Constable was acknowledged as one of the founders of modern art. He pioneered outdoor sketching, carrying his oil paints in animal bladders, but they were never intended as finished pieces to be exhibited. Uniquely, Constable used to paint 6-foot canvas studies outdoors, and today, they are regarded as great works of art in their own right, many of which are exhibited in London's Victoria and Albert Museum.

There is a denouement to this story which adds to the enduring fame of the Haywain. In July 2022, The Haywain appeared in the news. Two climate-change activists had superglued their hands to the ornate, gold gilt picture frame of the Haywain in the National Gallery in London. Over the original painting, they had superimposed a copy of it, photoshopped to warn the world of impending doom: emaciated trees, Willy Lot's dilapidated cottage and green gooey sludge in the water, as a result of acid rain, solar wind, greenhouse gasses and so on. If it had been an art installation, it wouldn't have been half-bad, a 'living sculpture' reminiscent of Gilbert and George. I think the National Gallery missed a trick, they should have left them there and sold tickets. The demonstrators were removed from the Constable by *a* constable while protesting their innocence even though they had gilt on their hands. They stuck to their story… they'd been framed.

Queen of the Iceni

What do you think would happen to someone responsible for burning the towns of St Albans, Colchester and London to the ground? And this was in her own country! She has been rewarded with a statue near the Houses of Parliament, showing her aboard an equestrian chariot in a dramatic pose. We are talking of Boudica, Queen of Iceni. She was born in Norfolk in the first century AD, and most of what we know about her life is derived from the famous Roman historian Tacitus. There is a strata of ash under Colchester from a timeline which concurs with the writing of Tacitus.

Boudica is thought to have been a pagan Druid Princess, tall with flowing red hair, who wore lots of jewellery. She was the wife of the King of the Iceni tribe, who maintained good relations with Rome, mainly by paying tribute money. In ancient Britain, women could have power, prestige and position, and after her husband died, Boudica assumed the position of ruler queen. However, the Romans thought otherwise. She was cruelly whipped, and her two daughters were raped in front of her. Subsequently, an enraged Boudica became the Warrior Queen and organised guerrilla tactics against the Romans. She would address her troops from her war chariot and galvanised mass support. Her raids inflicted numerous casualties and death to the Romans.

Rome did not regard Britain as a particularly important part of the Empire; it was more of a backwater, the cold northern limit of the known world. However, military prestige was important to Rome, and a Roman army defeated Boudica at the Battle of Watling Street. Boudica's fate is not known; she disappeared not only from the battle but from history. Modern historians have argued that if Boudica had stuck to her guerrilla tactics, the Romans possibly could have given up on bleak, cold, uncivilised Britain and withdrawn their legions. One battle too far could have changed the course of history dramatically. Some fifteen centuries later, during the Renaissance period (i.e. The re-birth of classical values), Greek and Roman statues were excavated in Italy, influencing Leonardo and Michelangelo. At the same time, Roman writing emerged from obscurity, including the works of Tacitus, which included stories of Boudica.

In England, during Tudor times, these stories became known. Queen Elizabeth related to this previous warrior queen, and inevitably, stories became embellished into legend. Boudica became Boudicea, meaning victorious, and in the 19th Century, Queen Victoria picked up the baton. She instigated the famous statue of three queens pioneering modern-day girl power.

Queen Boudicea of my school days has gradually morphed back to Boudica, the original Celtic spelling. The same has happened to King Canute, who is now known as King Cnut, which I suspect could be a potential problem for users of predictive text.

Southend

Southend boasts the longest pier in the world, which stretches for over a mile into the Thames estuary. There is a pier train, which opened in 1890, and we walked the length of the boardwalk and caught the train back after enjoying a wide view of the long seafront. The Britannia Hotel displays a sign saying 'Where Fish and Chips Rule', which probably sums up every resort in the country. I would describe Southend as retro, with its bright arcades with names like Las Vegas, Monte Carlo and New York. The seafront is busy with traffic while the rather bland town centre is mostly pedestrianised. Southend has always been a traditional day out for Londoners. We did it the other way and used Southend for a day out of London, on the train to Liverpool Street Station.

London

We've been to London countless times and considered by-passing it. However, our motorhome journey would feel incomplete if we missed out one of the world's great cities, so we took the train from Southend for a tourist day out.

We started off in Trafalgar Square and the National Gallery. In particular, we wanted to see paintings by Gainsborough and Constable since they were so fresh in our minds from East Anglia. It was fascinating to look with fresh eyes at The Haywain, having stood on that very spot a few weeks previously. Gainsborough's Blue Boy is larger than life, and up close, the brushwork on the fabric seems disorganised and random but magically transforms into a sumptuous colour and form from a distance. X-rays have discovered that there is a previous painting underneath, confirming that this *wasn't* a commission since Gainsborough would never have used a second-hand canvas. The identity of the boy remains a mystery, but it is almost certain that the artist was experimenting with techniques.

Trafalgar Square was originally a Royal Mews until the horses were transferred to Buckingham Palace, and architect Charles Barry was commissioned to design a square. The National Gallery was purpose-built in 1824. Nelson's Column is 5 metres high, and the granite statue of the Admiral was carved by E.H. Bailey. Around the base are depictions of Nelson's famous battles in bas-relief sculptures using metal from captured French canons. The lions guarding the column were sculpted by Edwin Landseer, whose most famous painting, The Monarch of the Glen, we had seen in Edinburgh. Landseer had never actually seen a lion, so after one had died at London Zoo, it was delivered to his studio.

Trivia Alert... He sculpted the head and mane, but the body and legs had started to de-compose. So he used his Golden Retriever for the body and a kitten's paws.

Admiralty Arch and the Church of St. Martin-in-the-Field complete the square. How did the church get its name? When it was first built in 1222, it was in... a field. Simple.

From Trafalgar Square, we walked to Covent Garden. This was originally *Convent Garden*, where Monks grew vegetables, but following the dissolution of the Monasteries, Henry VIII gave it to one of his Earls. Today, it is a major tourist attraction of craft stalls, street performers and musicians.

To complete our day out, we caught an open-top tour bus with head-phone commentary. There are 30 bridges across the Thames, the most famous and iconic being Tower Bridge, often confused with London Bridge. Indeed, rumours still persist that when an American entrepreneur bought London Bridge to resite it at Lake Havasu in America, he thought he was buying Tower Bridge. It was designed by architect Horace Jones and opened in 1894. It was designed to look much older, like a Medieval Castle, to complement the adjacent 11th Century Tower of London.

The original Houses of Parliament, otherwise known as The Palace of Westminster, was destroyed by fire in 1834. The artist JMW Turner went on to the Thames in a boat to make preparatory colour sketches for a painting. Gothic revival architecture was popular at the time, and Charles Barry's design for a new Parliament is based on late Gothic Perpendicular, creating cathedral-like splendour. Augustus Pugin assisted with decorative features, notably the Big Ben Clock, and it is now a UNESCO World Heritage Site.

Marble Arch was designed by architect John Nash and incorporates Graeco/Roman Corinthian pillars. It was originally intended as the entrance to Buckingham Palace. Despite being lavishly decorated, the designer overlooked one minor detail... The arch wasn't big enough for a horse-drawn carriage to pass through. This falls into the category 'You had *one* job to do.'

Our tour covered most of the famous sites, ancient and modern, but perhaps the most iconic symbol of London is St. Paul's Cathedral, designed by Christopher Wren following the Great Fire of London in 1666.

We were told that the Postal Museum has a carriage from The Great Train Robbery of 1963 when £2.6 million was stolen from a Royal Mail Train. The movie 'Buster' starring Phil Collins, tells the story of Buster Edwards, a local flower seller and petty criminal who escaped, 'going loco, down in Acapulco.' Eventually, he gave himself up, served his sentence and went back to his old job. The rest, as they say, is floristry.

From Southend, we drove back to London, crossed the Thames over the Dartford Crossing and followed the motorway to our next site near Canterbury in Kent.

Canterbury Tales

We had pre-booked a motorhome pitch on a farm, and we were surprised to see three modern chalet-type houses adjacent to the 200-year-old farm. The farmer greeted us and told us that the evening meal and breakfast were in the farmhouse, a communal meal with other guests.

Later, as we set off for our evening meal, we caught a glimpse of two dark, floating entities gliding around in one of the chalets, like Daleks. We realized that they were nuns and assumed they must be here for a visit to the Cathedral.

"Looks like we've got company over dinner," I said to Norma. She squeezed my elbow to emphasise a point and whispered,

"I don't want you to be flippant with comments about habits or nuns on the run."

"As if I would."

I wondered what conversation we could have. I think I would have been more comfortable sitting at a table of Trappist Monks.

However, we had an enjoyable evening. The homemade meal was unbelievable, and our conversation was very interesting. One introduced herself as Sister Madeleine, to which I replied,

"That was my mum's name, and she was named after a nun." She and her colleague, Sister Anne, smiled warmly, and that seemed to set the tone. They were very interested in our tour, in particular the Cathedrals and churches we had visited. We talked about architecture, stained glass, and religious art. The subject of football or rugby league never cropped up.

When I asked the farmer where we could catch the bus to the Cathedral the following morning, the nuns told us that they were being picked-up and we could have a lift with them. I'm not sure what is the collective noun for a group of nuns, but 'a minibus of nuns' sounds about right.

Trivia Alert... I've looked it up, and it is a Superfluity of Nuns.

On arrival at Canterbury Cathedral, we were met by an official party, all resplendent in their regalia. Each nun was greeted individually, but the Dean seemed taken aback when we stepped out of the bus. He shook our hands, and as I stood in a polo shirt and jeans, fashionably torn at the knees, I was tempted to say I had crawled on hands and knees as a pilgrim paying penance. But I decided to keep that thought to myself.

Canterbury Cathedral, a world Heritage Site, was founded in the year 597 AD by St. Augustin, a monk sent by Pope Gregory 1st to convert pagan Britain to Christianity. The original church was destroyed by fire, and the Cathedral we see today was built by the Normans in the 1070s. The exterior and the interior are awe-inspiring, and, as we entered, a choir was practising, demonstrating the superb acoustics. The huge stained glass windows are stunning. A thousand years of history is represented right up to the modern day. A figure by sculptor Anthony Gormley is made of iron nails and 'floats' from the ceiling. There is an exhibition of artefacts discovered during a 1938 excavation, which includes goblets, plates, and chalices. An unusual discovery was a small 10th Century personal sundial, which was probably used by a monk.

St. Augustin was the first Archbishop of Canterbury, but the most famous is Thomas Becket, who was murdered in the Cathedral in 1170. Becket was a friend of King Henry II, who appointed him as

Archbishop of Canterbury, expecting him to continue his allegiance to the crown. However, Becket was more loyal to the Pope, and he was constantly in opposition to Henry.

The famous quote, 'Who will rid me of this turbulent priest?' was overheard by four of his Knights, who took it literally. The knights, Reginald Fitzhurse, Hugh de Morville, William de Tracy and Richard Le Breton, rode to Canterbury and murdered the Archbishop. Pilgrimages began, miracles were claimed, and just three years later, Thomas Becket was Canonised by Pope Alexander III. King Henry II walked barefoot wearing sack cloths to beg forgiveness, while the four knights were sent by the Pope to the Holy Land to fight in the Crusades.

The shrine of St. Thomas Becket is still a destination for pilgrims, and it is ironic that the most famous are fictional characters in Geoffrey Chaucer's Canterbury Tales. Written at the end of the 14th Century, the author cleverly brings together representatives of different stratas of society, nobility, clergy, and peasantry, and using humour, satire and ridicule, he exposes the hypocrisy and many human traits. The basic premise is that pilgrims meet by chance at The Tabard Inn near London, and the Landlord, Harry Bailey, suggests a storytelling competition to alleviate the boredom on the route. The Knight's Tale is first, and there is the Friar, Clerk, Yeoman, Merchant, Doctor, Miller and others. The stories are funny, vulgar, and tragic, all based on many of the author's own experiences across all levels of society.

So what has all this got to do with Canterbury Cathedral? Very little. Chaucer uses the pilgrimage merely as a means of drawing different characters into one narrative. He got the idea from an Italian writer earlier in the Century, Boccaccio, who wrote the famous Decamaron about travellers escaping the plague. As we were marvelling at the sculptures, arches and decoration, a voice echoed along the aisle.

"Norma, John!" We looked round to see Sister Madeleine gliding along the aisle to greet us. "We're leaving at six o'clock. Meet us at the same place," she whispered.

And off she floated. We both became aware that we were being looked at by groups of nearby visitors, wondering why a nun would come over to us. Perhaps they *really did* think my distressed jeans were a sign of flagellation. As we drove away, the nearest hotel was called Hotel Chocolat. This reminded me of a quote: 'The religious significance of Easter is gradually being superseded by commercialism.' The Archbishop of Cadbury.

Jolly Boys' Outing

Our next booking was also on a farm near Botany Bay. No, we haven't been transported to Sydney; we were on the eastern tip of Kent, handy for Margate, Broadstairs and Ramsgate.

We took the bus to Margate, a pleasant journey along the Kent coast. Margate is somewhere I feel as though I know. It was the destination in the 'Jolly Boys Outing', one of many classic episodes from the BBC comedy series Only Fools and Horses.

It is one of the oldest resorts in the country, at one time attracting the well-to-do and becoming a rival to Brighton and Bath. Margate's faded glory is in evidence, but it seems to be making a comeback. The wide sandy beach is excellent, and a popular man-made feature is the walled areas that fill as shallow tidal pools. The water replaces itself at every tide. Nature is its pool attendant.

A stone clock tower is in front of the seafront façade of low-rise buildings, retaining architectural styles going back over a hundred years. Margate's signature building is 'Dreamland', a beautiful example of the Art Deco style, which was re-furbished and reopened in 2015. It accommodates a roller disco, a roller coaster called the Scenic Railway, and vintage fairground attractions. A coffee bar has seating in old fairground Waltzer cars. I kept expecting a leather-jacketed greaser to spin us around, take the money, and, as I remember, never came back with any change. There was a timeline with a display of posters, including Bill Haley and his Comets and The Rolling Stones.

The once-famous lido, now neglected and derelict since its heyday in the 1920s, has been taken over by street artists.

In the town, there are lots of pubs and wine bars amongst the cobbled streets, and most drinkers were outside enjoying the sunshine in a party atmosphere. There are indoor markets with quirky shops selling everything from antiques to vinyl records, and an interesting feature was a double-decker bus, which had been converted into a café.

The only modern glass building is at the harbour, the Turner Gallery. Arguably, Britain's greatest painter, JMW Turner, had a great affection for Margate. The son of a Covent Garden barber, it was here that he first saw the sea, and his love of marine painting developed. He returned many times, producing masterpieces such as Sunrise at Margate and Fishermen at Margate.

Although he never married, he is believed to have two daughters with a local widow. There are unsubstantiated rumours that he also had a similar assignation in London and commuted between the two 'families'. If so, it reminds me of the incident in Chile some years ago when miners were trapped underground. Families gathered anxiously at the surface, but one miner had *two* families arrive who had no idea of each other's existence. The world's media picked up on this, and the news soon filtered underground. Guess who was last to emerge into the sunshine?!

Talking of the underground, another final Margate attraction is the Shell Grotto. In 1935, some children were playing when they dislodged a paving stone to reveal a gaping hole. They had stumbled, literally, upon underground chambers. Exploration by experts revealed a grotto, including a niche thought to have been an altar. The astonishing thing is that the walls and ceiling were adorned with over 4 million seashells, each individually stuck on in intricate patterns, swirls and geometric shapes. No-one knows who made this mysterious place, when or why. It reminded me of catacombs in Italy or fabulous tile patterns in Islamic Mosques in the Middle East. The grotto is near the town centre, helpfully on Grotto Hill. It could date back just a couple of centuries or even a millennium, and it has been suggested that carbon dating could give the answer. However, this has been declined on the grounds that it could be expensive or disruptive. In other words, keep the mystery, keep the tourists.

Broadstairs

Broadstairs seemed timeless and gentile. Perhaps it was the lack of arcades or the bucket-and-spade shops selling swimming pool inflatables. The Victorian atmosphere was accentuated by the clock tower standing on a small clifftop, an ostentatious, sumptuously decorated clock on top of a gazebo. It is strangely attractive in its traditional seaside setting as it overlooks Viking Bay, a curved sandy beach with rows of slightly dilapidated and individually painted quaint beach huts.

Victorian and Edwardian buildings combine to create an elegant sea-front promenade, and the Carlton Hotel, in particular, attracted my attention. A Blue Plaque informed us that it was built in 1899, and members of the British athletics team stayed there before travelling to Paris for the 1924 Olympic Games. They ran on the beach, as portrayed in the movie Chariots of Fire, accompanied by the inspirational soundtrack by Vangelis. Incidentally, if I may digress, Bebbington Oval on the Wirral in Cheshire doubled as the Olympic Stadium and Cowley School in St. Helens was used for interior scenes. As a teacher there in the early 80s, the headmaster announced that a film crew would be coming into school. "If anyone is free, they are asking for extras." As we went for lunch, we saw some actors in straw boaters and 1920s striped blazers, but we weren't too bothered about being in some obscure TV programme. Cowley School was chosen as a location because it was built in the 1920s and retained many of the original features, such as tiles and a heavy wooden clothes stand. The staff changing room was used as the Olympic changing room. So, I missed out on an appearance in an Oscar-winning movie. One consolation was that when we went to the cinema, I whispered proudly, "Harold Abrahams is using *my* clothes peg." Queen Victoria occasionally stayed in Broadstairs on holiday, at the Piermont Hall.

The person whose name is ubiquitous throughout the town is Charles Dickens, who lived and worked in Broadstairs and visited regularly. Dickens lived in a turreted grade II listed building called Fort House, where he wrote David Copperfield. The name has since changed to Bleak House. There are lots of pubs, with names inevitably sprinkled with Dickensian references. We came across The Old Curiosity Shop tea rooms and the Dickens House Museum, which is black and white with decorated balustrades and was the inspiration for Betsy Trotwood's house in David Copperfield. There is an annual parade of Dickensian characters through the town. One nice touch was a house which had a plaque saying, 'Charles Dickens *never* lived here.' Dickens was actually born in Portsmouth in 1812, where his father, John, was a clerk in the Royal Navy Pay Office. Ironically, for someone who worked in finance, John couldn't organise his personal affairs, and his life went into a downward spiral. It's just as well that he didn't work in a brewery. He was an amiable character, constantly expecting 'something to turn up', and he was the basis of the character Mr Micawber. The family moved to London when Charles was three years old, and this is where he observed people from all levels of society who would become Mr Pickwick, Fagin, Miss Haversham, the Artful Dodger and Scrooge. John Dickens ended up in prison for a year and eventually got another job as a clerk at the Naval Dockyards at Chatham, and Charles fell in love with Kent, Broadstairs in particular.

A Blue Plaque on Chandios Square is in memory of Oliver Postgate. Not quite in Dickens' league, he was the creator of Ivor the Engine, Bagpuss and the Clangers.

Ramsgate

Ramsgate has a delightful harbour full of boats and yachts. It has an interesting history going back to Anglo-Saxon times and a collection of blue plaques commemorating famous people who have lived there. Let's start with Van Gogh, who lived in Spencer Square in 1876 and taught at a boys' school. For any pub quizzers, let me quote Basil Fawlty in the TV comedy series Fawlty Towers… 'Specialist Subject; the bleedin' obvious.' What subject did Van Gogh teach? Hands up everyone who answered 'art'. Wrong. He taught French, German and Arithmetic. It's like asking Jimmy Hendrix to join a band and putting him on the drums. Seriously, Vincent didn't start to paint regularly until a few years later, but there exists a drawing he did from a school window. I wonder if the headmaster looked at it and said, "Not bad, but don't give up your day job."

The raised promenade provided a panoramic view of the harbour, and there is a row of pavilion-style Victorian booths with cafes, bars, restaurants, ice cream parlours, a circular boating lake, and a croquet club.

There are no high-rise seafront buildings, preserving the authentic Victorian ambience. Indeed, what could be more authentic than the *actual* house where Princess Victoria lived briefly before she succeeded her uncle, King William IV, in 1937?

A plaque at The Grange commemorates Augustus Pugin, who designed the interior of the Houses of Parliament. There is a much-photographed flight of steps in the town on which the facing risers are decoratively tiled with designs by schoolchildren inspired by a visit to the Grange. Why didn't Van Gogh think of that?

During the Napoleonic Wars, the Duke of Wellington was a regular at the Falstaff Hotel, no doubt plotting Bonaparte's downfall. There is a Wellington Crescent, Plains of Waterloo, and Waterloo Road. During the Second World War, Ramsgate played a significant role in the evacuation of British troops from Dunkirk, and tunnels still exist built during the war to protect residents.

My final blue plaque discovery is perhaps the most surprising; Karl Marx, the founding father of Communism, stayed in Ramsgate in 1879. His daughter Jenny Marx lived in Artillery Road.

Trivia Alert... Karl Marx never once set foot in Russia.

Finally, The Victorian Pavilion, with its Greek-style columns supporting a balcony overlooking the sandy beach on one side and the harbour on the other, now boasts a significant achievement. Wait for it... it is the largest Wetherspoons Pub in Britain.

We continued our coastal tour of Kent through Dover and Folkstone. BBKing must be the only motorhome travelling through those ports without crossing the channel. Dover has an impressive castle which we had visited many years previously, so you'll be pleased to know we gave it a miss this time. Our next site was Hastings.

1066 and all that.

The most famous of many in British history is the Battle of Hastings. In 1066, when the country changed forever. William the Conqueror and the Norman Dynasty have been mentioned several times, and now we were able to visit the battle site, located conveniently at a place called Battle.

It was far from being a straightforward foreign invasion. The English King, Edward the Confessor, died childless in 1066, leaving rival claimants to the throne: Earl Harold Godwinson, Duke William of Normandy, and Harald Hardrada, King of Norway. William had been promised the throne by Edward, who later changed his mind and also offered it to Godwinson. Furthermore, Hardrada claimed family connections and a historical right to rule England. Harold Godwinson wasted no time to claim the Throne as a fait accompli. The newly consecrated Westminster Abbey in London held Edward the Confessor's funeral and Harold Godwinson's Coronation on the *same* day.

In 1066, Harold Hardrada and his army sailed across the North Sea into the Humber Estuary and along the River Ouse to take York. The new English King, Harold II, had no option but to march his troops north to confront the invading Vikings. They covered the 180 miles in four days, more than a marathon a day, with armour and weaponry! The English met the Norwegians at Stamford Bridge, a crossing on the River Derwent near York. Harold's army was held back by just one fearsome Viking defending the bridge. He killed about 45 men with his axe until an English soldier got under the bridge and killed him by thrusting a spear upwards into his groin. The English were victorious, and Harold Hardrada was killed. After centuries, the Battle of Stamford Bridge is regarded as the end of the Viking era.

The English troops had no sooner recovered when word came of the Duke of Normandy's landing on the South Coast. They were again marched south, which is about eight consecutive ultra-marathons with a blood-bath of a fierce pitched battle in between and another to follow. Those elite soldiers of a thousand years ago must have been the SAS of their day.

The Norman Conquest is well-documented on The Bayeux Tapestry. We had been to see it in Bayeux during an earlier motorhome trip. Although called a Tapestry, it is, in actual fact, a 70-metre-long embroidery. It is very informative and, like a movie story-board or comic strip, it describes the narrative in pictures annotated with written text.

The English army formed a shield-wall along the ridge of a steep slope, with the Normans attacking uphill. Basically, the exhausted English troops were overpowered by more modern warfare by the Normans, who utilized archers and Cavalry. Famously, Harold was killed by an arrow in his eye.

William was crowned at Westminster Abbey on Christmas Day 1066. He brought over nobility from Normandy and gave them land, property, and titles. He commissioned the famous Domesday Book to itemise property and land. King William was brutal and ruthless in consolidating his conquest. Executions were common, and rebellious uprisings were put down without mercy. The north, in particular, suffered massacres and burning of villages during an infamous period known as 'The Harrying of the North'. On a more positive note, the legacy of Norman rule is still evident today in the Norman architecture of churches, cathedrals, and castles.

Research and modern radar technology are beginning to question the actual location of the battle. Each army had roughly 7000 troops, but there seems insufficient evidence to suggest an all-day pitched battle had taken place at the acknowledged site. Researchers suggest nearby alternative sites are Crowhurst, Cenlec Hill and even the town centre of Battle. However, changing accepted writings is a long, slow process. It was an uphill battle, as it were, just like the Battle of Hastings.

From Hastings, the drive along the south coast took us past Pevensey Bay, where William the Conqueror actually landed, through Eastbourne, passed Beachy Head along the Sussex Heritage Coast to our next caravan site near Brighton.

Brighton

Brighton is the quintessential seaside town with its traditional pier, funfair, elegant seafront Georgian buildings, brightly painted beach huts, shops, cafe, stylish restaurants and pebble beach, fantastic street art, a myriad of colours, The popular Lanes area has specialist music shops, craft stores and interesting bric-a-brac. It reminded me of Greenwich Village in New York and the Paddington area of Sydney.

Along the seafront, we came across an 'upside-down house,' and my first thought was of the 1987 hurricane! There is the famous Grand Hotel and a splendid Victorian bandstand, a Grade II listed building on a small pier which still hosts concerts. Brighton's Pier has its famous Victorian clock tower, a helter-skelter, a ghost train and even a waterlog flume at the end of the pier. This is Brighton's only remaining pier since the west Pier burnt down. The skeletal wreck stands defiantly in the sea like a sculptural installation or the remains of a beached prehistoric creature from the deep. To me, it seemed a dreadful eyesore, a blot on the seascape, but it can't be removed because it is (or was) a grade1 listed building.

Brighton's signature building is the Royal Pavilion, a pastiche of an Indian Royal Palace. In my book 'Ten Camels for My Wife', while travelling through northern India, I described the hilltop palaces of Rajasthan as 'like a wedding cake with marble latticework as delicate as sugar-sprayed lace. They seemed to have been designed by confectioners rather than architects. More Mister Kipling than Rudyard Kipling.'

The Royal Pavilion masquerades as such a place since it is a pick'n'mix of Hindu, Islam, and Mughal. Neither architect John Nash nor The Prince Regent ever visited India. It is the architectural equivalent of a police artist's identikit drawing based on a vague description. George was advised to spend time in Brighton as the sea would ease his gout. Royal patronage caused the town to expand, and fashion and Dandyism soon followed. George's friend Beau Brummel was a fastidious, dedicated follower of fashion and influenced the Regency period. George was Prince of Wales, who ruled as Prince Regent in 1811 before being crowned King George IV in 1820. It was an age of architectural follies where country estates would have a classical temple, a grotto or a pagoda to enliven a landscape. George went one better and built a folly actually to live in and to entertain, a perpetual party, which I doubt did his gout any good.

The interior décor is meant to be Chinese, arrived at the same way as the exterior. Westernised Chinese figures, lacquered furniture and a huge chandelier. Everywhere is embellished and decorated in lavish colours. Willow pattern was everywhere, but even that design didn't come from China. It originated in Stoke-on-Trent by Thomas Minton. George's lifestyle inevitably ballooned his weight to 22 stone. 'Georgie Porgy, pudding and pie'. Cartoons in the press lampooned him mercilessly, especially when he tried to dress like Beau Brummel. Pink tights and purple satin pantaloons did nothing for him. These days, the Pavilion is used for a variety of events. ABBA won the Eurovision Song Contest there in 1974 with Waterloo. So, pink tights and purple satin pantaloons finally made a triumphant comeback.

Brighton is the setting for the perennial Christmas television favourite, 'The Snowman,' by Raymond Briggs. When the Snowman and the little boy are flying, or should I say, 'Walking in the air,' Brighton Pavilion can be seen below. A fantasy overlooking a fantasy since George's folly is about as authentic as a flying snowman.

King George V was advised by his doctor to visit Bognor Regis to ease his ailing health. His famous last words were, "Bugger Bognor." So we did. We can't stop everywhere.

Portsmouth

Portsmouth is the cradle of British Nautical heritage and has been home to the navy since the 13th Century. It's ironic that the city, so steeped in history, should today be defined by a 21st Century modern structure overlooking the harbour. The Spinnaker Tower opened in 2005 and is based, as its name suggests, on sails. It is bold and simple, and yet it fits in well with its maritime surroundings.

Portsmouth Point is a small outcrop, once nicknamed Spice Island, where the Spice Island Inn is located. It was thought that this name originated from unloading spices, but it seems it refers to 'the spice of life.' It was once a lawless, dangerous area where sailors on leave would frequent the numerous brothels and taverns. Also, it is thought that Portsmouth Point is the origin of the nickname for Portsmouth: Pompeii. Naval logbooks abbreviated locations, and Portsmouth Point was P.o.m.p.

Due to its strategic position, the town has always been heavily fortified, and the Round Tower, built in the 1490s by Henry VII, is linked to The Square Tower by a wall known as the Hot Wall, which these days accommodates artists' studios under the row of arches. The Square Tower has the Sally Gate through which thousands of sailors have passed to board ships, hence the term, 'to Sally Forth.' The Portuguese Princess Catherine of Braganza arrived ceremoniously at this gate in 1662 when she came to marry King Charles II at the nearby church Domus Cei.

Close by is a statue of one of the most famous Englishmen of all time, Vice Admiral Lord Nelson. He stands on a plinth looking out to Southsea from where he set sail on HMS Victory for Trafalgar in 1805. Nelson was about 5 feet 4 inches tall in life, while his imposing statue is close to 11 feet high. By my reckoning, that's Horatio of 2:1. Nelson was actually born in Norfolk in 1758 and went to sea at the age of only 12 as a midshipman.

Trivia Alert... Throughout his life, he suffered from an unfortunate ailment, especially for a sailor: seasickness. That's like a surgeon who can't stand the sight of blood.

We visited the Historic Dockyards, where ships are open to the public. Built in Portsmouth, the Mary Rose, Henry VIII's flagship, sank in 1545 during the Battle of the Solent against the perennial enemy, the French. The Mary Rose was eventually raised in 1982 and is a time capsule of Tudor England. Artefacts on display included weapons, hour-glasses, plates, cutlery, pottery, longbows and arrows. Gruesomly, there is a skeleton of a crew member known *for certain* to have been an archer. This is because of the distinctive shape of his shoulders and the slope of his upper back. They were immensely strong men due to years of pulling powerful longbows.

Trivia Alert... In Medieval England, all able-bodied men were required *by law* to practise archery. They reported to a Butts Arena for training, and this name survives to this day in many towns as, for example, a street name or a shopping centre.

HMS Victory, Nelson's flagship, is preserved and painted in horizontal stripes of creamy yellow and black, like a bee. To borrow a quote from Muhammed Ali, it could 'Float like a butterfly and sting like a bee.' In its day, it was the most advanced warship in the world.

Naval terms have developed an almost secret language, for example, aft, for'ard, futtock shrouds and lubbers' hole. Signal flags were on display, and we were told that it was common for ships to fly false flags to confuse the enemy. However, there was a strict code of practice that ships could not fire without first showing their true colours.

Trivia Alert... This is the origin of the expression and a song by Phil Collins when someone reveals their 'true colours.'

There are 104 guns with the capacity to devastate enemy ships with a broadside. Unbelievably, we were told that from an out-of-range distance, cannonballs could fire at certain angles to skim across the sea like pebbles on a lake, the original bouncing bombs. Could this have been the inspiration for Barnes-Wallis and the Dambusters in World War Two? There were over 800 men on board, all sharing just *two* open toilets. I thought that's what the Poop Deck was for. Discipline in the Royal Navy was notoriously severe, and on display were examples of the Cat O' Nine Tails, a vicious-looking whip consisting of 9 knotted lengths of rope.

*Trivia Alert...*This is the origin of the saying, 'Not enough room to swing a cat.' Nothing to do with the feline variety.

Numerous crimes were punishable by hanging or flogging. Now, here's the thing: The most common offence was drunkenness and *yet* each man was allocated 8 pints of beer per day, or half a pint of rum mixed with lime juice to prevent scurvy; the famous Navy grog. The sailors must have had a daily dilemma: grog or flog? If it was someone's birthday, they probably had a whip-round.

On display was a list of the crew from Admiral Nelson and Captain Thomas Hardy, down through the hierarchy of ranks as low as ship's boys and even those pressed into service by the notorious press gangs ashore. Midshipmen, as Nelson started out, were Cadet Officers who trained in seamanship, sails, navigation, maths and trigonometry.

These midshipmen were, in actual fact, *children* as young as 12 or 13 years of age, the equivalent of today's 1st or 2nd year High School pupils, and *yet* they had the authority to discipline and issue orders to rough and ready, battle-hardened, hairy-arsed sailors. Selection and promotion for officers was ostensibly on merit, but crucially, any social or political connections carried great influence. Indeed, when Nelson applied for the rank of Lieutenant, he was assessed by a board of Naval Captains, one of whom just *happened* to be his uncle. As the saying goes, 'Britain waives the rules.'

At the Battle of Trafalgar off Spain's Cape Trafalgar, the British fleet defeated the combined forces of France and Spain. Nelson was killed by a French sniper, and a plaque on the Quarter Deck marks the spot where he fell. It's a well-known quote that his last words were, 'Kiss me Hardy.' (One theory is that he actually said kismet, meaning 'it's fate.') Either way, an item of *obscure trivia* is that Captain Thomas Hardy was, in fact, a direct ancestor of none other than Oliver Hardy, of Laurel and Hardy fame. Perhaps Lord Nelson's famous last words should have been, 'That's another fine mess you've gotten me into.' There is a turn of phrase which I have often said jokingly, but now I could say it quite literally as we stood next to HMS Victory. "The sun is over the yardarm… it's time for a drink."

Nelson's body was returned to Portsmouth aboard the Victory, preserved in a barrel of brandy. The level mysteriously dropped... Sailors scooped up brandy to 'have a final drink with the Admiral.' There is no truth in the rumour that his ghost got out three times to go to the toilet or the Poop deck. The poignant image 'Victory Returning From Trafalgar' is a painting by Turner. As a denouement to this, Turner's most famous painting is 'The Fighting Temeraire,' which we saw in the National Gallery, which depicts a scene which the artist actually witnessed first-hand. Bathed in a dramatic sunset, it shows HMS Temeraire being towed up the Thames in 1838 to be broken up. An ignominious end for a ship that had fought alongside The Victory at Trafalgar 33 years earlier.

Back in town, we explored Camber Quay, a picturesque natural harbour around which the town originally grew. As we have seen in other towns, it has been redeveloped to incorporate a shopping mall, a cinema and restaurants. I liked the way historical and naval relics and artefacts have been placed almost as sculptures to enhance the area: a torpedo, a crane, and figure heads from ships, while the Old Customs House is now a popular pub.

Much of the town was bombed by the Luftwaffe during the Second World War. Consequently, there are many modern buildings, but the 800-year-old Cathedral survived. Lombard Street is an attractive row of pastel-coloured historic town houses which gives a glimpse into the past.

Residents of Portsmouth have included Rudyard Kipling, Arthur Conan Doyle and H G Wells. Charles Dickens was born there in 1812, and his birthplace is now a museum, even though he moved to London at the age of three. The renowned civil engineer Isambard Kingdom Brunel was born in Portsmouth in 1806, and, like Nelson, he was only 5ft 4 inches tall. Could it be something in the water?

Isle of Wight

From Portsmouth, we made the short drive through Southampton to a site near Lymington, which was handy for the Isle of Wight.

The following morning, we boarded the ferry as foot passengers for the short crossing of The Solent to Yarmouth. Several guides were touting for business, and we joined a group for a sightseeing tour. One of the island's top attractions is Osborne House, which was Queen Victoria's holiday retreat. She bought it from the Blatchford family in 1845, and Prince Albert practically re-built the house, mainly in an Italian architectural style, after he had visited Naples in 1845. Indeed, this had an influence throughout England and became known as the Osborne Style. The gardens are laid out in a geometric form, and we walked around manicured lawns, plants and colourful flowers. We didn't go into the house as our tour was a whistle-stop.

The Needles on the Western tip of the island area row of 3 stacks of chalk, like sharp white teeth emerging from the depths. At the southern tip is St. Catherine's Lighthouse, and further along the coast, we stopped at the Botanic Gardens at Ventnor, which recreates the natural environments from different parts of the world, such as Australia and South America. After walking around, we were looking forward to visiting the Eden Project in Cornwall.

Shanklin is a beautiful village lost in time, full of thatched cottages, while the Shanklin Chine is an experience which takes us into the heart of nature. A chine is a ravine created by a waterfall which has cut through softer sandstone, making a gully to the sea. The surrounding sounds of cascades and waterfalls conjured up the atmosphere of a rainforest. We didn't have time to stay until nightfall, but we saw pictures of how the chine is transformed into a magical fairytale scene with subtle lighting and gradual colour changes.

We turned inland and stopped at the model village of Godshill, which downsized the village and Shanklin village to a remarkable degree of accuracy. Our final stop on the way back to Yarmouth was at Carisbrooke Castle, which dates from the 12th Century and once held prisoner King Charles 1st during the Civil War.

Our 'taster tour' of the Isle of Wight was excellent, and back in Yarmouth, we explored the quaint gift shops and had a drink in the beer garden of a pub next door to the ferry terminal.

New Sarum

From Lymington, we diverted from the coastal itinerary to visit Salisbury.

The Cathedral dominates the town and surrounding countryside. Standing like a beacon, its spire is 123 metres high. Constructed in

1258, the cathedral is a replacement for an earlier church, which was situated about two miles away on a hill called Old Sarum. Over the centuries, this strategic position had been occupied by an Iron Age hill fort, a Roman garrison, and a Norman Castle. It is thought that priests wrote the Domesday Book of 1086 there.

Life in Old Sarum became overcrowded, and the clergy were constantly at loggerheads with the garrison soldiers. The bishop sent representatives to the Pope in Rome to apply for permission to build a new Cathedral. The story goes that the wealthy, landowning Bishop, with the ironic name of Richard Poore, shot an arrow to mark the spot for the new church. It hit a deer, which ran wounded and died, conveniently enough, on the Bishop's land near the River Avon. He certainly hit the bull's eye with that one. The town which built up New Sarum is now Salisbury. The inhabitants of Old Sarum gradually migrated to the new town until, eventually, there was no-one left. Bizarrely, it still had two members of Parliament… and no voters. But then again, why should that come as a surprise? Eight centuries later, Parliament still has hundreds of members of an upper chamber with not a single vote between them.

What makes Salisbury unique is that it was completed in 40 years. Therefore, it is built entirely in the Early English Gothic period style rather than incorporating evolving styles over subsequent centuries. The West Front has a magnificent façade with quatrefoil windows, tall, narrow lancet windows, and buttresses. Niches with statues descend in order of importance: Archangels, Angels, Old Testament Patriarchs, Apostles, Martyrs and Priests. Christ in Majesty sits above them all.

The famous spire was added to the tower in the 14th Century, which made Salisbury Cathedral the 3rd highest in Britain, after Lincoln and the old St. Paul's in London. It became the tallest structure only when their spires collapsed due to the weight. Obviously, the same fate would befall (literally) Salisbury Cathedral's spire, so they brought in a consultant in the 1660s, Christopher Wren, architect of St. Paul's Cathedral. He recommended load-bearing buttresses and an internal cross-beam construction, like a giant game of Kerplunk. The spire leans slightly, but this was easily straightened and made a little higher in the 19th Century by John Constable… in his painting, that is.

Due to its height, the pinnacle of the spire is required by law to have lights as a warning to aircraft. If workers had been told in the Middle Ages that the spire would be a hazard to metal flying machines of the future, they would have laughed, perhaps with the exception of Leonardo de Vinci.

A copy of the Magna Carta is on display. Forty copies were created, but only four remain, the best-preserved being this one.

The Cathedral's three-metre-wide font is the largest in England, a modern piece which fits well into its Medieval surroundings. Designed by renowned water sculptor Willian Pye, it operates on the same principle as a hotel's infinity pool with an overflow, creating a reflective surface as smooth as glass. A perfect reflection dramatically doubles the effect of stained glass windows, and you can study the splendour of the ceiling without getting a stiff neck.

Within the walls of the close are Elizabethan and Georgian houses. Mompessor House has appeared in many movies and television productions, notably the 1995 version of Sense and Sensibility.

Inadvertently, Salisbury Cathedral played a crucial part during the Second World War. The Nazi blitz resulted in black-outs throughout the country. Hitler decided not to target Salisbury Cathedral because the light on its spire acted as a navigational aid. When a Spitfire factory in Southampton was destroyed by bombing, production was moved to Salisbury in a top-secret operation. The British intelligence service knew it wouldn't be targeted, and Spitfires were built in Salisbury throughout the war. A stained glass window in the Cathedral commemorates this significant episode in its history.

The town is a picturesque collection of Victorian, Georgian and half-timbered Tudor buildings, with a wide variety of traditional pubs. Inevitably, there are ghosts in residence. The Blue Boar Inn is on a site where the Duke of Buckingham was beheaded on the orders of King Richard III. Buckingham was a co-conspirator with Richard and was involved in the murder of the Princes in the Tower of London. He knew too much; a classic example of 'I know where the bodies are buried.'

When we were in Salisbury, it was in the news about the poisoning of a Russian double agent, Alexander Litvinenko. Two officers of the Russian Intelligence Service had travelled to Salisbury to poison him with Novichok, a nerve agent manufactured in Russia. Their modus operandi was to smear the poison on door handles, and the general public was warned to be vigilant.

"Don't touch any dodgy-looking knobs," I advised Norma, earnestly.

"That's always been my policy," she replied.

Stonehenge

The bus from Salisbury to Stonehenge took us on a scenic, meandering route. The driver pulled over along a woodland road and pointed us in the right direction. We still couldn't see Stonehenge. The path took us through a cobbled courtyard of a farm, and up ahead on either side were rows of vehicles. We walked between rows of caravans, campers, converted ambulances, ice cream vans and tents. There were washing lines, wood burners, guitars, and other musical instruments. The demograph seemed to be a mixture of travellers, bikers, hippies, and druids, and we felt as thought we had stumble through a timewarp to the Woodstock Music Festival. Everyone gave us a smile and a friendly greeting. The bus driver had obviously dropped us at the tradesman's entrance.

As we approached Stonehenge, we felt a sense of awe on seeing it for the first time and took numerous photos. We picked up some information leaflets at the visitors' centre and browsed the exhibition.

There are 85 stones in this mysterious, magical structure. There are many theories as to the original purpose of Stonehenge, none of which can be proved or set in stone, so to speak. The most recent radio carbon dating indicates that it was built 4000 years ago. A theory is that Salisbury plain would have been ideal for creating a gigantic structure where The North and South Downs converge as a route for travellers. In the Kevin Costner baseball movie Fields of Dreams, there is a line, 'Build it and they will come.'

The larger Sarson stones were brought from the Marlborough Downs near Avebury, about 20 miles away, and the Bluestones were transported from the Preseli Mountains, 150 miles away in Southwest Wales.

The obvious question is how 'primitive' humans managed such a mammoth task. Perhaps that is it! They used woolly mammoths as beasts of burden. Now, come on, admit that you've just thought of Fred Flintstone in Bedrock's quarry operating a dinosaur as a crane. I wonder if the Loch Ness monster knows something we don't.

Numerous experiments have tested the theory by transporting stones using only the technology available at the time: pulleys, levers, logs and a sled. The Bluestones from Wales were probably chosen because they could be polished to a lustrous shine. The favoured theory is that the stones were floated along the Severn estuary and River Avon and then transported overland to Salisbury Plain. Hollowed-out logs supported a platform, like a catamaran, carrying a stone weighing about 4 tons, or the equivalent of 5 elephants, as we were informed. (I'm unsure what the conversion rate is from elephants to woolly mammoths.) This has been proved to be possible. Other suggestions have included a race of giants called Nephilim's, supposedly wiped-out by Noah's flood. The Brut Chronicle of the 12th Century, written by Brutus of Troy, has an illustration of one of these giants building Stonehenge. Stories of Arthurian legend by Geoffrey of Monmouth had the medieval population believing it was Merlin's work. We mustn't forget aliens, presumably the same ones who moved the statues on Easter Island.

Stonehenge is a calendar aligned with the sun, moon and stars, in common with many other civilisations such as the Mayans, Aztecs, Incas and Egyptians. It was thought it had been built by Druids (Celtic priests) for centuries, but we now know it stood for two thousand years before the Celts arrived from Europe. To this day, Druids celebrate the summer and winter solstice. The clock still keeps good time, but I pity the people who have to move the stones to the right or left twice a year when the clocks go back or forward. I still struggle with my central heating timer.

Trivia Alert... In 1915, millionaire Cecil Chubb bought Stonehenge at auction as a gift for his wife. She had actually sent him to buy some dining chairs. She hated Stonehenge, and consequently, Cecil bequeathed it to the nation. The story has a touch of Jack and the Beanstalk about it.

To Neolithic and Bronze Age people, the sun simply appeared at certain times on the horizon, crossed the sky and disappeared at sunset. They would wonder where it had gone... then it dawned on them. There was no concept of a rotating earth orbiting the sun. Membership of the Flat-Earth Society must have been at an all-time high in those days. It's dwindled steadily since the time of astronomer Copernicus (pronounced in his native Polish as Copper Knickers). Some members still have a recruitment slogan: Flat Earth Society; we have branches all around the globe.

Corfe Castle and Swanage

From Salisbury, we took the A38 south to the coast at Bournemouth, Poole through Wareham, and Corfe Castle, the village which takes its name from the ruins of the castle towering above. The word picturesque could have been coined specifically to describe the village. All the houses, pubs, and shops are built of local Purbeck stone, with slate or thatched roofs. Initially, we drove through the village because we wanted to continue a few miles further to Swanage. I had been down this way only once before on a field-trip from school as part of my A Level Geography course. The programme included a visit to Chesil Beach to study the movement of sand cliff erosion and a study of fossils. This was all topped-off by lessons at the hotel. Now, I'm sure you must be finding this as enthralling as we did... a lethargic group of 17 and 18-year-olds. After a particularly mind-numbing day, I and a mate Brian came up with the idea to escape. One of our other A Level subjects was art, so we approached our geography teacher, Mr Hargreaves, and asked if we could be excused from the following day's excursion so that we could visit Corfe Castle and spend the day painting and sketching. I had always suspected that he never trusted me, can't understand why. He stroked his chin suspiciously. There was a long pause before he agreed to our request, with the proviso that he would inspect our day's work. As if we would waste such valuable time!

The following morning, we waved the coach off, and I've got to say some of our mates weren't using *all* their fingers. We bought a sketchpad and some art materials at a craft shop, plus a selection of postcards. We estimated that the bus to Corfe Castle village would take an hour, and the walk up the hill to the castle would take up even more time. A couple of hours to play with as part of our cunning plan. As you will have guessed by now, we had not the slightest intention of leaving Swanage. Our first stop was a sea front bench where we could enjoy the magnificent view, 'Sitting in the morning sun, watching the ships roll in and

watch 'em roll away again, sitting on the dock of the bay, wasting time.' Otis Redding beat us to that one in that very same year, 1967, the Summer of Love.

Unlike the song, we couldn't waste any more time. We copied some sketches from our postcards in charcoal and coloured pencils until the sun was over the yardarm. We found a pub with a beer garden and set out our stall at a table. I should mention that we had both turned 18 and, therefore, not transgressing any licensing laws or putting the school in an awkward position regarding underage drinking on a school trip. We produced some watercolour paintings over a couple of pints and a pub lunch. Some customers and the landlord came over with encouraging comments.

Before returning to the hotel for the evening meal, we shared a pack of extra-strong mints. Mr. Hargreaves summoned us to his table.

"Have you two had an enjoyable day?" he asked with a teacherly undertone of sarcasm.

"Yes, thank you, but we were disappointed at missing a day at Chesil Beach," we lied.

Mr. Hargreaves gave us that teacher's withering look and said, "I can't wait to see what you have produced today."

We deliberately prevaricated to give the impression that he had caught us out.

"They're in our room."

"Well, go and get your sketches and bring them here, now," he ordered with a self-satisfied smirk.

We returned with our pictures rolled up and started to make excuses.

"We weren't able to do as much as we thought because the bus was late, and it was harder than we thought hiking up to the castle."

"Next, you'll be telling me that your dog ate your homework," he answered, clearly believing that he had caught us bang-to-rights.

Hesitantly, for effect, we laid out our paintings and sketches. Brian and I exchanged knowing glances as the teacher and most of our mates looked at the work. His attitude changed, and he even complimented us.

"I like the way you've used yellow ochre and burnt umber on the castle walls," he observed as a gesture of conciliation.

"Thank you, sir."

I thought it wise not to tell him that they were actually beer stains.

Time to fast-forward half a century to the here-and-now as Norma and I drove into Swanage, a quiet bay, harbour and quaint wooden pier with a backdrop of cliffs. We spotted a little café advertising Swanage Tea, another addition to our foodie theme. We set off back to Corfe Castle village, and this time, I *really would* visit the castle.

The lovely historic pubs, such as the Greyhound and the Fox Inn, look straight out of the Pickwick Papers, while the Bankes Arms is named after a former owner of the castle. There is the Parish Church of St. Edward the Martyr, who was murdered in the 10th Century, and the smallest town hall in England, now a museum. The model village recreates the village and castle as it was before being destroyed by Oliver Cromwell's Troops.

The site of the castle was originally a hunting lodge built by King Alfred as a defence against the Danes. It was further fortified by William the Conqueror in the 11th Century. It remained a royal residence, which housed the Crown Jewels, until the reign of Queen Elizabeth 1st. In the 17th Century, the then owner, John Bankes, supported Charles 1st against Cromwell, which resulted in the destruction of his castle. So, a belated thank you to Oliver Cromwell for creating such a picture-postcard ruined castle, which helped me to pass A Level art three centuries later. By the way, Brian and I passed Geography as well. Luckily, beach erosion didn't crop up.

Weymouth

Our next stop was The East Fleet Farm site, a short bus ride from Weymouth, a typical, traditional British seaside resort which will have changed little since Georgian times. Indeed, there is a Grade I listed statue of King George III on the sea front. His many visits to the town helped to popularise Weymouth. Another landmark is an elaborately decorated Jubilee Clock Tower, erected in 1887 to celebrate Queen Victoria's Golden Jubilee.

The palm trees and the pastel-coloured hotels frame the beach and harbour. Fishing is still important to the local economy and is reflected in the number of fish markets, restaurants, and fish and chip shops. The beach has been voted Britain's best on many occasions, with its sweeping bay and soft golden sand gently sloping into the clear sea. Tradition seems to be a byword, with rows of deck chairs for hire and even donkey rides along the beach. An old-fashioned helter-skelter dominates a fairground.

I would describe Weymouth as 'genteel', but further along the beach, a rowdy altercation attracted a crowd. A man was hitting a woman with a stick. He must have been on something because he had red cheeks and menacing, bulging eyes. The woman was manic but fought back, shouting abuse at her attacker. The onlookers, including us, were transfixed, and some very young children began to cry. Thankfully, a policeman intervened and tried to break up the melee, brandishing his truncheon. Shockingly, the man and woman both turned on the policeman and began assaulting him. Then, totally out of nowhere, a crocodile appeared and chased them off. It was the first Punch and Judy show I'd watched in ages. A sign proudly stated that it was Britain's oldest continuous Punch and Judy Show. That's the way to do it.

Our next destination was the Jurassic Coast. The area is often referred to as Thomas Hardy country. He was born in 1840 near Dorchester and wrote novels mainly about local rural life with atmospheric descriptions of Dorset. Many locations in his books are recognizable, such as Lulworth Cove and buildings in Dorchester. Indeed, Bathsheba Everdene in Far From The Madding Crowd is based on his wife, while Casterbridge in the Mayor of Casterbridge is clearly a fictional version of Dorchester.

Jurassic Coast

A UNESCO World Heritage Site, the Jurassic Coastal Path stretches nearly 100 miles from Studland Bay near Swanage as far as Exmouth in Devon. There is evidence of 185 million years of geological history, covering the periods Triassic (desert), Jurassic (tropical seas) and Cretaceous (swamps). Fossils of creatures have been unearthed by erosion of the cliffs. Incidentally, fossils are formed by a process called petrification over millions of years as bones are literally turned to stone by chemical activity, atom by atom. The study of rocks is called Petrology, which is why someone who is paralysed with fear is petrified.

Lulworth Cove is a circular inlet of the sea, surrounded by cliffs and formed by sea erosion. A walk along the cliff-top path took us to the Durdle Door, famous natural arch of limestone, which looks like Dragon dipping its nose into the sea.

The Jurassic Coast is very popular, and the name has become familiar through the Jurassic Park movies. We passed Chesil Beach. I wish I could explain its formation to you, but, as you know, I skived off that day. We parked at Charmouth at the Heritage Centre, and I told Norma I could remember from school ammonites and trilobites.

"Ammonites and trilobites? Never heard of em," she said, "But if you talk to me about megabytes and gigabytes, I'll know what you're talking about."

"I thought they *were* fossils."

"Yeah, I can see only one fossil here... and I'm looking at him!"

We were fascinated by a remarkable story. Remember the tongue-twister, 'She sells sea shells on the sea shore?' It's about a young girl called Mary Anning, who was born in Lyme Regis in 1799. Her father was a cabinet maker by trade, and to supplement the family income, 12-year-old Mary scoured the beaches searching for interesting shells and fossils, which she sold to tourists. Mary researched and educated herself to become an expert. She discovered some of the very first dinosaur (literally: 'Terrible Lizard') fossils and unearthed a complete Ichthyosaur, a marine reptile, which a museum bought. The new science of Palaeontology had begun due to the work of a 12-year-old child! However, the Geological Society gave no credit to Mary. Even though she had meticulously excavated, experts regarded it as a 'lucky find'. Some wrote pamphlets and reports and stole the credit for themselves. But Mary was tenacious, and in 1823, she excavated a Plesiosaurus. The tide was turning, so to speak, and some scientists began to support her. Mary went on to uncover a Pterodactyl, bringing the realization that some of these pre-historic creatures could actually fly. As a clever young woman, Mary Anning had catalogued sea creatures, fish and ammonites before she was 30.

There is a story that when Mary was a baby, she was looked after by a woman. Caught in a storm, lightning killed the lady holding her. Miraculously, Mary survived, and many felt that she had been energized, like the Duracell Bunny. Could this have been the source of her energy and cleverness? I wonder if Mary Shelly had ever heard this story before writing 'Frankenstein' in 1818. Just a thought.

Mary died in 1846 and finally got the recognition she deserved; The Geological Society of London made her an honorary member and commissioned a stained glass window as her memorial.

Inspired by Mary Anning's story, we decided to hike the coastal path to her birthplace of Lyme Regis, about 5 miles away. We walked along Marine Parade and noticed that the street lights incorporated a wrought iron spiral design to represent an ammonite. The low-rise, individual buildings included private houses, cafes, bars and restaurants. The Jubilee Pavilion looks out on a beautiful bay of yachts, pleasure crafts and fishing boats. We walked the famous harbour wall, known as the Cobb, which was featured in the movie The French Lieutenant's Woman. We stopped at Mollie's Seafront Ice Cream shop before heading back along the coastal path, which is quite undulating.

Like many great inventors, scientists, artists or musicians, the secret to success is a belief in yourself, determination, and tenacity. Mary had many setbacks, but her father encouraged her with his life-affirming motto; 'When one door closes, another one opens'. That's good advice, but obviously, he wasn't a very good cabinet maker.

After a short rest at BBKing, we set off for our next stopover, visiting friends for a garden party at the village of Branscombe. We crossed the River Axe a couple of miles down from Axminster, famous for its carpets. We had pre-booked a campsite, which was formerly an airfield.

The following morning, we strolled along the wooded path, dappled with sunlight, past a gorgeous village church and terraced cottages in full bloom with hanging baskets and window boxes. We arrived at the beautiful village of Branscombe, where we had arranged to meet my good friend Steve Frost at the Masons Arms Pub. He lives in Australia and was over in England for a biennial family reunion at his sister Barbara's house in Branscombe. It was like a gathering of the clans as family members came from far and wide: Liverpool, London, Germany and Australia. As the only 'outlanders', we were very flattered to be invited and treated with fabulous hospitality. Barbara's cottage in the village centre is like something from a Jane Austen novel, and we enjoyed a barbeque, endless drinks, guitars and a singalong.

We spent the following day at the beach. The towering cliffs set us wondering about what monstrous creatures had been at this very spot during the Jurassic epoch.

English Riviera

We skirted south of Exeter to our next stop at Twelve Oaks Farm near Newton Abbot, a small market town dating from medieval times. The main feature of the town centre is St. Leonard's Church, popularly known as The Clock Tower, which dates back to the 13th Century. We wandered around and browsed casually before catching the bus to Torquay at the northern end of Torbay. With palm trees along the harbour full of sailing boats, pleasure cruisers and luxury yachts, and numerous outside bars and cafes around the marina, it's not surprising that the area has become known as the English Riviera. A lavish, ornate clock tower looks like a miniature Albert Memorial.

There are exclusive properties along the hill tops, but a blot on the landscape is three brown, featureless, square apartment blocks looming over the town, looking more like North Korea than North Torbay. We stopped for a drink at the Pier Point pub, taking in the atmosphere of this popular holiday resort. Along the beach are many painted wooden kiosks advertising boat trips and watersports. Torquay was involved in Operation Overlord, the D-Day landings, and the embarkation ramps are still there.

The Princess Theatre is very popular and hosts shows, pantomimes, and concerts opened in 1961 by Morecambe and Wise. The Princess Gardens are beautifully maintained, a central feature being the English Riviera Wheel, which lights up spectacularly from dusk. Steep wooden steps zig-zag up the hillside to the top.

The famous crime writer Agatha Christie was born in Torquay in 1890 on Barton Road. The grand house where she was born and grew up has been demolished, but a blue plaque commemorates her. She lived amongst a country house society; many of her murder mysteries and characters draw on these experiences. Her first novel in 1916, The Mysterious Affair at Styles, is such an example and introduced the Belgian detective Hercule Poirot.

Plymouth

Our next port of call was Plymouth, which, like Portsmouth, has played a significant role in England's naval heritage. This is emphasized by the names of pubs in the Barbican Area of the docks: The Crown and Anchor, The Navy Inn, The Maritime Inn, and The Ship. Cap'n Jasper's is a wooden building on the waterfront with a mural of a pantomime pirate looking through an eye-glass out to sea. Plymouth's answer to Portsmouth's Spinnaker is a modern metal sculpture of a giant, fantasy crustacean on the harbour called Leviathan Sea Monster by Brian Fell.

Plymouth has the distinction of having elected the first-ever female member of Parliament, Nancy Astor, in 1919. Artist Joshua Reynolds was born in Plymouth in 1723 and went on to become the first President of the Royal Academy in London. Captain Bligh, notorious from The Mutiny on the Bounty, was also born in Plymouth in 1754

As with other dockyard cities, the Luftwaffe caused extensive damage, but Plymouth has revitalized and re-purposed to breathe new life into a bygone era while retaining the cobbled ambience of a labyrinth of narrow alleyways once frequented by pirates and smugglers. Warehouses have been redeveloped into pubs, restaurants, galleries and apartments. The Tudor House Pub is an over-hanging, black-and-white building, and Southside Street is full of 'olde worlde' gift shops and galleries. To misquote Humphrey Bogart, 'Of all the gin joints in all the towns in all the world, we had to go into this one.' Of course, the world-famous Plymouth Gin Distillery opened in 1793 and is the oldest in England. It is located along a terraced street in the Barbican district. Originally, it was a Dominican Monastery called Black Friars after the cloaks the monks wore. Thomas Coates bought the property in 1793 and began production of Plymouth Gin from his secret recipe.

Quote: 'Drink, the scourge of the working class. Work, the scourge of the drinking class'.

Oscar Wilde.

Gin can be traced back to the 11th Century across Europe when monks created a medical liqueur, and they must have thought this was a good habit to get into. Over time, it was modified in the Netherlands, and the origin of gin is attributed to Franciscus Sylvius, a 17th Century Professor of Medicine who distilled the juniper berry with grain mash. The Dutch for juniper berry in genever, which in English becomes gin. In the 18th Century, there was a gin craze in England, and homemade gin became the scourge of the lower classes, as exemplified by the engraving of 'Gin Lane' by William Hogarth in 1751. It was published as a campaign against uncontrolled drinking, and the government restricted the production of gin to licensed companies only. Thomas Coates and Company produced gin; each bottle carries a label with a logo of The Mayflower, and the reverse has a monk with a gin. The distillery is like a museum in itself, using 19th Century copper pots, and the roof has a magnificent, wooden vaulted ceiling. There is an excellent cocktail bar and a tasting session.

Plymouth Gin was appointed official supplier to the Royal Navy, and it *had* to be 'super strength.' For some strange reason, ships stored gunpowder *next* to the gin. If normal-strength gin happened to slop over on to the gunpowder, it couldn't be lit to fire the canons. However, if Navy strength gin of 57% alcohol happened to dampen the gunpowder, there was still enough alcohol to light and fire. In view of what we found out in Portsmouth about drunkenness and floggings, I think the sailors were hiding nothing.

The impressive harbour bobs with boats of all sizes, and it was from here that famous names have embarked over the centuries: Captain Cook on the Endeavour in 1768, convict ships bound for Botany Bay, Charles Darwin on the Beagle in 1831 and even Napoleon in 1815 aboard the Bellepheron on his way to exile on the island of St. Helena in the South Atlantic. By far, the two most famous sailings were Francis Drake commanding the Victory in 1588 as part of the English fleet, which defeated the Spanish Armada and The Mayflower taking the Pilgrims to the New World in 1690.

The Mayflower

A commemorative monument marks the Pilgrim Steps, where they boarded the Mayflower. The Pilgrims have become synonymous with Plymouth, but I was surprised to learn that the connection is tenuous, almost accidental. They were from Nottinghamshire and Lincolnshire, a religious group within the Church of England. Originally, they were called Separatists because they wanted to change and simplify (purify) ceremonies and rid them of all vestiges of grandeur not mentioned in the Bible. They moved to Holland and lived for 12 years with religious freedom. However, they still felt as though they were foreigners. The Pilgrims wanted their own homeland where they could be in control of their own destiny in terms of religion and democracy. A song by Neil Diamond called 'I am, I said,' has a line; 'L.A.'s fine but it ain't home, New York's home but it ain't mine no more.' This sums up the Pilgrims' attitude to Holland

and England. They decided on the New World, paid for passage on The Mayflower in England, and sailed from Southampton but returned due to bad weather. Later, they were accompanied by The Speedwell, which started to take on water, forcing them to return to Plymouth, the nearest port. Finally, The Mayflower embarked alone and landed at Cape Cod after a horrendous, dangerous crossing. Initially, they had to fight hostile local Native American Indians, but eventually, they made peace. Surprisingly, some of the locals could speak English because, previously, other ships had sailed and settled, and it had been 13 years since the first English settlement had been founded at Jamestown. Crucially for the Pilgrims, the indigenous tribes helped them plant corn and other food, but only half of the settlers survived the first winter. After the harvest, the Pilgrims invited the Indians to join them in a Thanksgiving feast, a tradition which continues to this day.

Trivia Alert... It was only in 1863 that President Lincoln declared that Thanksgiving could be a public holiday. An important date to look forward to, except for turkeys.

The Pilgrims called their settlement Plymouth, and although they weren't the first to arrive in the New World, they were the first to draw up a democratic charter according to their beliefs. The original 13 colonies grew from this, which is why the Pilgrims are recognised as the Founding Fathers of America.

Spanish Armada

Another momentous event in Plymouth occurred in 1588 when the English fleet sailed to confront the Spanish. Elizabethan Britain was a society of intrigue and spies, and the English ships were ready and waiting for the Armada. The famous story is that Francis Drake insisted on finishing a game of bowls even though bonfire beacons warned of the approaching Spanish Galleons. The invasion plan was that the Armada would sail up the channel to pick up Spanish soldiers in France and transport them across to England. However, the English fleet, under the command of Lord Effingham, the bad weather and a lack of communication between the Spanish forces conspired against

King Philip of Spain's plan. At the Battle of Plymouth, Drake captured two Spanish ships. Harsh weather forced the Spanish to shelter in Calais harbour, but Drake attacked with fire ships, which caused panic and the Armada scattered. The wind, known as 'The Protestant Wind', forced the Catholic Spanish into the North Sea, having abandoned any hope of invasion. No doubt the Spanish were Effingham all the way. The only way the Armada could get back to Spain was to sail around the north of Scotland and the west coast of Ireland. Fierce winds and mountainous seas caused even more devastation, and even today, there are Spanish shipwrecks off the wild Atlantic coast of Ireland. This marked the beginning of Britain's world-wide naval dominance led by men from the Plymouth area: Hawkins, Frobisher and Drake. They were basically 'legal' pirates, approved by the Queen and called 'Privateers', who plundered Spanish treasure ships.

Nutty Walt

Walter Raleigh, who was born near Plymouth, was a writer, politician and explorer. On the Beatles' White Album is a song called, 'I'm so tired', which contains a unique line: ... 'I'll have another cigarette, and curse Sir Walter Raleigh, he was such a stupid get...' What more can be said about the man who introduced tobacco to England and the world? I'm reminded of a satirical routine by the American comedian Bob Newhart called 'Nutty Walt' in which he imagines how Raleigh would try to pitch his discovery in modern times over the phone: 'A tobacco leaf that you can roll into a tube? You put it into your mouth? Then, you *set fire* to it?! You breathe in the smoke to fill your lungs?! And you become addicted to a drug called nicotine?! Don't phone us, Walt; we'll phone you'.

Walter Raleigh was invited to the Court of Queen Elizabeth 1st and quickly became one of her favourites. He was tall, dark, handsome and charming. He liked to dress fashionably, and a famous story is that he extravagantly laid out his cloak over a puddle so that the Queen could step onto it. Raleigh had a 'roving eye for a wench' and could have had his pick of any woman. So what did he do? He made pregnant and secretly married Elizabeth Throckmorton, who just happened to be the Queen's Lady-in-Waiting. When the Queen found out, she felt betrayed and imprisoned them both in the Tower of London. Not the smartest move by Raleigh.

Eventually, they were released, and Walter Raleigh was free to embark on voyages of discovery. He founded a settlement in North America and called it Virginia in honour of the Queen. Under the reign of Elizabeth's successor, James 1st, he sailed to South America in search of the fabled El Dorado, the City of Gold, as told by earlier Spanish explorers. Unwisely, Raleigh attacked a Spanish outpost, which violated an international peace treaty, and Spain demanded his execution. To avoid further war, James appeased the Spanish and had Raleigh beheaded in front of a huge crowd in London. Again, not the cleverest course of action by Walter Raleigh. I think Lennon and McCartney were spot on.

Eden Project

Next on our itinerary was a site neat St. Austell, from where we walked to the Eden Project, an awesome first impression with space-age domes emerging from a natural bowl. It was the brain-child of co-founder Tim Smit, who was inspired by the novel 'The Lost World' by Arthur Conan-Doyle. The book is about a closed environment in which the world is treated with respect and in harmony.

The site was originally a clay pit that looked like an alien world's surface. It was used by the BBC as a location for the planet Magrathea in Hitchhiker's Guide to the Galaxy.

The Eden Project was opened in 2001 and houses in a Biome, 'The Largest Rainforest in Captivity.' A Mediterranean Biome is linked to create a fascinating walk-through experience. The structure of the domes was inspired by bees, comprising honeycomb, interlocking hexagonal 'bubbles.' Imagine a gigantic roll of bubble wrap. Consequently, the Biomes are 1% the weight of glass and can re-adjust as the ground shifts.

There are waterfalls and rope-bridges straight out of Indiana Jones, and even a cool room, like walking into a fridge. There are information displays, such as 'Rain makes rainforest, and rainforests make rain,' which explains the weather cycle. We walked through an actual cloud, so now l know where my photographs are kept.

The word Mediterranean in this context refers to the climate types, not just the geographical area of the Med. The Biome also includes California, South Africa and Western Australia, all of which have a Mediterranean climate.

There are plants from different countries along with displays and art work. Sculptor Tim Shaw has created a large installation of Dionysus, God of the Vine. There are many sculptures in the outside gardens, set amongst beautiful floral displays: giant bees, surreal metal flowers, butterflies and sculptures of horses made entirely of driftwood.

Here is a jaw-dropping statistic: 99.9% of all species of plants and animals to have *ever* lived on Earth are extinct! The most famous cosmic impact was 65 million years ago, which killed the dinosaurs and half of all living things.

There have been five mass extinctions on Earth. The most devastating was 250 million years ago when 95% of plant and animal life was killed. This was caused by a low-oxygen atmosphere, acid rain and volcanic eruptions resulting in carbon dioxide and global warming. Where have we heard all this before? Not everything can be blamed on human activity, but the human race must play its part and respect the planet. Furthermore, there have also been 5 Ice Ages, the earliest about 2.4 billion years ago when the entire globe became a complete ball of ice.

Climate change has been happening on earth for 4.5 billion years due to a variety of reasons and will continue for the remaining 4.5 billion years until the sun's batteries run out and it takes its solar system planets with it, including earth.

The Eden Project site looked like a prototype for human colonization of other worlds. Perhaps it is. I learned that an award-winning Spanish architect, Emilio Perez Pinero, pioneered the idea of portable domes in the early 1960s. The US Navy were interested in domes for Antarctica, and NASA planned to build greenhouses on the moon. They wanted lightweight, flat packs which could be transported and assembled. I don't know if they went ahead, or if it is top secret, or if they went to IKEA instead. Coincidentally, in 2022, it has been reported that scientists have succeeded in growing plants in the moondust brought back to Earth by Armstrong and Aldrin in 1969. Furthermore, NASA has announced that it is planning to send a manned mission to the moon for the first time since 1972. The mission is to deliver units for future construction.

Rather than having guides, the Eden Project has storytellers. One began by asking us what we would choose to take to a desert island. Naturally, gramophone records came to mind, but we were assured that plants and seeds were the only guarantee of survival. Many millennia ago, Polynesian people sailed north in dugout boats from the South Pacific. They took with them 27 types of seeds, plants, shoots and bulbs to provide staple food crops, bamboo as building materials, and even medicines. The rainforests are like a giant pharmacy, full of medicinal plants, of which we only know about 10%. They found a remote deserted island to settle, which today is known as Hawaii.

A day at the Eden Project is fascinating, educational, thought-provoking, and enjoyable. The Eden Project 'brand' is expanding worldwide: Costa Rica, China, Lake Chad, Australia and New Zealand. One is proposed for Morecambe in Lancashire, which means, unlike when I was growing up, families can go there on holiday, *guaranteed* tropical or Mediterranean weather.

Personally, l think Morecambe is an excellent choice as a trial run before colonizing the Moon, Mars, infinity and beyond because they all have something in common… no atmosphere. Sorry for that joke; I don't wish to offend any citizens of Morecambe… especially Tyson Fury.

End-to-Enders

From St. Austell, we followed the A390 to Truro and continued to Penzance via Penryn and Helston and on to a site at Treyloy Farm. The following morning, we walked to the village of St. Buryon, which consisted of a post office, a small convenience store, some cottages and a stone cross opposite the village pub. Three jolly ladies of ample proportions were sitting on the plinth of the cross.

"Excuse me, where do we catch the bus to Land's End," I inquired.

"It's from here, dear. It's due about now, but it's *never* on time."

Right on cue, the bus arrived, and they laughed and stood up. They joked and pushed each other playfully as they got on. It was a Beryl Cook painting come to life.

The journey to Land's End was along narrow roads with hedgerows on either side. The bus driver had to occasionally reverse for quite a distance to give way to on-coming traffic. A high level of skill indeed, not to mention courtesy. Having been to John O'Groats, we felt a sense of achievement as we approached Land's End... we were now End-to-Enders. We've seen plenty of Neo Greek/Roman columns and architectural features, and even the entrance to Land's End has a row of fluted Doric columns leading to a white-painted courtyard, which is a small shopping mall including The West Country Shopping Village, Land's End Clothing Company, and the Land's End Doughnut Company. They were yummy and another box to tick... Land's End is the most westerly point on mainland England.

Trivia Alert... For quiz buffs, Ardnamurchan Point in Scotland is the most westerly point on Great Britain.

The costal cliffs are rugged and dramatic, with white waves crashing, carving out caves and coves. The Longships Lighthouse has stood on an offshore rocky outcrop since 1795, warning ships of the perilous waters between Land's End and the Scilly Isles. The main attraction for tourists is, of course, the famous sign post. This was first installed by a local family who owned the land and charged visitors for photographs. As we found out at John 'O'Groats, they set up a second franchise up there.

After a couple of hours, we caught the bus to St. Ives, along the dramatic Penwith Heritage Coast, Poldark country, where remnants of Cornish tin mines can be seen along the way.

St. Ives

St. Ives is a beautiful, traditional Cornish fishing village with a compact semi-circular harbour protected by a wall and a small white lighthouse. Smeaton's Pier dates from 1770 and is named after the designer. There are no high-rise buildings, and the quaint, narrow, cobbled streets are thronged with visitors browsing the galleries, craft shops, souvenir shops, cafés, and bars.

St. Ives is synonymous with art, and Tate Modern opened there in 1993. The light has a unique quality, shimmering and reflecting the sand and sea, and artists have been inspired by this since the 1920s. The founding father was a retired fisherman called Alfred Wallace, who unwittingly became an inspiration with his untrained, naïve style. At the beginning of the Second World War, several artists moved from London, ostensibly to be inspired by St. Ives, but the blitz probably influenced their decision. Ben Nicholson produced geometric, abstract seascapes, and Victor Pasmore and Patrick Heron added to their growing reputations. Barbara Hepworth made large sculptures inspired by the rugged, rocky surrounding landscape, and one of her monumental pieces stands outside the United Nations Building in New York.

The worldwide influence of St. Ives should not be underestimated, and much of the work from there influenced modern art in Britain. Today, there are many local studios where artists work in a wide range of media, including montage, found objects and printmaking. Also, there are traditional studios and galleries selling paintings of local scenes. The Sloop Studio occupies old fish cellars, and the St. Ives Society of Artists is located in a church.

For such a small town, there are a surprising number of varied beaches; for example, Porthminster Beach is reminiscent of the Mediterranean, Bamaluz Beach is secluded, while Porthmear Beach is windy and ideal for surfing.

There are, of course, numerous Cornish Pasty Shops to add to our list of named foods. We saw a sign advertising Cornish Cock which turned out to be a craft cider.

We caught the bus back to St. Buryon from St. Ives, completing the circle and a fantastic day. The joys of an OAP Bus pass!... living life in the bus lane. The bus stopped right outside the pub, so of course, we were drawn in. I asked the landlady about a taxi since it was quite an uphill walk to the farm. She said she would ring when we were ready, but after a pint and a couple more, she told us not to worry about a taxi as her husband would drive us home. Fantastic Cornish hospitality.

Newquay

Our next booking couldn't be a greater contrast. From the hamlet of St. Buryon, we got back on to the beaten track and followed the major roads to Newquay.

We went to Newquay to meet up with long-time friends Graham and Julie, who were on holiday from Wigan. As with meeting Steve in Branscombe and Keith and Sue in Cullercoats, we appreciated the freedom and flexibility of life on the road in a motorhome. Our site was about half an hour away by bus, and we met them on Fistral Beach for a great reunion and a few drinks on this popular, beautiful beach of golden sand.

Newquay was originally a fishing village and is now known as the Surf Capital of the UK. Although Fistral Beach is the most famous, others have different characters, such as Towan Beach, the Great Western Beach and the classy and exclusive Tolcarne Beach. There is also Lusty Beach in a secluded rocky cove, and one can only imagine how it got its name. Perhaps it's the origin of the popular cocktail, Sex On The Beach. Just a thought.

The town centre is mainly pedestrianised to accommodate the hordes of visitors, but Graham and Julie, being regulars, were able to give us a guided tour, mainly of side-street pubs. Lunch was, as usual, fish and chips in an impressive terraced chippy overlooking the sea. We found a karaoke bar that evening, and Graham and I re-lived memories of many a great night out in Wigan. One Christmas some years ago, Norma and Julie clubbed together and bought Graham and me some studio time to record an album mixed by a professional recording engineer. On the C.D., we called ourselves The Symbolics, but we had to abandon that name because we couldn't agree which one of us was Sym.

King Arthur

We made our way along the spectacular coastal route to Tintagel.

Most of us know the Legend of King Arthur from movies, television, and not forgetting Monty Python and The Holy Grail. He isn't included in any history exam curriculum simply because no-one knows if he actually existed. So where does Tintagel fit alongside the mythology of Camelot, Guinevere, Knights of the Round Table, Lancelot, Merlin and Avalon? What is the attraction for tourists?

Tintagel is an 'almost island' linked by a small causeway, and there are no crumbling ruins of a once magnificent castle, just some foundations and walls. It is thought to be the place where Arthur was conceived… not born, or lived there, but conceived on a one-night stand. That's it. The story goes that his father, Uther Pendragon, was a King who fancied the wife of the Duke of Cornwall at Tintagel. The King sent the Duke away under some false pretence and ordered the Wizard Merlin to magically transform him into a clone of the Duke. He was then able to seduce Igraine, the Duke's wife. There is no record of her comments about any improvement in performance. She became pregnant, and the baby Arthur was given to Merlin as part of the deal.

The seeds of the Arthurian legends were probably sown during the period which has become known as the Dark Ages. The Romans left Britain in 410 AD because the empire was falling, and troops were needed elsewhere. However, the exodus also included civil servants, government administrators, builders, and other stalwarts of a civilized, well-ordered society. Consequently, the economy in Britain collapsed, and everywhere became lawless with tribes at war.

Quote: *'Apart from the aqueduct, roads, a monetary system, education, law and order… what have the Romans ever done for us?'*
Monty Python.

Writing and recording of history finished abruptly, and consequently, modern-day historians and archaeologists know very little about the 5th and 6th centuries, hence the name Dark Ages. War leaders came to prominence, and one of these, or an amalgam of several, is probably the beginnings of Arthurian tales, embellished and fantasised over-time.

The Romans left a power vacuum which attracted Germanic people: Angles, Saxons, and Jutes. Ancient documents in the British Museum describe the Battle of Badon in the 5th Century AD, in which a military leader named Arthur defeated Saxon invaders.

The Welsh Monk Geoffrey of Monmouth wrote 'The History of Kings of Britain' in the 12th century and mentions Arthur, Tintagel and Caliburno (Excalibur). The legend of a hero warrior riding a horse is an enduring ancient tradition from many cultures. In 1485, Henry Tudor defeated Richard III at the Battle of Bosworth, and many people actually believed that the prophecy had come to life. This was in the news quite recently when Richard's body was found at a car park in Leicester. I don't know if his descendants have received a fixed penalty for an over-stay.

The Cornwall Archaeological Unit has been excavating Tintagel recently and has discovered foundations of 100 buildings and artefacts which indicate high-status, wealthy inhabitants. Its location was an ideal international port for ships from as far away as Constantinople bringing glass and buying Cornish tin. Tintagel is a dramatic setting with rugged cliffs, patterned rock formations and crashing Atlantic waves. On a cliff top is a mysterious sculpture in bronze of a hooded Arthurian knight. In formal pose with head bowed, he was wearing a ghostly, shredded cloak, with both hands resting on a double-edged broadsword. There is an Italian saying, 'Se non ē vero, è ben trovato'... It may not be true, but it's a great story.

Clifton Suspension Bridge

Our next destination following our tour of the West Country was Bath via the iconic Clifton Suspension Bridge in Bristol. The slight side-wind made me a little apprehensive since the Avon Gorge is 700 feet wide and 250 feet deep, with sheer rock on either side with the River Avon flowing below on its way to the Severn Estuary. It was an exhilarating experience.

The bridge was designed by the celebrated Victorian engineer Isambard Kingdom Brunel, whom most will be familiar from the quintessential photograph of him wearing his distinctive stovepipe top hat, smoking a trademark cigar, and standing in front of gigantic metal chains. An image which exemplifies the spirit of the Industrial Revolution. He was born in Portsmouth in 1806, but how did Brunel acquire such an exotic name? His father was Marc Isambard Brunel, a French refugee and civil engineer; his English mother was Sophia Kingdom.

The problem of how to span the Clifton Gorge had been around for hundreds of years, and in the 19th Century, a competition was launched. Brunel had never designed a bridge before, but he won the commission. Rather than build free-standing towers, Brunel used the natural rock to build on, and as the suspension bridge took shape over 33 years, he was so proud that he called it 'my first child, my darling.' Unfortunately, his 'child' became an orphan because Brunel died five years before the bridge was completed in 1864.

In its dramatic setting, the stupendous Clifton Suspension Bridge was described as audacious and visionary, which also describes Brunel himself. It has become his lasting legacy, but let's not forget that this genius of the Industrial Revolution designed and created many ambitious projects: The Great Western Railway linking London and Bristol, Paddington Station, tunnels, bridges and ships, including Great Britain and the Great Western. He was at the forefront of the Industrial Revolution, which transformed Britain from an agricultural society into the mechanised world we know today. A great man.

Aquae Sulis

Founded by the Romans, Bath is one of Britain's most beautiful cities, and a stopover in Somerset was an ideal link between the West Country and the Cotswolds. Standing on the River Avon, Bath is a UNESCO World Heritage site, and the thermal spring is the reason the city exists.

The spring and earlier settlements had existed long before the Romans arrived. In Parade Gardens in the city centre is a statue of King Bladud, who is said to have *originally* founded a settlement in 836 BC.

Trivia Alert... King Bladud was the father of King Lear, whose name has been kept alive by Shakespeare.

Their love of a Mediterranean Climate and Roman baths made it seem like a Godsend, an oasis of warmth in cold Britannia. They named it Aquae Sulis in honour of Sulis, the Goddess of the Springs, and the town built up around it. Most Roman structures are still intact, with classic statues lining the balcony overlooking the baths. Guides dressed in Roman costumes informed us of artefacts, coins and mosaics. The greenish water didn't look particularly inviting, and we were instructed not to touch or drink it. There was a water fountain of treated water from the springs, but it tasted of rust.

From certain vantage points, there is a familiar view of the Baths, columns and balcony, while looming behind is Bath Abbey. This is of historical significance because it was where the first English King, Edgar, was crowned in 973 AD. Later, Coronations transferred to

Winchester Cathedral and Westminster Abbey, but the first in Bath established much of the pomp and ceremonial rituals still followed at King Charles III's Coronation in 2023.

Although Roman culture underscores Bath, it is primarily a Georgian and Regency city. That is approximately the 18th Century, the period covered by the consecutive reigns of four King Georges, the latter ruling as Regent during the madness of George III prior to becoming King. It was a period of elegance, fashion and polite society culminating in the Regency Period, exemplified by Beau Brummel, a friend of the Prince Regent.

The buildings are made of Bath stone, a honey-coloured limestone mined locally. The solid Georgian buildings are perfect examples of harmony and proportion, as can be seen at The Royal Crescent, which opened in 1774 and The Circus. Many of Bath's buildings were inspired by Palladian architecture. This means the influence of the 16th Century Italian architect Andrea Palladio and a style of architecture incorporating proportion based on mathematical ratios. Palladio himself was influenced by Classical Roman architecture, but he didn't just copy; he used its elements, such as columns, as a basis for his own style.

The Pulteney Bridge over the River Avon is probably Bath's most famous architectural feature. Designed by Robert Adam in 1774, it is, in effect, a street over a river incorporating shops built into the structure. The closest comparison I can think of is the Ponte Vecchio over the River Arno in Florence.

The writer Jane Austen lived in Bath from 1801 to 1806, and her books, such as Sense and Sensibility, Emma, and Pride and Prejudice, describe the intrigue within the social world of high society. The films of her books used Bath as a location, along with other period pieces like Bridgerton, Harry Potter and Russel Crowe's version of Victor Hugo's novel Les Misérables.

The rich and famous were attracted to Bath not only for the social whirl and to take the health-giving waters but also to become part of polite society. But what exactly *is* polite society? A real-life Mr. D'Arcy was a man called Beau Nash, who created this notion. Not long before, Bath had been a hotbed of gambling, drinking and duels. It was a real party town, more Aya Napa than Aquae Sulis. Nash was given the title Master of Ceremonies and set about changing Bath's raucous image. He introduced a Code of Conduct for behaviour and good manners, hence polite society. The Assembly Rooms were opened in 1771 with a Grand Ball. It was a meeting place for the rich, influential, famous and elegant, including Jane Austen and Charles Dickens. No wonder artist Thomas Gainsborough moved to Bath from East Anglia for prestigious portrait commissions.

Today, much of the city centre is pedestrianised with many restaurants and pubs. Still, a place we definitely wanted to visit was the home of the Bath Bun, Sally Lunn's Eating House of 1680, which has a Regency-style café downstairs. The famous Bath Bun is similar to a French brioche, which isn't surprising since Sally Lunn was a French refugee. The bun was sugary and delicious, and they sold like hotcakes. It went straight on to our legendary list of geographical foodie places.

Apart from tourist pamphlets, we found that the best local information sources were taxi drivers or local newspapers. We picked up free papers regularly, but one in Somerset was particularly enlightening. A section was called 'The Farmer Takes a Wife', which I presumed referred back to a children's playground/street game. (For younger readers, this was a time when kids actually played together before the zombification of mobile phones took hold.) Basically, it was a dating site for the agricultural community and reminded me of a joke; 'Gentleman farmer with own tractor seeks to meet lady farmer with combined harvester, with a view to friendship and possible matrimony. Will be happy to meet. Please send photograph... of the combined harvester.'

Cotswolds

The Cotswolds is designated as an Area of Natural Beauty and covers an area between Bath and Stratford-upon-Avon. To many people, especially foreign visitors, it is the epitome of the perception of rural England with its thatched cottages and ancient village pubs. It's almost like a theme park full of charming places with names straight out of a children's storybook: Chipping Sodbury, Great Coxwell, Tiltups End, Wyre Piddle and Chipping Norton. As we drove through these sublimely picturesque places, I was reminded of the joke about the confused tourists who were lost because they had seen a sign by the road which said Loose Chippings, but they couldn't find that village on the map.

Most of the quirky names are derived from Anglo-Saxon words, but two villages in particular seemed to stand out: Upper and Lower Slaughter. I assumed this must refer to an abattoir or butcher shop, but it is nothing of the sort. The name is derived from the Anglo-Saxon word 'slohtre', meaning muddy place. I remember as a child that mud was often called slutch. It's not a word you hear these days, but I wonder if it is from the same derivation. The term Cotswolds is also derived from Anglo-Saxon Cots, meaning sheep pens, and Wolds, gently rolling hills. The woollen industry was vital to the economy after the Romans brought sheep to the area.

Bourton-on-the Water, on the River Windrush, has been dubbed 'Venice of the Cotswolds' by virtue of its shallow streams and low stone bridges. Having been on a gondola on the Grand Canal in Venice, I doubt if one would fit under any of the bridges in Bourton. The name of the village derives from two Anglo-Saxon words: Burgh, meaning camp or fort, and ton, which means village, hence Bourton, village by the camp.

There are craft shops, cafes, galleries, historic pubs, and the Cotswold Motoring Museum and a Toy Collection. The Cotswold Perfumery in the village is regarded as the finest of English fragrances, and visitors can make their own. Norma couldn't resist this, having worked in the Beauty Therapy business, and she enjoyed experimenting to produce her own unique label.

The fact that there are 114 listed buildings speaks for itself. A general description of the village probably sums up everywhere in the Cotswolds: a warm ambience conveyed by the creamy, honey-coloured or pinkish Cotswolds stone. A golden village of thatched cottages or deep-pitched tiled roofs surrounded by rolling hills, valleys and streams.

A few miles north on the A429 is Stow-on-the-Wold, located at the junction of Roman roads, including the Fosse Way, which linked Exeter and Lincoln. My description of Bourton-on-the-Water applies equally here, and its Market Charter was granted in 1107 by Henry II. It thrived on the wool industry, and local sheep farmers donated to churches, hoping to secure a place in heaven. These churches, such as St. Edward's Parish Church, became known as 'wool churches'.

Trivia Alert... John Entwistle, bass player with The Who lived in Stow-on-the-Wold and his funeral was held at St. Edward's Church. So he achieved his wish of 'Hope I die before I get old'.)

Yew trees were traditionally planted in church graveyards because they are poisonous to many animals and discourage them from digging. Two yew trees on either side of a door have intertwined with the masonry to blend in and become an integral part of the structure. (A similar effect to what we have seen at Angkor Wat in Cambodia.) This church door inspired JRR Tolkien's Doors of Durin in Fellowship of the Ring.

The market square has the expected coffee houses, galleries, old book shops, antique shops and pubs, including The Talbot, which opened in 1714. The Porch House dates from the 10th Century and claims to be the oldest Inn in England. Other contenders will dispute this claim. Two places which attracted our attention were The Cotswold Cheese Company and The Cotswold Chocolate Company, two more to tick off on our food trail.

In the 13th and 14th Centuries, the main sheep breed was the Cotswold Lion, and most wool was sold to Italian merchants. Wool trading in Bourton-on-the-Water took place in the Market Square, and passageways led onto the square. They become progressively narrower to enable sheep to be funnelled in and then forced into a single file as they emerge onto the square. This made it easier for shepherds to count the sheep as they went by one by one. Here's a question to ponder: How many sheep could a shepherd count before he fell asleep? Narcolepsy must be an occupational hazard when you count sheep for a living.

Some descriptions of individual places can sum up the outstanding natural beauty of the Cotswolds. Victorian designer William Morris of the Arts and Craft Movement described Bibury as the most beautiful in England. A row of cottages called Arlington Row takes 'dilapidated picturesqueness' to another level of chocolate box art. They were originally occupied by poor weavers, and the river alongside was where the wool was washed. It's ironic that most of these, and elsewhere in the Cotswolds, are now second homes and worth a fortune, a world away from the lives of the original occupants. Broadway is known as the Jewel of the Cotswold, and the nearby village of Snowshill was featured in the movie Bridget Jones' Diary. Many other villages have been described in equally glowing terms.

Blenheim Palace

Our next stop was a caravan site; it was just a short walk to Blenheim Palace, a World Heritage site and ancestral home of the Dukes of Marlborough. According to an urban myth, when John Lennon was once asked if Ringo Starr is the best drummer in Britain, Lennon supposedly replied, 'Ringo isn't even the best drummer in the Beatles.' It was actually coined by a comedian. You must be wondering what this has got to do with Blenheim Palace. A similar question can be asked in a different context: Was Winston Churchill England's greatest wartime leader? Answer: Winston wasn't even the greatest wartime leader in his *own* family! That accolade could go to his 18th Century ancestor, John Churchill, the first Duke of Marlborough and head of the army.

Under Louis XIV, France attempted to take Spain's Empire in the War of the Spanish succession. Spain was part of a Grand Alliance (a NATO of its day), and when France, with its ally Bavaria, moved to capture Vienna, Marlborough commanded the allies. The victory at Blenheim in Bavaria in 1704 crushed the ambitions of Louis XIV to rule Europe. A grateful Queen Anne gave Marlborough land near Woodstock in Oxfordshire and a huge amount of money to build Blenheim Palace.

Renowned architect Sir John Vanburgh was commissioned. Vanburgh was an intriguing character who had had a variety of occupations, including political spy! The French had imprisoned him, and he had become familiar with the new Baroque style of architecture: sumptuous decoration, classic columns, niches, and sculptures. This influenced his design for Castle Howard in Yorkshire, famous for the television series Brideshead Revisited.

The saying 'you don't get a second chance to make a first impression' would be highly relevant in the 18th century, when first impressions meant everything. The classical facades and symmetry of Blenheim Palace are awe-inspiring, and this is accentuated on entering the Great Hall, embellished with classical Greek columns. The spectacular ceiling painting is by James Thornhill. As we walked through the Palace, it was evident that the over-riding theme was the glorification of John Churchill, as we see him portrayed as a Roman General: statues, paintings, tapestries, and inscriptions highlighting heroic moments in his career.

Subsequent Dukes have made additions and collected works of art. The 8th Duke installed an imposing organ in the Long Library in the 1890s, and organ recitals were prestigious invitations.

Trivia Alert... On one occasion, the Duke wanted to impress the audience with his (*non-existent*) musicianship. He had the organ set up on automatic so that he could *pretend* to play. He made his way towards the organ, but unfortunately, he tripped and fell over, and the music started while he was lying on the floor. How embarrassing. It went off prematurely, the biggest organ malfunction of all time.

There is a statue of Queen Anne sculpted in Italian marble. Her robes are delicately carved to emphasise the intricate woven patterns as a tall, elegant monarch looks imperious. Apart from one *tiny* detail… In real life, she was 4ft 10ins tall and weighed over 20 stones. All this was supported by her Queen Anne legs.

The fourth Duke of Marlborough commissioned the pre-eminent landscape designer, Capability Brown, to re-model the surrounding grounds. Capability? What kind of a name is that to give a child? It was actually a nickname because he had the habit of saying, 'It has capabilities,' when assessing a commission. His real name was Lancelot, which presumably his parents thought would have a nice ring to it should he ever be awarded a knighthood.

Previously, gardens of the 17th century tended to be formal, patterned layouts, but in the 18th century, Brown changed this fashion as he embraced the natural surroundings. He would create lakes and rivers, accentuate hills, remove trees, and plant others to create views from the house or the grounds. He created over 130 commissions, including Alnwick, Chatsworth and Longleat. At Blenheim, he dug out a valley, lined it with clay and flooded it to enhance the pre-existing stone bridge and view of the palace.

His signature tree was the Cedar of Lebanon, which he planted at Highclere House, the setting for the television series Downton Abbey. Gnarled trees with imagined human features have always been a standard cinema cliché in the horror or fantasy genre. One of the trees at Blenheim featured in Harry Potter and the Order of the Phoenix. It has its own plaque and is as popular as the Palace itself. It has a gaping hole, which reminded me of 'The Scream', but I don't know if Edvard Munch ever visited.

It's well known that Winston Churchill was born at Blenheim Palace in 1874, and the bedroom in which he was born has been preserved. His mother didn't live there, and she was attending a party and perhaps over-exuberant dancing induced baby Winston to make an appearance. He always liked to make an entrance. He is buried at Bladon nearby, and I well remember his funeral in 1965 when the Dock cranes on the Thames lowered in unison as a unique emotional guard of honour.

The Churchill and Spencer families have been closely related for centuries by marriage. The two families were intertwined on a complicated family tree, and the surname Spencer-Churchill was often used. Lady Diana Spencer and Winston Churchill were distant cousins.

Stratford and Shakespeare

As we have seen, many places have maximised connection with specific individuals. I can't think of anywhere as inextricably linked as Stratford-upon-Avon and William Shakespeare.

In ancient Celtic, Strat means street, Ford is a riverbed, and Avon means river, giving this beautiful city its name. Half-timbered buildings are everywhere, some in black and white while others have an ochre hue. The Shakespeare connection is everywhere: Anne Hathaway's cottage still has its original furnishings. William's mother, Mary Island, had a farm which still functions. His birthplace in Henry Street, the schoolroom, and the Holy Trinity Church where he was baptised are all close together. There is an impressive monument with a sculpture of a seated William Shakespeare, surrounded by some of the most famous characters from his plays.

William was born in 1564, a year in which there was an outbreak of the plague, but fortunately he survived. (Or, *unfortunately,* for students who have struggled through set-books for English Literature exams!) His father, John, was a prosperous glove maker catering for the fashionable well-to-do, and he became mayor when William was a child. John Shakespeare's business collapsed, and he was later forced to take William out of school at fourteen. These were turbulent times, and Queen Elizabeth Ist had spies everywhere reporting on religious conspiracies and tax evasion. John was dealing illegally in wool and money- lending, for which he was fined, while William was *actually* jailed for poaching deer. I wonder if he used slings and arrows to create an outrageous fortune.

For such a prolific writer, relatively little is known about William Shakespeare's life, leading to conjecture and theory. He married Anne Hathaway in 1582 and became a father at 18. He referred to the book A History of Kings as source material, and his writing was inspired by his favourite author, the classic Roman poet Ovid (my dreaded predictive text tried to change this to Covid! As if the plague wasn't enough.) I prefer old-fashioned methods like mnenims... Rhymes to remember lists or grammar. Probably the most commonly-used is i before e except after c. But this has been disproved by science.

In 1587, a group of travelling actors, The Queen's Men, visited Stratford, and one theory is that Shakespeare joined them and travelled with them to London, where a theatrical community was beginning to emerge. Playhouses had been recently built, whereas previously, performances had been in yards or houses. Shakespeare was in the right place at the right time. He wrote 37 plays and numerous sonnets and became a shareholder in the company that built the Globe Theatre in 1599. He returned to Stratford regularly and built a second home after his first house was destroyed by fire. What did Shakespeare, the greatest wordsmith in the English language, decide to call his new house?... The New Place. He must have agonised for hours before coming up with that name. I would have expected something like Dun Bardin', at the very least.

Shakespeare has left an amazing legacy of phrases and one-liners: Vanish into thin air, fight fire with fire, made of sterner stuff, cruel to be kind, a sorry sight, wearing your heart on your sleeve, there's method in my madness, too much of a good thing, heart of gold. The world is your oyster was created for Falstaff in Henry IV part 1, and let's not forget Arthur Daly in Minder, 'The World is your lobster, my son.'

Aldous Huxley took the title of his book Brave New World from the Tempest, and John Steinbeck took The Winter of our Discontent from Richard III. This was also used to describe a winter in the 1970s in Britain when there were power cuts, soaring inflation and strikes. (Has anything changed?) An enterprising outdoor pursuits store advertised, 'Now is the winter of our discount tents.'

Many of Shakespeare's plays were based on Kings, and it seems appropriate that the King himself, Elvis Presley, should get in on the act. The song 'Are You Lonesome Tonight' has Elvis quoting, ' Someone said that all the world is a stage and each of us play a part.' Willian died in 1616 and, intriguingly, in his will, he left to his wife, quote: 'My second best bed.' I wonder if he added, 'per chance to dream?'

It has been suggested that Shakespeare didn't write the works attributed to him and that others wrote them, Edward de Vere, the Earl of Oxford, being one of the favourites. Furthermore, it's been argued that William Shakespeare could not have written about intrigue at court because the son of a glove maker who left school at 14 could not know about such things. Well, as far as I know, Gene Roddenberry, the writer of Star Trek, never went into space and was never beamed up by Scotty.

Trivia Alert... The catchphrase 'Beam me up, Scotty' was *never* said in any TV episode or movie.

Like the da Vinci code, some believe that there is a Shakespeare code containing hidden messages in the text. The arguments proposed have about the same logic as the old television gameshow 3-2-1, where solving idiotic, tenuous clues can win a prize or Dusty Bin. I think that's where these Shakespeare theories belong: in the Dusty Bin of History. Me thinks the conspirators have lost the plot. It's much ado about nothing.

Bridgnorth

From Stratford, we travelled north-west to our next booking at Bridgnorth in Shropshire, founded in 1101 AD. The town got its name, funnily enough, because it was a new bridge *further north* than the original one spanning the River Severn. There are two distinct sections, high and low, linked by the Castle Hill Funicular Railway, opened in 1892, and which poet John Benjamin described as 'being lifted up to heaven.' The booking office retains its original Victorian style and signage, and the view over the bridge and the Severn is impressive.

The town suffered from the ravages of Cromwell's troops during the English Civil War, but today, it is a charming place built mainly of local red sandstone complemented by timber-framed black and white buildings. The Old Market Hall is an example of grand Victoriana at its proudest, and the Old Town Hall, with its impressive clock, has a market underneath. Bridgnorth's North Gate is the only original one left, and its castellated design is like a miniature castle. The Georgian Quarter is elegant, while the ruins of a 12th Century castle emphasise the town's history.

Trivia Alert… Here's something that's hard to believe. Recently discovered documents have revealed that if the German invasion of Britain (Operation Sealion) had been successful, Hitler had decided that Bridgnorth would be his headquarters due to its central location and high vantage point.

Coalbrookdale

Ironbridge Gorge was granted World Heritage status in 1986, and ten museums are located along the River Severn. In the 18th Century, Coalbrookdale was the centre of the iron industry, and barges were used to transport raw materials across the river. This mode of transport became untenable, and it was decided that a bridge was essential. Abraham Darby owned the Coalbrookdale Iron Works, and he had perfected the smelting process of iron ore. Being an entrepreneur with a flair for marketing, Darby took advantage of this opportunity to demonstrate to the world the potential of cast iron. He collaborated with a local architect and opened the world's first iron bridge in 1779. The bridge is a work of art with its semi-circular arch and intricate tracery, and the whole effect is enhanced by the reflections in the river, which creates a circle. The town expanded and is regarded as the birthplace of the Industrial Revolution, and Britain became a world technology leader. It is a pleasant town with plenty of cafes, pubs, and shops, and there is a hotel called, you've guessed it again, Bridge View.

We visited the Coalbrookdale Iron Works Museum and toured the factory and foundry. A huge brick-built viaduct with 26 arches still stands, brought raw materials to the ironworks. We were able to view the original blast furnace, a very interesting insight into the industry of the past. I have actually worked in an iron foundry as a student in the 1970s, and it was hot, grim and smoky, so life for the factory workers in the 18th Century must have been like something from a Hieronymus Bosch painting.

Standing on a hill overlooking this scene are two mansions, Dale House and Rose Hill House, both grade II listed buildings. These were the homes of the Darby family, and it takes the saying 'living over the shop' to another level. With his fabulous wealth and influence, I would have expected Abraham Darby to look out on a landscaped garden designed by Capability Brown rather than Dante's Inferno. It was more like a scene from 'Brass' with Bradley Hardaker smoking a huge cigar, looking down smugly on the source of his wealth. The interiors of both houses have been lovingly restored, and many original items have survived: carpets, paintings, intricate plasterwork, furniture and all the trappings of a comfortable life, apart from the view through the windows.

Blists Hill

Nearby is the Blists Hill Museum, a UNESCO World Heritage Site, a recreation of a Victorian town, which opened in 1973. It was built on a former industrial area, and some existing buildings have been restored. Some have been brought brick by brick and rebuilt, while others are exact replicas of buildings of the period. Lloyd's Bank was obtained from a few miles away, and the interior recreates cashiers' counters sourced from around the country. Blakemore Grocers opened in 1917 in Wolverhampton, and the one at Blists Hill is an exact copy. The New Inn Pub was originally in Walsall and was transferred in 1981 to be rebuilt. It is fully licensed, and of course, we went in for a drink. I didn't make the same mistake I made at Beamish, asking if the prices were the same as in Victorian times. This was a lively place which had regular music hall singalongs. Great fun. The village seems alive and authentic, with 'local' people in period costume everywhere, from policemen to chemists, shop assistants, and blacksmiths, all acting out their roles enthusiastically.

The Bates and Hunt Druggists supplied medicines and drugs. They were very important in the days when working people couldn't afford to go to a doctor. Things seem to have gone full circle because it has been suggested recently that pharmacists could ease the pressure on the National Health Service by holding consultations. One thing which I don't think will come back are travelling dentists. Decoratively engraved on glass panels on the door of Bates and Hunt was the reassuring sign, 'Teeth Carefully Extracted.' It was the word *carefully* which made me shudder. What's the alternative? The well-worn dentist's chair and the accompanying implements looked straight out of a chamber of horrors. There was a working post office and a fish and chip shop. These started around the 1860s due to the introduction of the railways, which enabled fish from the North Sea to be transported quickly inland. Fish and chips became a cheap, staple food for the working classes. This is hardly a statement that could be made today regarding the prices at the seaside towns we have visited. However, they are still a cheap food source for kamikaze dive-bombing seagulls.

The industrial part of Blists Hill has original buildings from hundreds of years ago and a coal and clay mine from the 1780s. The world's first steam engine was built in Coalbrookdale in 1802, and a replica travels back and forth along the side of the Shropshire Canal. It was fascinating to watch cogwheels of all sizes meshing together as it puffed along, looking like Heath Robinson designed it.

There were many enamel posters throughout the village and a sign which said, 'Saggar Makers Bottom Knocker', which sounds like a village in the Cotswolds, probably near Loose Chippings. I first heard this on a TV programme called 'What's My Line', hosted by Eamon Andrews. Members of the public would be invited to sign in, with chalk on a blackboard (very hi-tec), and then mime what they did for a living. A panel of 'experts' would then question the contestant on a yes/no basis to try and guess their occupation. That was peak-time television entertainment in the 1950s. Older readers might remember it and the sheer thrill of finding out that someone was a postman, hairdresser, or baker. Younger readers, you don't know what you've missed!

I can't remember the mime for a Saggar Makers Bottom Knocker, but I'm sure you're anxious to know more. Rather than keep you in suspense, I've looked it up… It is an occupation in the pottery industry. Saggars are made to support pottery during kiln firing. Saggar making was a skilled job. Making bottoms for the saggars was done by lesser-skilled workers who knocked them into shape. I'm glad I've cleared that up for you.

Chester

Arriving in Chester took us back to our familiar home territory, but we decided to look at everything through fresh eyes as tourists. We stayed near Ellesmere Port, opposite the popular Cheshire Oaks shopping centre and commuted by bus into Chester.

Chester thrives on its Roman heritage. Founded in the 1st Century AD as Deva Victrix, it has the largest Roman Amphitheatre in Britain and the most complete city wall with a walkway. The focal point along the wall is the beautiful, elaborately decorated clock above the Eastgate arch. The year 1897 features prominently on the design as it was built to commemorate Queen Victoria's Diamond Jubilee.

Adjacent to the wall in the Roman Gardens are exhibits of artefacts and architectural pieces unearthed locally. Columns are re-sited in rows, and a mosaic welcomes us at the gate. There is even a reconstructed hyper-course which provided underfloor heating, probably an absolute necessity for Romans transferred from the Mediterranean sunshine to one of the northernmost outposts of the Empire.

The amphitheatre was un-earthed in 1929. A Roman show of power, it was built about 70 AD as a 7000 seater, bigger than today's Deva Stadium, the home of Chester Football Cub. Guides dressed as Roman soldiers or gladiators explained and demonstrated the drama during games in the amphitheatre. The word gladiator takes its name from the short sword, the gladius. There were many different types of gladiators whose weapons, shields and armour were derived from their original culture within the Empire. For example, those from fishing communities were trained to fight with a net and a trident. Spartacus, a real-life historical figure portrayed by Kirk Douglas in the movie, was from Thrace, the quintessential image of a gladiator.

A common misconception is that gladiatorial combats were *always* to the death. This wasn't necessarily the case since much time and money had been invested in training, housing and feeding these men (and also women at one time). Often, an arbiter would decide a winner, taking account of the mood of the crowd. As with modern-day boxing, divisions were based on weight categories. Gladiators were sub-divided based on armoury, weaponry and experience. This extended the longevity, however brief, to appease the owners of the training schools. Wild animals such as crocodiles, lions, giraffes and elephants would be let loose on each other and often on criminals sentenced to death. Roman battles would be recreated for the entertainment of the crowd, including, we were told, Boudica and the Iceni Tribe from East Anglia.

Trivia Alert... To briefly digress, here's a sports question: Taking into account monetary inflation, who was the richest sportsman to have *ever* lived? A boxer? A Formula 1 champion? An American footballer or basketball player? What about a European Footballer? Not even close. Remarkably, he was actually a Charioteer in Ancient Rome, the Formula One of its day. He was the most famous sportsman in the known world, a sort of Muhammad Ali, Pele and Michael Jordan rolled into one. In my mind's eye, he *must* have looked like Charlton Heston in Ber-Hur. His name was Gaius Appuleius Diocles, who lived in the 2nd Century AD. He was worth, in today's money, 15 *Billion* dollars! The rival chariot teams were named after colours and toured the Empire to entertain massive crowds.

The outfits worn by our guides reminded me of a joke, more of a conundrum: A Roman citizen went into a clothes shop in the Forum and bought a tunic as a gift for his wife. She looked at the label and wasn't too happy.

"What makes you think I'm a size L? I'm not that big. Take it back and change it for a smaller size."

So he did as he was told and gave her the new tunic, size XL.

"That's more like it, thank you."

Modern Chester is built around the original four streets of Deva: Bridge, Watergate, Eastgate and Northgate. It has many different facades in which Roman ruins are complemented by Medieval stone, black and white Elizabethan and imposing Georgian and Victorian buildings. Some of the half-timber Elizabethan structures are not quite as old as they appear to be. Many date from the late 19th Century when the Tudor style became fashionable again. A unique feature is the Chester Rows, a second walkway a level up from the ground floor pavement, linking shops, cafes and galleries.

No one knows for sure the origin of such an arrangement. There is also a modern shopping precinct called, appropriately enough, The Forum. Many shops, pubs, and offices expose Chester's historical heritage behind toughened glass incorporated into walls or floors.

In common with many northern towns, Chester Town Hall is a towering Victorian edifice. Dating from 1860, it is modelled on the Cloth Hall in the Belgian town of Ypres, or as British soldiers in the First World War called it, Wipers. Nearby is the White Lion Hotel, formally a major coaching inn for journeys to London, Ireland and a hub for many routes. A 700-year-old stone cross was a rallying place for Oliver Cromwell's Parliamentary troops during the Civil War and still acts as a popular rendezvous point in the town centre.

The magnificent Chester Cathedral stands on the site of the 11th Century Abbey of St. Werburgh, the Patron Saint of Chester. It took over 400 years to build, incorporating elements of architecture, embellishments, and stained glass from the intervening centuries.

Around the town, the name Grosvenor seems to crop up frequently. There is Grosvenor Park, Grosvenor Street, Grosvenor Museum and the Grosvenor 5-star Hotel. The family had come to England as part of William the Conqueror's entourage, acquiring land and property in Cheshire.

As born-again tourists, we decided to try something new: a cruise on the River Dee. The river rises in Snowdonia and flows through Wales to the Irish Sea. Since Roman times, it has changed its course. Chester Racecourse is Britain's oldest, dating from 1539, and the site was once under the river. The going was described as water-logged. We crossed the river via the impressive Queen's Park Suspension Footbridge and booked on one of the pleasure boats. One boat was called The Mark Twain, which I thought was more Mississippi than Dee. The leisurely sightseeing cruise was tranquil as we passed impressive-looking hotels and some fabulous houses overlooking the river.

"No wonder many Premiership footballers live here," I heard someone say.

Actually, a friend of mine who suffered from a severe stammer had to move house because he could no longer afford to live in Chester… Taxi drivers kept taking him to Chichester. On that note, I think it's time we moved on.

Port Sunlight

On the Wirral, we visited the delightfully named village of Port Sunlight. Built in 1889, it was purpose-built to house factory workers. Its black and white mock-Tudor buildings, cobbles, theatre and art gallery look like a Hollywood version of a typical English village. The focal point is the Lady Lever Art Gallery, in the style of a Greek Temple with its Ionic Columns, pediments, porticos and architectural details.

The village and gallery were the vision of William Lever, a businessman and philanthropist born in Bolton in 1851, the son of a grocer. In Victorian times, people used to buy soap in chunks cut off a huge slab by the grocer. Lever had the simple idea of cutting small bars of soap, wrapping them and selling them as a brand; Sunlight Soap by Lever Brothers was born. Unlike most Victorian industrialists, William Lever was concerned with the welfare of his workforce (similar to what we have seen with Titus Salt at Saltaire), and he built the village. He became the First Lord Leverhulme and built the Lady Lever Art Gallery in memory of his wife, Lady Elizabeth, who had died in 1913. William had been an enthusiastic art collector, which began with his admiration for Wedgwood Pottery. The Gallery has a domed skylight, and the eclectic collection includes Chinese lacquerware, marble sculptures, tapestries, furniture and paintings. He was an admirer of Napolean, and there are several Napoleonic artefacts, including Bonaparte's death mask. There are paintings by Turner and Constable and Pre-Raphaelite paintings. This means simply a group of artists who took inspiration from Medieval, chivalrous times before Raphael and the Renaissance.

The most famous of these paintings is the Scapegoat by William Holman-Hunt. He travelled to the Holy Land, bought a goat and tethered it to a post at the Dead Sea. He painted it whilst it was exposed to the unforgiving climate. He produced a masterpiece, but the poor goat died. A scapegoat indeed!

Birkenhead and Mersey Tunnel

On the way to Birkenhead, as mentioned earlier in Broadstairs, we drove past Bebbington, whose sports ground doubled as the Paris 1924 Olympic Stadium in the movie Chariots of Fire.

The main architectural feature of Birkenhead is the magnificent Hamilton Square, a Georgian wonder dominated by a town hall with a towering clock tower and a Graeco/Roman portico supported by six columns with capitals of Corinthian-style acanthus leaves. The square opened in 1847 and was designed by Edinburgh architect James Gillespie-Graham, commissioned by the Scottish Shipbuilder Hamilton Laird, of Cammell-Laird fame.

Also opened in 1847 is Birkenhead Park, the world's first public park, which became the template for New York's world-famous Central Park.

The Mersey Tunnel was opened in 1934 by King George V, and a second tunnel, the Wallasey Tunnel, was opened in 1971 by Queen Elizabeth II. The Mersey Tunnel has been used as a location in several movies, notably Harry Potter and the Deathly Hallows, and a chase scene in Fast and Furious 6. An interesting feature at both ends are the ventilation shafts, built in the Art Deco style of the 1930s. These and the tunnel entrances are now Grade II listed. There is even an annual Mersey Tunnel 10K run from Liverpool to New Brighton, where competitors can be heard gasping to each other, 'Don't worry, there'll soon be light at the end of the tunnel.'

Liverpool

Emerging from the Mersey Tunnel, we headed for Bridge Farm in Rainford, on the outskirts of St. Helens. The working farm had a barn, outhouses, greenhouses and a farmyard of hens roaming free. The owners had a licence for a limited number of motorhomes, caravans and tents with pitches looking out on horses and cows in the fields.

The following morning, we went to the adjacent station to catch the train to Liverpool. The Liverpool waterfront is one of the most impressive and most famous worldwide.

Trivia Alert... The waterfront of Shanghai in China is based on that of Liverpool, and the Liver Building has a sister on the other side of the world. We have been to Shanghai, and the similarity is quite uncanny. The only difference is that Liverpool looks out to a low-rise Birkenhead, as Shanghai has a vision across the water, which is more like the Emerald City in The Wizard of Oz. At night, even the lights are coordinated between buildings to move and dance in unison. I can't see that happening to Birkenhead any time soon. Incidentally, Liverpool was the first place to be settled by Chinese immigrants in Europe, and consequently, it has Europe's oldest Chinatown. The traditional arched gateway is the largest outside of China and was imported piece by piece from Shanghai. Today, Liverpool is officially 'twinned with Shanghai.

The Three Graces are Liverpool's jewel in the crown: The Liver Building, the Cunard Building and The Port of Liverpool Building. Each is an architectural masterpiece and a triumph of harmony and proportion with beautifully detailed classical adornments. Opened in 1911, the most famous of the three is the Liver Building, on top of which stands the emblem of Liverpool: The Liver Birds. It is believed that these stone mythical creatures guard the city, and if they ever fly away, Liverpool will crumble. The Cunard Building was opened in 1917 as the offices of the Cunard Shipping Line and is now home to 'The British Music Experience.' The domed Port of Liverpool Building opened in 1907 and is the administrative centre of the port, which has gone from strength to strength since Liverpool became a cruise ship terminal relatively recently.

Liverpool waterfront was awarded World Heritage Status in 2004, but unfortunately, this was rescinded in 2021 due to the addition of ultra-modern angular buildings not in keeping with the classical, elegant surroundings. One modern feature which does fit well is a statue of the Beatles. Passengers disembarking from cruise ships or Mersey ferries are greeted by a larger-than-life sculpture of John, Paul, George and Ringo in casual pose as if walking along the street. This is based on a photograph of the group arriving at the BBC in London, used as a cover for a compilation album.

The modern buildings are home to some very impressive exhibitions. The Museum of Liverpool opened in 2011 and traces the city's growth from its Irish settlers following the potato famine, destruction during World War Two, its two Cathedrals and much more. The Merseyside Maritime Museum and The Fab4 Store are also worth a visit.

As we have seen so far on our travels, former neglected, decaying harbour fronts have been given a new lease of life by re-purposing and gentrification. Liverpool is no exception. When I was growing up in the 1960s if someone had predicted that the docks area would one day be up-market apartments and tourist attractions, I would have laughed. It was grim and filthy. What a transformation.

As we approached the city centre, we saw a couple of Hop-On tour buses similar to those in most tourist destinations worldwide. Liverpool can also offer a Magical Mystery Tour Bus, which takes in all the Beatles connections such as Strawberry Fields, Penny Lane, Abbey Road and their childhood homes. A friend of mine joined one of these tours not many years ago. One of the passengers was a mysterious-looking character wearing a long overcoat and a wide-brimmed hat. He seemed familiar, but only when he spoke to ask the guide a question did my friend realise that he was none other than Bob Dylan. He had bought a ticket (to ride) like everyone else and joined the group pilgrimage like an ordinary fan. He could hardly be described as an ordinary fan. He had an influence on the Beatles, John Lennon in particular, and he does, after all, have the distinction of featuring on the album cover of Sgt. Pepper's Lonely Hearts Club Band, designed by Peter Blake.

The central shopping centre is mainly pedestrianised, and a new precinct, called Liverpool One, has all the usual chain stores and high street brands. Liverpool Football Cub has its superstore there and called it Liverpool One. The Everton Cub opened their store close by and called it Everton Two. A nice touch of Scouse humour, a trait well-known the world over. It is thought that the distinctive Scouse accent originally derives from the Irish who arrived in the 19th Century. The word scouse originated from a lob-scouse meal, consisting of a stew of meat, vegetables and potatoes. In nearby St. Helens, we called it lobbies. Another theory is that the name derives from the Scandinavian dish Labskaus. This was brought to Liverpool by sailors, and to this day, there is still a pub on the Dock Road called The Baltic Fleet.

Trivia Alert... Scousers refer to Lancashire folk who are not from Liverpool as Woollybacks. This refers to 19th Century strike-breakers who were brought to the docks from nearby towns to load ships with bales of wool.

Queen Victoria visited Liverpool in the 1850s and declared that many Neo-Classical buildings were worthy of ancient Athens or the Parthenon in Rome. Just up the hill from the main shopping area is a collection of buildings which could replicate parts of Rome: St.

George's Hall, the Walker Art Gallery, the Natural History Museum and the Library, all built in local sandstone standing majestically like classical temples.

St. George's Hall opened in 1854 and was restored in the 1980s. And is one of the finest of its type in the world. Charles Dickens has given readings there, and today, historians give talks to the public. It is a vast building with rows of fluted Corinthian columns, and Greco-Roman decoration is everywhere. Standing in front are equestrian statues of Queen Victoria and Prince Albert and a statue of the Earl of Beaconsfield (otherwise known as 19th Century Prime Minister Benjamin Disraeli) draped in ceremonial robes, looking like a Roman Emperor. The decorative Victorian street lamps acknowledge Liverpool's maritime heritage with their dolphin bases, while the entrance lights have a Mermaid theme. The hall's interior is fabulous with its sumptuous decoration from floor to ceiling, cathedral organ, and heritage centre.

Inlaid marble floors and huge crystal chandeliers add to the splendour, enhanced by the stained glass windows of St. George and the Dragon and myths of the sea. A final acknowledgement of ancient Rome is a sculptured sign above an interior door. In Biblical epics featuring Roman soldiers, the sign SPQR always translates roughly as Senate and People of Rome. Russell Crowe had the tattoo in Gladiator. In the same style of font, St. George's Hall has SPQL.

Behind St. George's Hall are St. John's Gardens, an oasis of calm in a busy city, a beautiful setting for statues and memorials. Not to be outdone by his rival Prime Minister Disraeli, there is a Gladstone Monument commemorating Liverpool-born William Gladstone.

Adjacent to the gardens is a row of classical buildings which complete this impressive area of the city. We didn't go into the library or the National History Museum. I think our walk along Dorset's Jurassic Coast satisfied our fossil curiosity.

The Walker Art Gallery was founded by former Mayor Andrew Walker, who made his fortune in Brewery and was opened in 1877. The collection ranges from Medieval Art of Italy, Spain and France to Rubens, Rembrandt and Gainsborough. There is an outstanding collection of Pre-Raphaelite paintings of the 19th Century and French Impressionists, notably Monet. An interesting painting is Bathers in Dieppe by Impressionist Walter Sickert, who was actually English.

Trivia Alert... Sickert is one of the short-list suspected of being Jack the Ripper.

Modern paintings are included, but most of the contemporary and experimental pieces are more likely to be seen at the Tate Liverpool at the Albert Docks. The Walker is home to the John Moore's Exhibition, founded and named after the owner of Littlewoods Football Pools, and intended as an answer to London's Royal Academy Summer Exhibition. One of the most famous winners was David Hockney's painting Peter Getting Out of Nick's Pool in 1967, set in California.

The Empire Theatre on Lime Street is also in the Neo-Classical style with Ionic Columns. It opened in 1866 and during its history, it has been extended, refurbished, bombed, and today, it is restored with a beautiful, sumptuous interior, what I call a proper theatre. The range of performers who have 'trod the boards' would grace any theatre in the world: Charlie Chaplin, Margot Fonteyn, Bing Crosby, Frank Sinatra, Judy Garland, Laurel and Hardy, The Everly Brothers, Tom Jones and, of course, The Beatles. A person who I think deserves a special mention is local comedian Ken Dodd. Many small provincial theatres owe Ken a debt of gratitude because he performed free-of-charge to save many from closure. He is immortalized in bronze as his life-size statue greets rail passengers with his tickling stick in Lime Street Station.

Next to the Empire Theatre is a French Chateau-style grade II listed building, dating from 1879, formerly the North Western Hotel. Remember when we were in Durham, where University students lived in a castle? Well, this comes close. This 'French Chateau' is home to Liverpool John Moore's University students.

A popular tourist area of Liverpool is the 'Cavern Quarter' based around Matthew Street, where once there was a fruit and vegetable market. The Beatles performed at the Cavern Club 292 times, and a statue of John Lennon leans against a wall, based on a photograph of him taken at the exact spot. I went to the Cavern just once in the 1960s, sadly after the Beatles, and I suffered from tinnitus for a week. There is a wall of fame outside, with the names of performers embedded in the brickwork, just another brick in the wall.

Trivia Alert... Acts from Liverpool have produced more number-one hits than any other city worldwide.

Bold Street is part of the 'Ropewalks Area', formerly the centre of the ship ropemaking industry. It leads up to St. Luke's Church, more commonly known as 'The Bombed-out Church', retained as a Second World War Memorial. Liverpool was Britain's second most bombed city after London.

Rodney Street dates from 1784, and the area is now known as the Georgian Quarter. Impressive terraced houses were built for affluent merchants and elite society. Number 62 was the home of a plantation owner and slave owner named John Gladstone. His son William Gladstone was born there in 1809 and became Prime Minister. Brian Epstein was born at number 34. Today, it is known as the Harley Street of the North as the classical, columned entrances are now home to many Doctors' Private practices.

A friend of mine once booked an appointment on Rodney Street. It was for a 'well man's clinic', an MOT test for humans. The doctor tested his heart rate, pulse, blood pressure, prostate, bodily fluids and temperature. Hoping for a clean bill of health, my friend asked, "So, what's the verdict, doctor?"

The doctor looked at him with a vacant expression and said, "I think Mercury is in Uranus,"

"Oh. I don't believe in any of that astrology mumbo-jumbo," he responded dismissively.

"No," said the doctor, "I think my thermometer has just broken!"

Standing high on St. James' Mount overlooking the city is Liverpool's Anglican Cathedral. This massive, brown sandstone edifice is one of the biggest cathedrals in the world. The architect, Sir Giles Gilbert Scott, also designed the traditional British red telephone box, and there is one located inside the cathedral. The stained glass, columns and decoration are spectacular, and the sheer size of the interior is awe-inspiring. The organ is one of the biggest in the world.

The Liverpool folk group The Spinners recorded 'In My Liverpool Home,' which has the line, 'If you want a Cathedral, we've got one to spare.' Liverpool has another one; Liverpool Metropolitan Catholic Cathedral was consecrated in 1967, and the contrast in architectural style could not be more different from the Anglican Cathedral. It is circular, made of concrete, topped off with a huge lantern of stained glass. The interior is bright and airy, and the colours of the glass in the lantern are designed to accentuate the sunlight at any given time of day. For example, the late afternoon sun comes in through reds and oranges. Being Liverpool, it has acquired a nickname; it is known as Paddy's Wigwam.

Liverpool has more galleries and museums than any other city outside of London and more parks than Paris. Sefton Park is perhaps the most famous, and its Victorian Bandstand is thought to be the initial inspiration for Sgt. Pepper's Lonely Hearts Club Band. Let's not forget Liverpool's Superlambananas. What? They are sculptures of a lamb's front and a banana's back end (and why not?) painted in a variety of bright colours in pop-art style. Over a hundred of them are dotted around, including a row at the Pier Head. They were first introduced when Liverpool was awarded the Capital of Culture in 2008. Liverpool does have an undeserved reputation for having more than its fair share of 'scallies' (Scouse name for scallywags), and when the Capital of Culture Award was announced, there was a cartoon in one of the papers. It was of a car, wheels missing, jacked-up not on bricks, but on a stack of books... The Complete Works of William Shakespeare.

Another Place

We caught the local Metro to Crosby, a leafy suburb on the northern outskirts of Liverpool, to look at Anthony Gormley's 100 statues which populate the beach.

The seafront at Crosby has rows of smart houses looking out on grassy sand dunes and a pleasant beach. The statues are spaced-out on a long stretch of beach, all looking out to sea, which is presumably why the whole installation is called 'Another Place'. From a distance, it's often difficult to distinguish the life-size figures from visitors standing nearby. I sensed a mystery about them, which I didn't feel with Gormley's Angel of the North. Manufactured at Siddon's Iron Factory, they were installed in 2005 as a temporary exhibition but proved so popular that they are now honorary Scousers.

As with all his figurative work, the models are based on the artist's body, but they are no longer identical due to different degrees of weathering and rusting. They have taken on various expressions, like a modern-day Terracotta Army, and Gormley has said that they 'symbolize emotion of emigration'. The combination of colours created by rusting ranges from greens to oranges, browns, and yellows, and the artist has described them as 'Industrial fossils ageing through passing of time and weathering'. Visitors have given some statues scarves and hats, but none seemed to carry it off with the panache of The Duke of Wellington in Glasgow wearing a plastic traffic cone. Crosby Beach is popular with photographers, and I remember seeing one memorable magazine picture of the silhouetted statues looking out to a dramatic sunset over the Irish Sea.

A bi product of Another Place is that the figures have proved helpful in scientific and marine research. The build-up of microbes can now be researched to measure the growth of organisms, with examples taken back to laboratories. The job of scraping barnacles off the bottom' could be the new Saggar Makers Bottom Knocker.

Isle of Man

Next on our itinerary was the Isle of Man. The following morning, we flew from Liverpool John Lennon Airport (why not Beatles?) to Ronaldsway Airport, then a taxi north along the coast to Douglas. It was as good as a guided tour because the driver, a proud Manxman, chatted cheerfully, giving us background information and useful recommendations. The Isle of Man is regarded as *the* Mainland, and Britain is known as 'Across'. The coastal landscape was dramatic, and we passed a sign; 'Rest Home for Old Horses', a well-earned retirement after pulling the unique horse-drawn carriages along Douglas Promenade.

We were dropped off at a guest house we had booked on-line. It was a converted Victorian terraced house that retained its stained glass front door and original tiles in the entrance vestibule. The reception was tucked away, almost invisible under the stairs, and our room was an attic on the fourth floor. There wasn't a lift, so we struggled up endless flights of stairs, a bit like going to the toilets in a Wetherspoon pub. There was no television or fridge, but the view from the skylight windows across the rooftops to the sweep of Douglas Bay was a plus point.

"I feel like Mrs. Rochester locked in an attic in Jane Eyre," said Norma ruefully.

The Isle of Man is 33 miles long and 13 wide, with a population of 80,000. The name is possibly derived from the Celtic word for Mountain or the Sea God Manannan. The actual origin is lost in time. The first inhabitants built megalithic monuments, as we had seen in Orkney and Stonehenge, and there was a distinctive Celtic culture by the Iron Age.

Immigration from Ireland in the 5th Century brought Christianity, and in the 9th Century the Vikings invaded. A lasting Viking legacy is the Tynwald, set up in 979 AD. It is the World's oldest continuous parliament. In 1266, the island became part of Scotland following the Battle of Largs, and rule alternated between Scotland and England until finally England from 1399. The Isle of Man never became part of Great Britain or later the United Kingdom but retained self-government as a Crown Dependency of the UK.

The island is famous for several things: The T.T. (Tourist Trophy) motorbike races since 1907, the Laxey Wheel, Manx kippers, the unique tail-less Manx Cat and The Three Legs of Man. The best explanation I could find for the origin of the Cats is that they were late boarding Noah's Ark and caught their tails as the doors shut! Sounds good enough for me. The National symbol of the Isle of Man is the Triskelion, three legs in armour with spurs. The origin is obscure. One theory is that this logo first appeared in the Mediterranean and was popular on the island of Sicily. A triangular shape with three points. It appears on the IOM National flag and could link with its Latin motto: Quocunque Jeceris Stabit: Whichever way you throw me, I will stand. The sea front is more of a wide boulevard than a typical seaside promenade, with a sunken landscaped garden with fountains and a wide stretch for pedestrians. There is a road and tramway lane in front of the rows of gloriously sumptuous Victorian grand houses, nearly all converted into hotels. Each building is overly embellished with classic Greek columns niches in a 'more-is-best' Victorian Style. It's easy to visualize the splendour of the past, accentuated by the clip-clop of the horse-drawn trams, which date back 150 years. At least the horses can look forward to a happy retirement home, as pointed out by our taxi driver.

My favourite building was the Gaiety Theatre and Opera House, one of Britain's best-preserved buildings. It is a riot of mix'n'match match architectural styles, and I was particularly impressed with the entrance portico, a superb example of stained glass art. The different seating categories are incorporated into the stained glass: Early Doors,

Gallery, Amphitheatre and Pitt. The names alone conjure up images of the days of the raucous Music Halls, as re-created in The Good Old Days on television. Indeed, the term 'early doors' is still used for a prompt start. Next to the theatre are the Villa Marina Gardens behind an arcade of classical columns. This is very popular for festivals, bike shows, concerts, etc.

On a more up-to-date theme, there is a bronze statue of the Douglas-born Bee Gees in the promenade gardens. In a similar style to the Beatles statue in Liverpool, the Bee Gees are walking along together. If my memory serves me correctly, it is taken from the video 'Stayin' Alive', in which Maurice Gibb is wearing excruciatingly tight trousers. Perhaps it helped his falsetto voice. The sculptor seems to have let them out a little.

Back at the B&B, after climbing the stairs, we felt as though we had conquered the north face of the Eiger and collapsed into bed. We couldn't resist the 'Full Manx Breakfast' of Manx kippers and scrambled eggs the following morning. Delicious, rivalled only by Whitby kippers, and we ticked yet another foodie box.

The Electric Railway is advertised like the famous Hollywood sign. We walked to the Derby Castle terminus and boarded the Electric Railway, which opened in 1893, to Laxey. The Victorian carriages are meticulously maintained in brown, varnished wood. The seats and backrests were of wooden slats, and once we got going, I started to feel every bump, creak and squeak. We saw a statue of Sir William Hillary, founder of the Royal National Lifeboat Institute (RNLI). Apparently, lifeboat stations all around Britain are numbered, and the one on the Isle of Man is the proud original Number 1. Out in the bay is a fairytale castle, The Tower of Refuge, built by Hillary in 1822 to take in shipwrecked victims before they could be transferred to the mainland. The railway trundled up the coast as I alternated buttocks, and the coastal views were magnificent. Occasionally, there would be unscheduled stops as the driver climbed down to shoo away sheep on the line. Incidentally, there is a breed of sheep unique to the island, the Manx Loxen, which can have six curved horns. A fierce look for such a gentle creature.

We arrived at the village of Laxey and transferred to the Snaefell Mountain Railway to ride to the summit, the highest point on the island at 2,036 feet. The name Snaefell is of Viking origin, and the term 'fell' refers to high land for grazing above tree level. This is a common term in the Lake District, where we will be visiting when we get back to the mainland, or should 1 say, *Across*. The spectacular views became increasingly magnificent. After coffee and cake at the Summit Hotel and photo opportunities, we caught the next train back down to Laxey. We had a cone of delicious Laxey ice cream (tick the box) and walked into the village to see the famous Laxey Wheel, the Island's most popular tourist attraction. It was built in 1854 to pump water out of the lead mines of The Laxey Mining Company. It has been fully restored, and the huge red wheel set in white stone housing is perfect for a Triskelion.

In the village, there is a group of standing stones, thought to be 5,000 years old and possibly a burial chamber. They are at the bottom of someone's garden, just over a small fence. This must be the world's best garden rockery.

Back at the station, we boarded the next train up the coast to Ramsey. The train stopped briefly at strategic points, providing views of Laxey Village and wheel, waterfalls and the former Laxey mine. We had a brief browse around Ramsey, which is different in character to Douglas in that it is more of a working fishing harbour, ideal subject matter for photographers and watercolourists. We had our obligatory pub stop, a Manx beer, and my gluteus maximus suggested we return to Douglas by bus and upholstered seats. The route more or less followed the railway track, and at the terminus, we went for a drink at an excellent pub called, appropriately enough, The Terminus.

At our bed and breakfast, I had noticed that morning that there was a television lounge on the ground floor. In our room, I remembered, as if by magic, that a rugby league match was on the TV, and my team, St. Helens, were playing.

"I'll just go down and watch the match before we go out," I said.

In the TV room, there were easy chairs and one or two people sitting there.

"Do you mind if I put the rugby on," I asked to no-one in particular.

"Er, no, not at all," mumbled an older gentleman.

I picked up the remote and made myself comfortable. While watching the match, one or two people came in and out, and a young boy opened a cupboard. He took out an electronic game and acknowledged the older man, his grandad. After a few comings and goings, it gradually dawned on me that this wasn't a television lounge at all. It was the owners' family room, and there was I, bold as brass, sat amongst them. There was an elephant in the room... me. I managed to bluff my way through, and each person thought one of the others had invited me in. After the match, I thanked everyone profusely, expressing more false humility than Uriah Heep. Back in our room, Norma was getting ready to go out, and I told her my tale. Her mouth dropped open, but before she could say anything, I said, "Saints won."

We wandered around Douglas town centre and noticed a café menu board advertising a bap (bun) with Manx kipper and *marmalade* filling! I had enjoyed the bizarre concoction of a deep-fried battered Mars Bar in Stonehaven in, Scotland, but this was a step too far. Whatever next? Tripe and trifle?! We were attracted by a lively pub, O'Donnell's, which had live music. A perfect end to a perfect day.

After breakfast the following morning, we explored the compact town centre. Strand Street is a pedestrianised main thoroughfare with a wide selection of high-street stores. Many of the streets are named in English and also Manx Gaelic, a language which became extinct in 1974 when the last native speaker died. It was revived in 2015 (the language, that is, *not* the body), and now 2% of the population can speak Manx Gaelic.

We took the short hop back to Liverpool and the bus back to the farm the following day. We relaxed for the rest of the day before departure tomorrow for Southport.

Southport

A comedian once said, 'Southport is so boring that the sea once went out and never bothered to come back.' It might have been a good line, and the sea does seem to be a distance away, but the joke couldn't be further from the truth. In my opinion, having by now visited numerous seaside holiday towns in Britain, Southport is one of the most elegant. It doesn't have a seafront promenade, but wide landscaped gardens, bandstands and one of Europe's largest man-made boating lakes, called Marine Lake.

The pier, which is Grade II listed, is the oldest iron pier in Britain and the second longest after Southend. The Promenade Express Train is very popular for covering the pier's one-kilometre length. Funland on the pier retains its charm and has hosted many world-famous performers, including Charlie Chaplin. In the arcade is an exhibition of old photographs of many piers around the country, all full of elegant Victorian, Edwardian or 1920s promenaders.

As a child, I've been many times to Southport Pleasureland, and as teenagers, a group of us would go to Southport sea-bathing pool, which sadly is no longer there. I remember the old wooden rollercoaster rattling alarmingly, competing with piercing screams. The first sand-sculptor I ever saw worked next to the rollercoaster, and I was fascinated watching him create animals. He was there for years. A ride on the miniature railway skirts the lake and a popular miniature golf course. Nothing seemed to have changed.

Along the main road, facing the gardens, lake, and sea, are rows of Edwardian buildings, mainly in white or creams, now occupied by hotels, B & Bs, pubs and cafes. The most famous street in Southport is Lord Street, a couple of blocks back.

Its pavement is covered by a walkway with a translucent roof and supported by Victorian Bandstand style metal columns, with details highlighted with gold paint. In one of the arcades is a bronze statue of Southport's very own Red Rum, the famous racehorse who won the Grand National 3 times. His regular training run was along the local Ainsdale Beach. On the opposite side of Lord Street, overlooking an avenue of park and trees are rows of imposing buildings combining the familiar Graeco-Roman columned facades with Victorian grandeur, including the Art Gallery, a cinema, and a Town Hall. Further into town are the railway station, modern shopping precincts, and a McDonald's. I mention this in particular because it was only the second to open in Britain, after one in London. I went there in the 1970s when it opened to reminisce about happy days as a student when I travelled around America by Greyhound Bus for 10,000 miles, sustained mainly by a Big Mac and milk shake.

Southport could be described as 'the town that time forgot', but, unlike some similar seaside towns we have seen, it hasn't decayed. Its only concession to modernism is Wesley Street, marketed as a 'village in the town' with a Carnaby Street overhead sign spanning the narrow road of terraced buildings. Similar to what we saw in Brighton, the buildings are brightly painted. It's probably an attempt to attract a younger clientele, but there is a bit of a giveaway as to Southport's true demographic profile: The Walking Stick Shop and The Hearing Aid Shop.

Before leaving Southport, I must mention the British Lawnmower Museum, the town's Coup de Grass.

Trivia Alert... There used to be an old saying, 'Who do you think you are, Stirling Moss?' when a driver was caught speeding. He was a famous British racing driver who was *never* a F1 world champion because his career coincided with that of Fangio, the great Argentinian. But Moss *was* a World Champion… at Lawnmower Racing.

Blackpool

Blackpool is the most famous seaside resort in Britain. The Tower is iconic, and the annual illuminations are world-famous with the televised switch-on ceremony. Blackpool retains much of its character from days-gone-by such as Blackpool Rock, kiss-me-quick hats, candy floss, Gypsy Rose Lee and donkey rides. It has one of the oldest tramways in the world and three piers, each offering entertainment and rides ranging from a suicidal-looking sling-shot bungee jump, helter-skelter, fairground rides, shows, bars and cafes.

In front of the Tower is the world's biggest mirror-ball, an art installation dedicated to the Tower Ballroom, one of the most prestigious in the world. Weighing over 4 tons, the glitter ball comprises 4,000 glass tiles and was designed by Michael Traynor in 2002. Also on the pavement is The Comedy Carpet, Blackpool's version of the Hollywood Walk of Fame. The carpet is laid out as posters and includes quotes or catchphrases from comedians going back many years.

The entrance building to the Tower has a sandstone façade in a Neo-Baroque style. Inspired by the Eiffel Tower, Blackpool Tower opened in 1894, and the iron structure stands just over 500 feet high. We took the lift up to the viewing platform and stepped out with trepidation on to the glass floor. We had fantastic views of North Wales, Southport, The Isle of Man, The Pennines and The Lake District. Breathtaking. Other attractions in the Tower include a Cinema Experience, which features a timeline of Blackpool, which brought back childhood memories. Also, a Virtual Reality thrill ride was authentic and exciting with awesome effects.

The ballroom is the 'Wembley Stadium' of the ballroom dancing world and has become even more famous through television's Strictly Come Dancing. It needs some attention, but nevertheless, it is sumptuous with richly decorated gold-leaf balconies, sparkling grand chandeliers, ornate ceiling, inlaid-wooden sprung floor and the famous Wurlitzer organ, which rises from the front of the stage. It retains that unique, timeless Blackpool sound. 'Oh, I do like to be beside the seaside.'

The Winter Gardens, a Grade II listed complex, is a vast entertainment centre which opened in 1878. It houses The Opera House and also the Empress Ballroom. The circular foyer gives pride of place to Morecambe and Wise, with a larger-than-life joyful sculpture. A roll of honour painted in the traditional style of gold on wooden panels, like in a sports club, lists stars going as far back as 1889. Early names included Lily Langtree 1901, Charlie Chaplin 1904, Anna Pavlova 1912 and George Formby 1939 through to Frank Sinatra and the Beatles. Theatre posters line the walls. An impressive conference suite had crystal chandeliers, and a bar was styled on the interior of a Spanish Galleon.

The Grand Theatre is a superb example of a small Victorian Theatre with its stained glass, chandeliers, ornate balcony and sumptuous soft furnishings. It has been described as Britain's most beautiful theatre, and as mentioned in Liverpool, it has Ken Dodd to thank for saving it from dereliction.

Being Blackpool, we had an evening meal of fish and chips and stayed for the illuminations. They were impressive and retained the timeless quality with the traditional trams, tourist train, horse-drawn, fairytale Cinderella pumpkin carriages, and lights spanning the road. The Tower lights were more up-to-date, with co-ordinated led lights changing colours on the front façade. The shops and arcades were well-lit, and the Golden Mile Casino is modelled on the famous Golden Nugget in Las Vegas. I went to have my palm read by Gipsy Rose Lee, but there was a sign saying, 'Closed due to Unforeseen Circumstances.'

After an invigorating day and evening, it was time to catch the bus back to our motorhome, already looking forward to returning the following day. We started off quietly in Stanley Park with a game of crazy golf and a ride on the miniature train. The 260-acre park is an area of calm with a marble fountain, bandstand, amphitheatre seating, a boating lake and a model village. A gentle start to the day, but we soon found ourselves at the Pleasure Beach with its screaming roller coasters and ghost train. A ride on the Big One involves a terrifying vertical plunge, increasing the vocal decibels. It cost me a fortune… all the loose change in my pocket cascaded out into space.

Madam Tussaud's is synonymous with Blackpool and has a prime location on the Golden Mile. As we entered, we were greeted by a wax model of Madam Marie Tussaud herself and a timeline biography of her fascinating life. She was born in Strasbourg in, France in 1761, where her mother was housekeeper to a Monsieur Curtuis, a waxwork modeller. Marie became his apprentice, and her first piece was of the philosopher Voltaire. To have one's head modelled in wax was quite prestigious at the time, and further commissions followed, including Benjamin Franklin and Marie Antoinette. During the French Revolution, Madam Tussaud was accused of being a Royalist sympathiser, and her head was even shaved in preparation for the guillotine. A reprieve saved her at the last minute. This reminds me of the movie, 'Carry On, Don't Lose Your Head,' when Kenneth Williams put his head on the guillotine block. A letter arrived for him… 'Drop it in the basket; I'll read it later.'

During the Revolution, Marie was assigned the gruesome task of picking through graveyards to make death masks of celebrities, including Marie Antoinette and Robespierre. Furthermore, she made models of executed criminals, where heads were displayed on spikes at Place de la Concorde in Paris, the origin of the Chambers of Horrors. Later, she moved to England and spent over 30 years on the road with her travelling waxwork museum, using portraits and marble busts as source material. She set up her first permanent exhibition in Baker Street, London.

The first category of waxworks in Blackpool featured reality television so-called celebrities I didn't recognise anyone. However, The Doctor Who exhibition was impressive, underscored by the famous theme by Ron Grainger. I remember watching the very first episode, starring William Hartnell.

Trivia Alert... This was overshadowed and hardly noticed at the time, in November 1963, due to something momentous which happened the day before… the assassination of President John Kennedy in Dallas.

There are lots of sports stars, and I couldn't resist having my picture taken with the greatest himself, Muhammad Ali. There are rock stars galore, from Tom Jones to Adele. I've often felt sorry for all the Adel-tribute singers. Imagine how horrified they must have been when she lost about six stone in weight. That's showbiz; well, almost.

Television 'Soap Operas' are well represented. The world's longest-running soap is Coronation Street, and many of the most popular characters since 1960 are included in street sets and the Rovers Return pub. I confess to being a fan, and the wax models are eerily accurate. The famous theme tune, written by Eric Spear, adds atmosphere and authenticity. Is it just me? But isn't the tune a rip-off (or let's be generous and say pastiche) of the wartime classic Moonlight Serenade by Glenn Miller? A personal observation.

Madam Tussaud's is now more interactive and atmospheric than in years gone by when the models were exhibited more like mannequins in a shop window. Kids can even ride a bike with E.T., or you can join the Beatles on the famous Abbey Road zebra crossing.

'If you can keep your head while all around are losing theirs...' wrote Rudyard Kipling. Marie Tussaud did *exactly* that and went on to fame and fortune. She was an exceptional entrepreneur with a flair for self-promotion, advertising and marketing. She could wax lyrical. She would be proud today that the Tussaud's brand has over 20 franchises worldwide, including Las Vegas, Shanghai, Orlando, New York, Amsterdam, Istanbul and the original in London.

Let's finish on an artistic, philosophical note. The perennial question is, 'Can these waxwork models be regarded as art, or are they merely novelties pandering to tourists?' Some would argue that art can be anything from Carl Andre's pile of bricks at the Tate Gallery to Marcel Duchamp's 'Readymades'. On the other hand, can Madam Tussaud's wax models be compared to a painted portrait or a Renaissance sculpture? Verisimilitude, a rarely used word meaning superficial likeness devoid of character or emotion, is probably the key. It is a concept with no definitive answer. The Irish writer George Bernard Shaw perhaps sums it up best: 'You use a mirror to see your face, you use a panting to see your soul.' I wonder what the famous French Philosopher Voltaire would say. He was, after all, Madam Tussaud's first sitter.

Traditional British seaside holiday resorts we have visited so far have a common denominator; they have re-invented, re-purposed, and up-graded. For nearly all the resorts, the heyday was undoubtedly the Victorian and Edwardian eras. Blackpool, a sleeping giant, seems to have been a little slow to wake up, but the amount of scaffolding, cranes and future plans suggests that it has a bright future and has the potential to outshine (literally) every other resort.

I mentioned earlier that Blackpool's Golden Mile Arcade models itself on the Golden Nugget in Las Vegas. I first went to Las Vegas in 1972 when working in America as a student. It was a tremendous experience, but not a particularly safe place. I went back about 30 years later… what a transformation. Fremont Street is now covered with a canopy of thousands of led lights, and the general ambiance is friendly, thriving with tourists from all over the world. The covering kept out the heat, and I believe Blackpool could do the same to keep out the cold. I read some years ago that Blackpool, Manchester, and

London were to be granted 'super-casino' status. Nothing came of it, which is often the case, but if this were to happen, Blackpool could become one of Europe's, if not the World's, entertainment destinations. It's got the glitz; all it needs is the glamour… and money. If Las Vegas can do it from scratch in the Mojabe Desert of Nevada, then Blackpool can. It is right on the motorway and rail networks and close to airports. Bugsy Seagal opened the first hotel in Vegas. He didn't have any of these amenities in the desert… just a spade. I don't know what a mafia gangster was doing in the desert with a spade, but that's another story.

Morecambe

Travelling north from Blackpool, we decided to have a lunch break in Morecambe, more out of curiosity. When we visited the Eden Project in Cornwall, we found out that there was to be another one built in Morecambe. As we arrived in the town, one of the first buildings on the coast road was the 4-star Midland Hotel, an impressive 1930s building refurbished to breathe life into its Art Deco heritage. It is so impressive that it has been used as a location for the television series Poirot, which epitomizes the period.

A very promising first impression, but after that, the rest of the town seems to be tired and faded. However, the site on which the Eden Project is to be located looks ideally suitable. The derelict area used to be The Bubbles Leisure Complex, right on the beach. Quite appropriate, really, since the new build will effectively be a collection of interlinked bubbles looking out over Morecambe Bay. The Eden Project in Cornwall was one of our most memorable and educational excursions. I expect that the new one will attract holidaymakers, day trippers, and educational groups, benefiting the whole town.

The town is the birthplace of Eric Bartholomew, who, along with Ernest Wiseman, we know as the immortal comedy duo Morecambe and Wise. There is a statue of Eric on the seafront in a typical comic-dancing pose unveiled by Queen Elizabeth II in 1990. The King's Arms Pub is opposite, where we decided on a pub lunch. Performing outside was a one-man band equipped with guitar, harmonica on a cradle, bass drum on his back and cymbals between his knees, all operated by knee jerks as if he was suffering from St. Vitas Dance.

Inevitably, as we approached the pub, he sang, 'Bring me sunshine in your smile…' we listened for a short spell, dropped some coins in his guitar case, and Norma whispered,

"Don't say it?"

"Say what?"

"He's playing all the right notes, but not *necessarily* in the right order."

As we drove north out of Morecambe, I noticed that one of the businesses was an Exclusive Dress Agency called East of Eden. Perhaps they will change the name to North of Eden in the future.

The Lake District

Leaving Morecambe, it was only about 30 miles north to Kendal, our first stopover in the Lake District. As was the case with Melton Mowbray, we just *had* to go to Kendal to buy an item of local food: Kendal Mint Cake. As an instant energy boost, it is so beloved by walkers, climbers and mountaineers that it has even been to the summit of Mount Everest.

The Lake District was awarded the status of National Park in 1951, a compact 900 square miles very popular with tourists. Billions of years ago, it was a huge dome, higher than the present-day Himalayas, and it has been scraped, carved and sculpted by glacial activity over millions of years. During one of the Ice Ages, Britain was covered by a glacier 2 miles deep. As it progressed south, at about the same rate that a human finger nail grows, it picked up everything in its path while carving out and smoothing off the Lake District under that unimaginable weight and power. The glacier reached as far south as present-day London, and archaeologists are able to accurately identify its most southerly point before it was reversed by global warming. (Where have we heard *that* term before?) As the glacier slowly melted and retreated, anything it held in suspension dropped on to the land below. Now, here's a personal observation to give this some context. In my home town of St. Helens, which is about 100 miles due south of the Lake District, there is a huge, smooth boulder standing like a monolith, around which a small space has been landscaped. It looks like a Barbara Hepworth sculpture. It was brought down by the glacier and deposited there. It's in Shaw Street, right opposite the railway station. If it is waiting for a train back home to the Lakes, I think it would be quicker to catch the next glacier.

Looking at a map of the Lake District, you can identify the footprint of the dome, with lakes and rivers radiating in all directions. Comprising 16 lakes, The Lake District could just as easily have been called the Water District since the majority of the lakes have this name: Coniston Water, Hawes Water, Ullswater, and Derwentwater, to name a few. The most famous, and at 10 miles long, the largest in England, is *Lake* Windermere.

When we were in the North East, the Viking imprint was evident everywhere, and I pinpointed some influences from the Viking language. Danelaw stretched across to the Lake District, and Viking terms underpin the identity of The Lakes. The term Fell derives from Old Norse for a rounded hilltop for grazing. Bekker is a stream, and Thwaite, originally meaning an isolated piece of land, is common in place names and family names.

Kendal stands on the River Kent, which flows down to Morecambe Bay, and the market town is an interesting introduction to South Lakeland. The market hall was granted a charter in 1189, the final year of the reign of Richard the Lionheart. Naturally, mint cake was available everywhere, in a range of varieties, but we went for a traditional Romney's Kendal Mint Cake. The market sold a vast selection of goods, as we have seen numerous times on our travels, but there seemed to be a specialism for fabrics, sewing goods, luggage, and handbags. As in York, the New Shambles was once an area where butchers slaughtered animals, and blood and offal slid down a sloping yard to the river. It's now full of gift shops, knitting shops, walkers' outfitters, antique shops, cheese and a bakery. The former public bath and wash house is now a Wetherspoon Pub. There are several information plaques dotted around. Did you know that author John Cunliffe lived in Kendal? Who? The creator of Postman Pat (and his black and white cat.) The stories are based on the nearby valley of Longsleddale.

Wainwright Walks

The Victorian Town Hall stands on the main street with its distinctive clock tower. We went in to see an exhibition of watercolour paintings by Lakeland artists, while at the same time, we discovered that a man whose name had become synonymous with the Lake District once worked in that Town Hall. It was Alfred Wainwright, author of the illustrated guides to walking the fells. His books have a personal, unique quality with their hand-written text and sketches of the mountains. Over one million copies have been sold due to their meticulous accuracy and notes from an author who has *walked the described routes*. What *is* surprising is that Alfred Wainwright isn't from the Lake District at all. He was born in 1907 amongst the dark, satanic cotton mills and factories of Blackburn in Lancashire. The grim, depressing prospect of a life of industrial drudgery filled the young Alfred with dread. His saving grace was that he was a clever pupil at school and managed to secure a job in accounts at the Town Hall.

At 23, he went on holiday to the Lake District, which changed his life. He said he was 'transfixed, unable to believe his eyes.' He went back there at every opportunity, and in 1941, he was offered a job at the Treasurer's Office in Kendal. His dream job, indeed.

He had been married since his early 20s, but unfortunately, it didn't work out even though they stayed together in a somewhat distant relationship. This probably suited Alfred since he seems to have been a dour character, unsociable with obsessive traits. He started writing his guidebooks in 1952, and his analytical mind calculated that he could write seven books over 14 years. This he achieved, mapping 214 fells. He once said his books were the first hand-written publications since Medieval Monks. Come to think of it, Alfred Wainwright would have been ideally suited to monastic life as a Medieval scribe in a previous life.

On his walks, he avoided speaking to anyone in case it interrupted his flow of concentration. His wife once asked him if she could join him. He answered, "Yes, provided you don't talk."

'I'll take that as a no then,' she probably thought.

It seems ironic to me that a character such as Alfred Wainwright should provide walkers with an intimate, personal guide, which is much more welcoming and user-friendly than accurate satellite maps. Nobody has interpreted the mountains better. When he died in 1991, his ashes were scattered on Haystacks, his favourite spot.

Windermere and Bowness

Windermere is the Lake District's most famous town, which expanded after 1847 with the arrival of the railway. Conservationists didn't want trains terminating at the Lake shore, and rich locals at Ambleside at the lake's northern edge were more concerned with preserving their exclusivity.

The first thing we noticed arriving by bus was a shop selling 'Windermere Ice Cream', an absolute must for our list of foodie places. As we found in the Cotswolds, a general description of one village tends to give a one-size-fits-all, identikit overview of all the others. In Windermere, grey Lakeland slate predominates, with Victorian buildings, walls and arches, occasionally punctuated with some in the Georgian style and half-timber Tudor buildings. Even the bus stops are built of local slate, like miniature cottages. Pavements are constructed in local flagstones, and many roads are cobbled in smooth stones rounded into shape by glaciers. One drawback to the stone cobbles is that it does tend to amplify the sound of traffic, of which Windermere gets more than its fair share.

Splashes of colour are provided by hanging baskets, window boxes and floral displays in cottage gardens, particularly a row of cottages called College Court. There are galleries, cafes, coffee shops, souvenir shops, bars, and pubs.

We enjoyed browsing for a while, and, sustained by Kendal Mint Cake, we set off on the short walk to Bowness, or to give it its official title, Bowness-on-Windermere. Lake Road connects the two with rows of elegant hotels. We turned off towards the lake to follow the Lakeshore Trail, known as Millerground and maintained by the National Trust.

How can I describe Bowness? I know… go back to my description of Windemere. We went for a delicious pub lunch at the Old John Peel Inn, chosen because we liked the name.

We made our way to Bowness Pier and negotiated the obstacle course of swans, geese, ducks, wading birds, and fowls. Hundreds co-habit and seemed unconcerned as we walked amongst them, even side-stepping a couple of sun-bathing swans. It resembled a Lake District version of Trafalgar Square or St. Mark's Square in Venice. The pier and buildings have retained a Victorian quaintness and charm, and the booking offices were doing a roaring trade selling tickets for lake cruises and rowing boats. We booked on a lake cruise on a double-decker boat called, appropriately enough, The Swan. We cruised north to Ambleside, and it was idyllic and sitting on the upper deck, admiring the stunning views. We disembarked at Ambleside, another beautiful Lakeland village, which I could say defies description, but it doesn't. It follows the same 'formula' described earlier. The town is a popular base for hikers and originally thrived as a textile centre with its fast-flowing streams and water mills. Its most famous building is Bridge House, which began life as a folly over a river and features regularly in tourist pamphlets.

We Wondered Lonely, as a Cloud

Our main focus for the day was Grasmere on the River Rothay, just a few miles away. We took a local bus which skirted the north shore of Rydal Water and Grasmere Lake. Quote, 'The loveliest spot that man hath ever found,' was William Wordsworth's description of Grasmere. Who could argue with a Poet Laureate?

Wordsworth is strongly associated with the Lake District, particularly Grasmere, where he lived from 1798. He was born in 1770 on the western fringes of the Lake District, in Cockermouth, on the River Derwent, and a significant moment in his life occurred in Somerset, where he met fellow poet Samuel Taylor-Coleridge. They became friends, and Coleridge moved up to the Lake District to live in Keswick. They collaborated many times, the most notable being the joint publication The Lyrical Ballads, which begins with Coleridge's Rime of the Ancient Mariner and ends with Wordsworth's Tintern Abbey poem.

Dove Cottage, where Wordsworth lived, is Grasmere's major tourist attraction, and it has been preserved to give visitors a taste of the ambience of his time there.

Trivia Alert... Dove Cottage is so called because it had previously been a pub called The Dove and Olive Branch Inn.

Not everything was plain sailing for Wordsworth. In 1807, a collection called Poems in Two Volumes was published, and a critic in the influential Edinburgh Review wrote, 'If the printing of such trash as this be not felt as a insult on the part of the public taste, we are afraid it cannot be insulted.' Brutal criticism, indeed. I would suggest that every creative person of note in any branch of the arts will have had to face fierce criticism at some point. One of the worst I can think of was about 70 years later when the French Impressionist painters were ridiculed to such an extent that the public would go to see their exhibitions in Paris just to laugh out loud. JMW Turner was lampooned in the press, and a cartoon showed him painting a canvas with a floor mop and bucket with the caption, 'Is this the death of painting?' Elvis Presley was advised not to give up his day job as a driver for Crown Electrics in Tupelo, and who can forget the Record Executives at Decca who rejected the Beatles? From Rembrandt to Picasso and Van Gogh, the list is endless, but most rode the wave of criticism and went on to achieve great things. However, the sensitive poetic soul of William Wordsworth was wounded, and a spark of creativity was lost. Even his publishers lost confidence and tried to sell the rights, but couldn't find a buyer. Eventually, the copyright reverted back to Wordsworth and his family. As is often the case, public taste gradually turned around, and Wordsworth's poems regained popularity, greatly benefiting the family. Poetic justice, indeed. Willian died in 1850 and is buried at the 14th Century St. Oswald's Church.

A cottage which dates back to 1630 is home to the famous Grasmere Gingerbread, made from a recipe invented in 1854 by Sarah Nelson, who sold her Gingerbreads outside her cottage. It went straight on to our foodie list. Sarah died in 1904 and is buried in the churchyard near William Wordsworth.

Hawkshead

From Ambleside, we took the Lakesider tourist bus back to Windermere and the local bus to the campsite in Kendal.

After breakfast, we set off on a short stage to our next booking on the other side of Lake Windermere. We chose this site at the edge of the small lake of Esthwaite Water as it is handy for hiking in Grizedale Forest and nearby Coniston Water. Another minor consideration was that it was a short walk to Hawkshead Brewery, another addition to our now-famous list.

We followed the A590 to the southern tip of Lake Windermere and stopped at the Lakeland Motor Museum near Newby Bridge. The Museum is in an idyllic setting surrounded by fells and next to a river. Adjacent is the Lakeside and Haverthwaite Railway, a heritage steam railway and popular tourist attraction.

The museum is a modern building of metal and glass plus traditional Lakeland slate and stone, and we began our visit in a separate annexe called Tribute to the Campbell Legend. Malcolm Campbell and his son Donald broke 21 World land and water speed records between them. Many were set in the Lake District, and Donald was killed on Coniston Water in 1967. The Bluebird exhibition has several full-size replicas of the famous Bluebird series. Also on display is one built for a movie starring Anthony Hopkins. Seeing newsreel footage on television doesn't convey the huge size of these jet-propelled machines. To describe them as boats and cars seems inadequate. There are lots of posters and paintings and an illustrated timeline. One of the jet engines was exhibited, and to me it looked like a work of art, a free-standing sculpture that wouldn't look out of place in the Tate Modern.

Trivia Alert... Incidentally, the jet engine was invented by Frank Whittle. As I've mentioned before, as a teacher, we had a lunchtime quiz in the staffroom. One of our colleagues was also called Frank Whittle, and a phone call came through for Frank one day. (Way before mobile phones.) "Frank Whittle?" shouted the person who had answered the call. Instinctively, a few shouted back, "Jet engine." A definite case of *over*-quizzing.

The entrance to the Motor Museum took us through, inevitably, a colourful souvenir shop selling everything connected to transportation: coffee mugs, key rings, photographs, paintings, and badges. In the museums, the cars weren't just shining; they were gleaming, and the light coming through upper windows and skylights caused them to dazzle. I was bedazzled, and not for the first time in this book. There are 30,000 exhibits, including cars, motorcycles, bicycles, nostalgic enamel posters, toys, petrol pumps and even a microlite aircraft hanging from the ceiling. Cars are arranged to create a meandering one-way system for visitors. The cars are parked, practically touching each other; I suspect some very nervous drivers did the parking.

One effect the motor museum had on me wasn't so much pangs of nostalgia but feelings of old age! Not only did I see cars that I remembered on the road, like an Austin A35 that Norma's grandma owned, but models I had *actually driven*, and here they are in a museum! An Austin A 40 on the show was the same model in which I passed my test. Pride of place was a Model T Ford van belonging to a Blackpool business. It was a square box of a vehicle decorated in Fairground-style lettering with Blackpool Tower on the side panel. There was no guided tour as such, but plenty of background information was on display. Some visitors were obviously enthusiasts who were happy to share their knowledge.

It would be impossible, not to mention boring, to give too much detail; reflecting on an overall view would be much better. Clive Sinclair might have been a computer genius, but the Sinclair C5 wasn't his brightest idea. Some tiny cars, like a 1960 Messerschmitt, made John Cooper's Special Edition Mini Cooper seem huge. A Delorean took me Back To The Future. Donald Campbell's car from the 1930s was, of course, the same Bluebird colour. A black Citroen with the distinctive chevron logo looked straight out of an Inspector Maigret movie, while a Cadillac and a 1933 Buick seemed more Al Capone.

Trivia Alert... I've seen a car that Al Capone actually owned. Not in a Chicago museum, but bizarrely, in the Salvador Dali Museum in Figueres in, Spain. Surreal.

Every manufacturer you could think of is represented, and the wall displays of enamels and garage signs enhance all these cars. There are vintage petrol pumps, many topped with the iconic Shell logo, models, cigarette cards and much more. An interesting feature was a row of shop windows from different eras, each displaying period clothes, children's toys, Dinky and Matchbox cars, most of which evoked childhood Christmas nostalgia.

The upper floor was reserved for motorcycles and bicycles, which included everything from a penny farthing to a mountain bike. There was an exhibition dedicated to the Isle of Man T.T. having recently been to the Isle of Man, we took particular interest. There was even a range of motorbike sidecars, but I couldn't get the image of Wallace and Gromitt out of my head.

Trivia Alert... Jaguar began life as Swallows Sidecars.

I mentioned in my book introduction that new words come into use over the years. I picked up one today… Automobilia.

From the Motor Museum, our Satnav lady guided us north along the western shore of Lake Windermere to our next campsite near Hawkshead. As we drove to our pitch, our attention was grabbed by a bizarre sight. One of the caravans had a bike rack attached, but stretched across it, drying in the sun, was a pair of the biggest knickers we had ever seen. I don't know how many Xs go before an L in size, but these must stretch it to its outer limits. They would have been loose on Nessie. The elastic must have been the same as on Medieval catapults during a Castle siege. A strong gust of wind could have propelled the caravan across Coniston faster than Donald Campbell.

We wondered if perhaps it was a Candid Camera wind-up to record the reactions of passers-by. I suggested that it could be a subliminal warning for potential burglars along the lines of, to borrow a quote from Dante's Divine Comedy, 'abandon all hope ye who enter.'

The following morning, we decided to go on a short walk, which took us to the Hawkshead Brewery as if by magic. Being in such a historical setting, I assumed it was an old traditional brewery dating back a couple of centuries, but I was surprised to learn that it was founded as recently as 2002. We joined a guided tour which took us through the various stages of production. The local water from the Lake District fells, which is filtered naturally through the rocks, created mineral-rich fresh water used in the brewing process. Some of the unused mash is added to local farms' cattle feed. Probably the happiest cows in the world. The pub at the brewery is conveniently called The Hawkshead Brewery, which is possibly a good aide memoir for customers suffering the after-effects of the range of Hawkshead beers. Excellent quality and another box ticked on our ever-increasing foodie list.

A Walk in the Forest

The following morning, we donned our hiking boots and set off to explore Grizedale Forest, in particular the famous sculptures. There are trails catering for mountain bikes, rally cars, hikers, and even one called Go Ape, where you can zip-wire across the tree tops. We took the Millwood Trail to contemplate the forest sculptures. Going under a huge wooden tripod arch was like entering War of the Worlds, and an ominous massive carving of a solitary figure seemed more like something from Arthurian legend. It reminded me of the statue of the Knight at Tintagel, but instead of a sword, the one at Grizedale was leaning on a huge axe, suggesting something like 'man at one with the forest.'

Further on, we were confronted by a wooden carving of a weird dog of no particular breed, with an outsized head and a scary, demonic face. A tree trunk had a large old-fashioned brass key, the type used on grandfather clocks or Victorian music boxes. On the other side of the trunk was a brass cylindrical drum. Norma pointed to the key and asked,

"Is this a wind-up?"

"No," I replied, "It *isn't* a wind-up, it's *genuine*." The artist was probably feeling stressed, so came into the forest to unwind."

So we turned the key, and sure enough, the clockwork operated the music box on the other side of the tree trunk. Now, if the artist thought that the gentle 'plinkety-plonk' music would create a tranquil atmospheric sound in the forest, I'm afraid it didn't work for me. It sounded more like an eerie soundtrack to a Stephen King story. I looked back along the trail and expected to see the two ghostly young sisters from the movie The Shining. Further on, more unearthly sounds began to filter through the trees. It came from an installation of bamboo totems called Aeolian Flutes by artist Dan Fox, and the wind created the sound. We passed under a living wooden archway carved by sculptor Antony Holloway and arrived at another piece by the same artist: a sculpted water wheel propelled by wooden water courses. The sound of running water was reassuring following some of our earlier experiences, and several artists followed this theme, or should I say 'went with the flow.' A wooden waterway sculpture by David Nash consisted of hollowed-out water spouts which pour out into a stream, Woman of the Water by Ban An T'ishka had carved figures appearing out of the water holding up a line of spouts along which flowing water cascading into the stream. All fascinating and thought-provoking, and installations which look as though they *belong* in a forest environment, except perhaps the wind-up. I even wondered if an artist had installed a pair of giant knickers between trees and called it something pretentious like Brief Encounter, but they had blown away and landed on a nearby caravan.

We continued our hike over to Coniston Water and reflected on our visit to the Campbell Exhibition. We finished an excellent day, would you believe, at the pub on the campsite. They were having a quiz night, so we joined in. We did quite well up to the interval, but I think the Hawkshead Beer kicked in, and the metaphorical wheels fell off. Besides, none of the trivia from our travels cropped up, and there wasn't a single question on Barbara Cartland or Barbara Castle.

Tales of Beatrix Potter

On our final day, we walked to the former home of Beatrix Potter, Hill Top Farm, at Near Sawrey. We discovered what a fascinating, clever, talented lady Beatrix Potter was. The interior meticulously recreates the Victorian ambience that Beatrix will have found conducive to original and creative thoughts. Her world-wide popularity was apparent in the number of foreign visitors, mainly from Japan. The house has an original Victorian fireplace, horse-brasses, and a spinning wheel, the original four-poster bed with a patchwork quilt, and many paintings and illustrations.

Although strongly associated with the Lake District, surprisingly, Beatrix Potter was actually born in London. Childhood family holidays to Scotland and the Lake District nurtured her love of the outdoor environment, prompting her to leave London. She was always a keen and talented botanical artist, and in Scotland, she met Charles Rennie MacIntosh, who encouraged her and gave her samples from his collection.

In the 1890s, Beatrix produced illustrated Christmas cards. A printing company bought some of her drawings and encouraged her to continue with her own illustrated stories, leading to her first publication in 1893. Tom Kittens, Peter Rabbit, Jemima Puddle-Duck and the rest were born. She wrote 28 books, bringing her fame and fortune. Infusing inanimate objects with character, personality and voices is called amorphism, and Beatrix Potter pre-dated Walt Disney by decades. In addition to all these attributes, she was also an astute business woman, scientific illustrator, environmentalist and farmer. When she died in 1943, she left all her property to the National Trust;

that's 4,000 acres, 16 farms, cottages, herds of cattle and flocks of Herdwick sheep, a breed she had developed. What a woman!

Keswick

We were back on the road after breakfast, heading for Keswick in the North Lakes. We took the B road from Hawkshead to Ambleside, picked up the A591, and passed Rydal Water and Grasmere through the Cumbrian Mountains along Thirlmere with Helvellyn to the east.

Trivia Alert... Thirlmere provides Manchester with its water supply.

The route of the pipes was cleverly engineered so that the entire flow is by gravity only.

Keswick is an attractive market town on the River Greta close to Derwentwater, where the weekly artisan market takes over the main square. The northern Lake District is less commercialised than the south, and Keswick seems more of a hub for serious fell walkers than browsing tourists. There are dozens of outdoor pursuit stores alongside the customary bars, craft shops and cafes. The Keswick Theatre By The Lake was built of traditional Lakeland stone and slate and opened in 1999. Hope Park and Fitz Park are popular with mini golf, traditional park cafes and local ice cream. Most of the town centre is pedestrianised with the familiar shops. There is a good selection of pubs, including a Wetherspoon, once the police station and courthouse. You can enjoy a pint in a police cell or in the dock. However, we opted for The Wainwright Pub, named after our old friend Alfred. There is now a Wainwright Beer, and the label is in the style of Wainwright's travel guides.

Beyond the Pleasure Dome

William Wordsworth's good friend, collaborator and co-founder of the Romantic Movement in poetry, Samuel Taylor Coleridge, lived in Keswick.

Coleridge suffered from ill health for much of his life, and his mood swings went from depression to manic activity. He took Laudanum, which contained opium, to which, unfortunately, Coleridge became addicted. It possibly opened his subconscious, creative, abstract thoughts. I suppose a modern-day comparison would be the drug culture of the 1960s in music, art and poetry. The San Francisco Flower Power, dropout hippy generation of LSD-induced psychedelic happenings and transcendental meditation. There is a saying, 'If you can remember the 60s, then you weren't really there.' Coleridge pre-dated all this by two centuries.

Indeed, Samuel Taylor Coleridge claimed he dreamed about Kubla Khan and woke from his opium-induced slumber with a poem formed in his head. Kubla Khan was a real-life historical figure, the grandson of the even more famous Genghis Khan. The renowned traveller Marco Polo brought back from China stories of a Pleasure Dome in Xanadu about 500 years before Coleridge was even born.

The following day, we decided to embark on a strenuous walk. We caught one of the ferries that circled Derwentwater and disembarked to follow a recommended hiking trail to the summit of Catbells, a popular route evident in the number of walkers along the footpath. We could feel thigh-burn as the climb became steeper over well-worn rocky sections. It was well worth the effort on reaching the top. The 360-degree view was sensational as distant mountains receded in atmospheric perspective of blues, purples, magentas and lilacs, a whole palette of colour. No wonder JMW Turner enjoyed visiting the Lake District.

Trompe-L'oeil

As you will know by now, I have a compulsion to visit any galleries or museums we happen upon. The Puzzling Place, the Museum of Illusions, in Keswick, was an interesting diversion. It is full of clever optical illusions that play tricks with your mind and make you question your perception of what you see. Artists have used many of these 'tricks of the eye' in the past, the most notable being the Dutch graphic artist MC Escher's impossible drawings of staircases. Pop artists such as Victor Vasarely and Bridget Riley in the 1960s created images with wavy lines, chequerboards and stripes to create movement and distance. Surrealist painter Salvador Dali often created double images, where you see one thing which changes into something else and back again as your brain processes the image. All of these are represented in the museum along with holograms, an old-fashioned fairground hall of mirrors and false perspective. A ball on a pool table appears to roll uphill, and most fascinating of all is a room in which you can walk from one side to the other and transform from being tiny into a giant touching the ceiling. I watched with fascination as kids thoroughly enjoyed swapping roles, and I'm still unsure how it works.

Also, in Keswick, there is a museum, the like of which I haven't seen before: the unique Pencil Museum. I couldn't resist. I was just drawn to it even though we hadn't pencilled it in as part of our itinerary. It opened in 1981 and draws 80,000 visitors a year. It is next to the derelict Cumberland Pencil factory, which opened in 1832 beside the River Greta. Production has been transferred to a modern state-of-the-art factory near Workington.

2B or not 2B

Entering the Pencil Museum is a bizarre experience. It is supposed to replicate a graphite mine, but the plaster walls and sprayed colour seemed more like the ghost train at Blackpool. There were figures of mannequin miners and weird sounds of picks, shovels and squeaky wheels on rail tracks. All it was short of was a chorus of 'hi ho, hi ho.' Having said that, and at the risk of sounding like a pencil nerd, the museum itself turned out to be interesting. Every visitor was given a quiz sheet to complete as they made their way through the museum. 2B or not 2B? that was the first question. (Ok, I admit I made that bit up.) Pride of place in the centre of the room, together with a framed certificate from the Guinness Book of Records, was the world's biggest pencil. Where else would it be? Having been an art teacher, I am familiar with the presentation tins of coloured pencils with the Cumberland and Derwent brands and the Lakeland scenes. I suppose fate decreed that it was inevitable that I would end up in pencil heaven one day.

A massive storm in Borrowdale in 1550 felled trees by the roots, unearthing the first discovery of graphite. Records are sketchy, but it's thought that slithers of this stone were wrapped in strips of sheepskin to create the first primitive pencil.

Trivia Alert... The word pencil comes from the French word 'pincel,' meaning small brush. In 1580, The Michelangelo School of Art in Florence used pencils made of Cumberland graphite taken there by Flemish traders. At one time, graphite was very valuable and sold illegally. This is the origin of the term 'The Black Market.'

There was an exhibition of tiny graphite carvings on pencils ranging from King Kong to Big Ben. The world's first Pb pencil was on display.

Trivia Alert... The name refers to the lead content, plumbum being Latin for lead. This is how plumbing and plumber got their names due to early use of lead piping.

Pay Attention, 007

A display which I found most fascinating was about secret wartime pencils. Being a James Bond fan, I was intrigued to learn more about a man who is thought to have been Ian Fleming's inspiration for the character Q. Charles Fraser-Smith worked for MI6, and during the Second World War, his department was developing ideas to provide assistance to servicemen trapped behind enemy lines; such as miniature maps and compasses. In 1942, Fraser-Smith visited the Cumberland Pencil factory, and, drawing on their expertise, they came up with designs for hollowed-out pencils that secretly twist open. Some of these ingenious ideas were on display. There is even a sign above which says, 'Now, pay attention, Bond.' I could just visualize Desmond Llewelyn chastising a bored-looking 007. So, let me see if I've got this right. The Secret Service sent agents on assignments with no lead in their pencils. James Bond must have been the exception to this rule. On the graphite scale of hardness, he must be a 4H at least. A denouement to this story is that in 2023, television news and front page headlines informed the public that secret documents relating to Nuclear Submarines had been found in a toilet in a Wetherspoons pub... in Cumbria! The head of M15 said, 'It's fortunate there were no Russian Spies in the area'. Probably too busy smearing knobs in Salisbury.

I completed my quiz sheet and got enough correct answers to qualify for a prize. I think I just shaded it. Guess what the prize was. That's right… a pencil. It was now time to draw a line under our visit and, you will be relieved to know, any more pencil puns. We went for lunch at the Pheasant Inn and had a Cumberland Ale and Cumberland sausages. That's another box I could tick… with my new pencil.

Our stay in the Lake District was one of our most memorable, but it was time to move on. We headed to the Cumbrian Coast, where the Solway Firth meets the Irish Sea. We followed the A66 following the western edge of Bassenthwaite Lake and passed Cockermouth, the birthplace of Wordsworth. We took the A595 along the coast, passing through Workington and Whitehaven towards Barrow.

Barrow-In-Furness

We had a brief stop in Barrow. In the 1840s, it was a small village near Furness Abbey, which was once one of the most powerful in England but now stands in ruins. Barrow-in-Furness Town Hall, built in 1886, is a great statement of civic pride, and there are Victorian architectural gems all over town. The prosperity of Barrow grew exponentially through the input of two industrialists: Henry Schneider, 'the Iron Man', and James Ramsden, 'The Railway Man'. They developed the iron and steel works into one of the largest in the world, and the railway tracks manufactured there were exported all over the world.

Shipbuilding became the main industry as the Iron Shipbuilding Company, which the Vickers Corporation later bought. Many famous vessels have been launched down Barrow's slipways, from cruise liners to battleships and aircraft carriers. Unlike many shipbuilding docks around the country, Barrow hasn't found it necessary to re-invent itself with bijoux apartments, cafes, galleries and museums because it still plays a vital role for the Royal Navy. It is the home of BAE Systems Nuclear Submarines, and the docks area has huge, cube-like, featureless buildings protected by perimeter fencing. It looks like the kind of facility that gets blown up at the end of a James Bond movie.

The high level of security makes it even more incredulous that secret nuclear submarine documents were found in a Wetherspoon pub toilet in the Lake District. I don't think it takes James Bond or M to work out that they *must* have come from Barrow. A government official reassured us that they were *not* classified documents. To borrow a famous line by Mandy Rice-Davies during a Political sex scandal trial in the 1960s, "He would say that, wouldn't he." Perhaps he should be transferred from MI5 to MFI, where he could decode the instruction pamphlets. I think this story would make a Bond movie, something like 'From Wetherspoons With Love,' or 'Wetherspoons Are Forever,' or 'Wetherspoonraker' or 'The Spy Who Loved Wetherspoons.' (Keep it going...)

Way Out West

On our way through Ulverston, we pulled over for a short coffee break to look at a statue of one of Ulverston's famous sons and one of Britain's most famous stars. It's the birthplace of Stanley Jefferson. Who? We know him better as Stan Laurel of Laurel and Hardy fame.

Trivia Alert... When Stan sailed across the Atlantic to America, he shared a cabin with none other than Charlie Chaplin.

We followed the coast near Cartmel, where we once spent a memorable day at the races. The town square becomes a huge street party surrounded by pubs, and horse racing takes place around the perimeter of the town. A great day out many years ago. As we drove past Flookburgh Aerodrome and Grange-over-Sands on Morecambe Bay, I shuddered slightly as I remembered that I had a bird's-eye view of the surrounding area from when I did a parachute jump for charity.

Picking up the A590, it was a short drive over to the M6 motorway and a leisurely drive south for another short stay at Bridge Farm in Rainford before embarking on the next stage of our journey around the coast of Wales.

Severn Bridge

A crossing over the River Severn estuary, linking England and Wales, had been a challenge for centuries due to the force of the river and the distance across.

The 1960s saw the first use of box girders, and the deck sections of the bridge are aerodynamic, based on aircraft wing technology, as we saw at the Humber Bridge. The result is a light, aesthetic suspension bridge. In 1966, it was opened by Queen Elizabeth II, who was accompanied by the Transport Secretary, Barbara Cartland, er, sorry... Castle.

The Full Moon and Stephen King

The River Severn is one of very few places on Earth to host a natural phenomenon of a tidal wave flowing upstream. Here, it is known as the Severn Bore, a major attraction for surfer in wet suits. Now, at the risk of becoming a Severn Bore myself, let me *very briefly* explain what happens: The full moon needs to be aligned so that its gravitational pull creates a 'super' high tide. This funnels into the river mouth against the river's natural flow, creating waves which travel at about 12 mph upstream. Surfers catch the waves, and the surfing record is about 9 miles long and is held by a man called, would you believe, Stephen King. Surely it can't be the *same one*!... I've never heard of a Stephen King horror story about surfing! I've seen photographs of the Severn Bore, but the colour of the water and surfer in wet-suits suggests that it isn't California. But hey, who needs Bondi or Waikiki when you can ride the Severn Bore?

Phase Three: WALES

Chepstow

We decided to stop at Chepstow in Monmouthshire primarily to walk along a section of Offa's Dyke path as far as Tintern Abbey. It was a long drive down the motorways, and we set up our pitch and had a meal at the restaurant. The following morning, we walked into Chepstow, famous for its racecourse, particularly its historic castle. There are over 600 castles in Wales, more per square mile than any other country in the world, but don't worry, we won't be visiting all of them. The Normans built the castle in 1067, just one year after the invasion. Chepstow Castle is a daunting, awe-inspiring structure perched on a cliff overlooking the River Wye as a stronghold between England and Wales. Originally, it was called Striguil, meaning river bend, a major crossing point and strategic position. An interesting feature is a magnificent massive wooden door dating from the 12th Century, the oldest in Europe, which has been moved inside for preservation. It is heavy and solid, with intricate carving and mechanisms for locks and levers. The vast castle has large windows, huge fireplaces and Norman round arches decorated in typical chevron designs.

In Chepstow town centre, we browsed casually around the usual cafes, souvenir shops, and bric-a-brac arcades. There are many historic pubs, and one in particular caught my attention because I had never before seen a pub with this name. It's called The Five Alls, and the distinctive sign comprises five paintings representing different sectors of society and what each contributes: A Soldier: fight all, an Archbishop: pray all, Queen Elizabeth 1st: rule all, a Lawyer: plead all, and John Bull: pay all. It's just as well that there isn't a picture of a Member of Parliament telling us what they do.

The following morning, we were out early in our hiking gear and rucksacks to walk along Offa's Dyke. The traditional boundary between England and Wales meanders from near Chepstow to

Prestatyn in North Wales, a town made famous by that classic song by the Moody Blues: Nights in Prestatyn. Offa was an 8th Century King in central England, known as Mercia, and his life is shrouded in myth and legend. We do know that he introduced the first English penny with the inscription Rex Angloram, King of the English. A gold coin from Offa's reign is in the British museum. The Dyke wasn't a strong, fortified boundary like, say, Hadrian's Wall, but more of a statement of power and prestige, a marking of territory. I suppose it could be described as a human equivalent of animals in the wild, like a lion peeing on trees. The Dyke was a massive earthwork, a mound with a V-shaped ditch on either side, from which the term dyke is derived. The path opened in 1971 and is popular with hikers, many walking the entire length. At a more modest level, we are just doing about seven miles to Tintern Abbey. Offa's Dyke could be a metaphor for the Dark Ages; sections disappear, then nothing discernible for miles until another section appears... Fill in the gaps with your imagination.

So, with that in mind, we set off along the footpath.

"Let's see what's on, Offa," I couldn't resist saying to Norma. Cue the usual pained expression.

Inevitably, the name of King Arthur cropped up, and legend has it that he is buried somewhere along the way. In the 17th Century, a skeleton was found in a cave called, you've got it, King Arthur's Cave. We came across a sign, 'Wintour's Leap,' which marks the spot where he jumped off the cliff into the river to escape Oliver Cromwell's. He must have been desperate to escape because, looking over the edge, it was like the leap by Butch Cassidy and The Sundance Kid in the movie. There is an outcrop of rock with a commanding view overlooking Tintern Abbey. It is known as The Devil's Pulpit, from where, according to myth, the Devil preached to entice the Monks to leave the Abbey and give up their religious calling.

Tintern Abbey was founded in the 12th Century by Cistercian Monks and stood in a beautiful setting by the River Wye. This masterpiece of Gothic Architecture fell victim to the dissolution of the Monasteries. The sandstone building began to decay and suffered further damage during the English Civil War the following century.

As a ruin, it retains its grandeur; a huge, impressive structure of columns and arches evokes a romantic, magical atmosphere. It has always been a popular subject for artists, the most notable being JMW Turner, perhaps the greatest of watercolourists, who created an atmospheric vision. When we were in the Lake District, I mentioned William Wordsworth's Tintern poem included in The Lyrical Ballads, his collaboration with Samuel Taylor Coleridge. Walking around Tintern, I could sense what moved Wordsworth to create his Romantic poem, with lines such as; 'the power of harmony' and 'beauteous forms of nature delight the senses.' Between them, Turner and Wordsworth encapsulated, visually, poetically and emotionally, the mystery and magic of Tintern Abbey.

Leaving Chepstow, we continued into Wales. This is probably a good time to explain some Welsh place names briefly. The most common word we will come across is Cymru (Wales), which derives from an early Breton word Camboges, meaning countrymen. The Welsh language survives from ancient Celtic times, and the prefix of many place names often refers to geographical features or local customs. For example, Llan (as in Llanelli and Llandudno) are named after a place of worship or a Saint. Aber (Aberystwyth, Aberaeron) is the mouth of a river: Rhos (Rhosneigr), a meadow, Mae (Maesteg), a pasture. Caern is a fortress, and Arfon is a river, hence Caernarfon. A good example is Betws (a small church) and Coed (trees) giving Betws-y-Coed its name. Llyn is a lake, Pen means at the head or the top of, and Bryn is a hill. That's enough to be going on with, and no doubt we'll come across others as we follow the coast of Wales.

The Red Dragon

As we drive towards Cardiff, the Red Dragon seems everywhere. This has been a symbol of Wales for centuries and can be seen on flags, badges, sculptures, and tourist souvenirs such as tea towels. But why would a mythical creature become such an emblem? The oldest recorded use dates back to the 9th Century, probably as a Battle Standard. As with many aspects of history from the Dark Ages, no one is entirely sure, but it is thought that it originated in Celtic myths or the legend of King Arthur. As we learned at Tintagel in Geoffrey of Monmouth's 'History of Kings', the Red was a prophecy. The wizard Merlin prophesied a battle between a White Dragon representing England and a Red Dragon representing Wales. The Red Dragon featured on the Battle Standard of Welshman Henry Tudor, who became Henry VII by defeating Richard III at the Battle of

Bosworth in 1485. Many believed that this was the prophecy coming true. Indeed, the Dragon is so intrinsically entrenched in the history of Wales that even the misty clouds swirling moodily around the peaks of Snowdonia are known as 'Dragon's Breath'. It seems a great anomaly that the Welsh dragon does not feature on the Union Flag. This is because when the flag was created in 1606, combining the Crosses of St. Andrew and St. George, Wales had been regarded as part of England since the 13th Century. These days, with devolved Governments, who knows what the future holds for the United Kingdom? Perhaps a modern-day Willian Wallace or Owain Glyndwr will emerge. I doubt if even Merlin the Magician could prophecy that.

Cardiff

Cardiff, the Capital City, is located where the River Taff flows into the Severn Estuary. The city and Cardiff Bay are two distinct parts, about 2 miles away. Like most British cities we have visited, Cardiff boasts an impressive infrastructure of solid Victorian buildings with Graeco-Roman facades. There seemed to be more classic columns than we'd seen in either Rome or Athens. The market and even Poundland are in grand, elegant buildings. A coal miner statue carrying a lamp is on the pedestrianized Queen Street, which has the usual array of chain stores. The Statue of Aneurin (Nye) Bevan, Member of Parliament and founder of the National Health Service, stands close to Cardiff Castle. Cardiff attracts 18 million visitors a year and, as to be expected, there are plenty of souvenir shops: a large store called Historical Wales and a shop called Great Welsh Gifts.

The largest Principality Stadium in Wales is near shopping centres and attracts big crowds for rugby matches and concerts. Cardiff Castle was originally a Roman fort and still retains some original walls. The Keep on the hill (motte) is the finest in Wales and displays the Welsh flag of the Red Dragon against a white and green background, while a large model of this iconic emblem stands in the castle grounds.

The 1st Marquis of Bute owned the Castle in the 18th Century and turned Cardiff into a coal exporting port. Successors to the title became the richest men in the world, and this fabulous wealth manifests itself in the lavish interiors. Halls and rooms have an unbelievable level of opulence, with murals, marble, stained glass, intricate wood carvings and gilding. Each room has a dedicated theme, such as Mediterranean gardens, Italian and Arabic decorations, and Moorish design, all inspired by the Marquis' travels. The Banqueting Hall has a wooden hammer-beam roof based on church architecture and a mezzanine level for musicians. The roof garden at the top of the tower is a re-creation from Pompeii, and, having been to Pompeii, I was impressed by its authenticity.

An interior walkway has an original Roman wall, called the Chariot Wall, and a sculptured golden mural is opposite. There are depictions of village life, a Roman invasion fleet, men at work in an armoury, and battles culminating in a magnificent Roman charioteer. It looks like a Roman or Medieval creation in copper or bronze. It is actually plaster and gold paint made by local sculpture Frank Abraham as recently as the 1980s.

We took the water bus from Bute Park to Mermaid quay at Cardiff Bay. The reddish-coloured Pier Head Building has all the hallmarks of Victorian architectural splendour. It stands isolated, surrounded by modern buildings, like a proud grandmother at the centre of a family gathering. There are impressive modern apartments with balconies looking out on cafes and bars and a vibrant atmosphere. The Red Dragon Centre is for exhibitions and shows. There is a Roald Dahl Plass monument dedicated to the Cardiff-born writer and even a Doctor Who exhibition. There is always a runt in every litter, and, in my opinion, the Senedd (National Assembly for Wales) building doesn't satisfy my aesthetic sensibilities. Perhaps the architects should visit the Doctor Who Centre and travel back to the drawing board.

Swansea

Swansea, or Abertawe in Welsh, is a gateway to the tranquil Gower Peninsula. It is a modern city, largely due to the fact that it was heavily bombed during the Second World War. The scars of war can still be seen on some surviving buildings, but regeneration and rebuilding have resulted in a well-designed modern environment.

The best overview of Swansea was from the top of the tallest building, the imaginatively-named Tower on Trawler Road. The ultra-modern architecture looks expensive and luxurious. We went into its Grape and Olive pub, then up to the Sky Bar on the 28th floor. The spectacular view takes in the surrounding countryside, Swansea Bay, several superb beaches, and the Marina. Rows of pastel-painted terraced houses cling to the hillside, the line of distinctive gable ends looking like the teeth of saws.

As we have found with most towns with a substantial student population, there is a vibrancy reflected in the range of pubs, cafes and restaurants. The original Pumphouse at the Marina is now a bar and grill, and there is the National Waterfront Museum, a square, glass modern building which is well worth a visit. There are vehicles dating from horse-drawn carriages, ice-cream vans, a Sinclair C5 and a Benz 7-horsepower single-cylinder car. There are toys through the ages. A twin-tub washing machine took me right back to washing day as a kid, and my memories pre-date this to a dolly tub and a scrubbing board, standard percussion for the early Skiffle Groups.

Walking through the Copra Bay Bridge was like entering a giant cheese grater, which took us to the impressive Leisure Centre, a rotunda more like a modern abstract sculpture. We noticed a survey boat called The Mary Anning, a name which would have meant nothing to us had we not visited the Jurassic Coast in Dorset.

The street horses and chariot-style vehicles offering city tours are a novelty in the centre. Traditional buildings are interspersed with modern and co-exist pleasingly. Little Wind Street is pedestrianised, meandering through gardens, verges, trees and outside cafes. During the Second World War, some American G.I's stationed in Swansea were having a drink in a pub around here. A big, loud-mouthed Australian soldier started an argument with one of the Americans. A fight erupted, and the Aussie was knocked-out cold by the young G.I, whose name just happened to be Rocky Marciano. So Swansea could claim to have started the career of one of the greatest-ever boxing champions.

Trivia Alert... To this day, Marciano still holds the record as the only World Heavyweight Champion with a perfect record: 49 fights and 49 wins. (Not counting Swansea).

A blue plaque on a house in Cundonkin Drive commemorates one of Wales' most famous sons, the poet Dylan Thomas. He is on the cover of the UK's biggest-selling studio album of all time, The Beatles 'Sgt. Pepper's Lonely Hearts Club Band' was designed by Pop Artist Peter

Blake. Dylan Thomas is next to Marlon Brando, and nearby is a fan and great admirer of his writing, Robert Zimmerman… who changed his name to Bob Dylan as a tribute.

Born in 1914 in Swansea, Thomas wrote over 100 poems, and he is probably best known for his 1944 radio script 'Under Milk Wood', a one-day chronicle of a Welsh village. In 1971, it was made into a film starring Richard Burton, Elizabeth Taylor and Peter O'Toole.

Dylan Thomas was once described as 'An un-made bed'. He loved a drink and pub sessions and even described a pint of beer in glowing, descriptive prose in a poem. So much so that he talked me into it. We went into the Slug & Lettuce, a black and white half-timbered pub opposite Swansea Castle. There has been a castle there since Norman times, and over the years, it has been a workhouse, prison, post office and newspaper office. Dylan Thomas worked there as a journalist for the South Wales Daily Post in the 1950s.

When leaving Swansea, we made a short detour around the bay of the Gower Peninsula, which became Britain's first 'Area of Outstanding Natural Beauty' in 1956. We stopped at Oystermouth Castle (didn't go in) and Mumbles Head, with dramatic cliffs, a lighthouse and magnificent beaches.

Pembrokeshire Heritage Coast

At St. Clears, we detoured to Laugharne. Dylan Thomas had a house perched on a hillside overlooking the sea, where he converted a boathouse into a writing studio. This has been preserved to show visitors the environment in which the poet worked. An interesting and timeless experience. Thomas wrote a poem about the nearby Laugharne Castle, which he described as the most romantic of all.

Pendine, situated at the western end of Pendine Sands on Carmarthen Bay, is a wide 7-mile beach used for highspeed racing. It is the equivalent of Daytona Beach and Bonneville Salt Flats in the USA for speed records. In the 1920s, Malcolm Campbell began his dynasty of expensive Bluebird cars and speedboats. His great rival was Welshman John Parry-Thomas, who raced in a car he called BABS, which had an aeroplane engine. The world record exchanged hands between them until Parry-Jones was killed. Hot-rods, vintage and sports cars have set records on Pendine Beach. Unbelievably, the record for a pushbike was set at 112mph! (Following the slipstream of a truck.) There is a museum of speed, but unfortunately, it was closed for renovation. But looks to be well worth a visit on re-opening.

We drove back along the same road passed Saundersfoot to our next campsite at Tenby. Tenby is a harbour town and popular holiday centre with beautiful co-ordinated pastel buildings nestling along the cliff-top sea front. We sampled some excellent pubs and were particularly attracted to a café selling Ginger Welsh Cakes, another addition to our ever-growing list of locally named food and drink.

Our main reason for staying a couple of days in Tenby was to enjoy the magnificent splendour of the Pembrokeshire Coast National Park and some of the Heritage Coastal Path, which stretches approximately 150 miles from Saundersfoot around the peninsula to Cardigan. We set off along a coastal path from Tenby. To call the Pembrokeshire Coast an area of outstanding beauty is an understatement. There are jagged outcrops, stacks, rocky cliff faces and inlets. The folds and formations of rocks exposed millions of years of history. We passed Giltar Point, Lydstep Point and the 12th Century Manorbier Castle and continued to Stackpole Head. Many movies have been filmed along the Pembrokeshire Coast, including Robin Hood Prince of Thieves, starring Kevin Costner.

We left the campsite the following morning towards Haverfordwest via Pembroke and towards our next stopover at St. David's. We parked up for yet another photo opportunity at Solva on St. Bride's Bay. This was an important trading centre during Medieval times, and today, it thrives on the popularity of the heritage path. Several stone steps were built into the cliffs for access to the beach. I'm running out of superlatives when trying to describe and do justice to many of the sights we have seen. Perhaps I should dig out a Thesaurus, but then again, Mary Anning has beaten me to it.

We arrived at our campsite on Whitesands Bay, on the Heritage Path.

St David's

St. David's is famous for being the smallest city in the UK. I'm unsure if the name should have an apostrophe because there were numerous signs of both versions. St. David, the Patron Saint of Wales, was born in the year 512 AD in the local area. He became a monk and preached in Wales and Europe, establishing an Abbey on the site where the cathedral now stands. He was appointed Archbishop of Wales, and during an outdoor sermon, a white dove landed on his shoulder, and the congregation interpreted this as a blessing from God, a miracle.

The Pope declared him to be a Saint 500 years after his death, and pilgrims pray at the Shrine of St. David. The grey stone cathedral was built between the 12th and 16th Centuries and combines architectural styles ranging from Norman to Gothic.

The cathedral has a plain square tower, and inside are round Norman arches, Gothic windows and impressive stained glass. The floor is decoratively tiled, while the Tudor wooden ceiling is intricate and spectacular. There is a wooden lectern, pulpit, Bishop's Throne, or cathedra. Adjacent to the cathedral, over a stream, are the ruins of the Bishop's Palace. They must have lived in some splendour because it was bigger than the actual cathedral.

Walking the short distance to the city centre is up stone steps, providing a superb view of the cathedral. This is quite unusual as most Cathedrals are sited in open spaces or on higher ground. The city centre is a small square, with a Celtic cross, lots of flowers and benches next to the Bishop's Pub, where, of course, we went for a drink. There are the usual gift shops, cafés and ice cream parlours, and the Pebbles Yard gallery.

Our motorhome site was a short walk back through the countryside, and we were overlooking the popular Whitesands beach of beautiful sand and sea framed by dramatic rocky outcrops.

Going Dutch

We enjoyed a day of tranquillity at BBKing. This was shattered the following day when a bright red fire engine came thundering up the pathway. We were startled, thinking a serious incident had occurred. However, the engine reversed into the adjacent site. We looked on bemused. It was gleaming and immaculate, like something from a Mack Sennet silent movie.

Two young men jumped out and seemed boisterous. Norma and I gave each other a woeful look. When they eventually noticed us watching them, they approached and introduced themselves enthusiastically with vigorous handshakes. They were Dutch and in their twenties. Johannes and Pieter were mechanics in a garage in Holland. They had spent their spare time on the restoration of a vintage fire engine, the same idea as Cliff Richard and his double-decker bus in the movie Summer Holiday.

That night, we returned late after a night out, and we were dismayed by the view ahead. All around, the fire engine was strewn with empty beer cans, and we knew the Dutchmen had gone to bed... one of them had his feet sticking out of the window. However, when we got up the following morning, everywhere was pristine. Not bad lads, after all. So much so that later, one of them stopped on his bike and asked if we wanted anything from the supermarket. They turned out to be perfect neighbours.

We had lunchtime drinks with our new Dutch friends. They told us the history of the renovation. It was a 1950s Regent Mk III Merryweather, complete with a ladder and hosepipe. And they had spent a couple of years on it. Their benevolent boss had allocated storage and workspace in the garage and allowed them to consolidate their holidays to enable them to go on longer trips.

"Have you been allowed to keep the siren and blue light?" I asked.

"I don't know about *permission*," answered Pieter, "we didn't ask in case we got the wrong answer, but we've kept them anyway and in full working order."

"Have you ever used them?"

"Only a few times," they answered gleefully, "we've frightened motorists with the siren, and the blue light has got us through many a traffic jam!"

Aberystwyth

From St. David's, we headed north, following the coast of Cardigan Bay through Fishguard, Cardigan and Aberaeron to the University Town of Aberystwyth. It was a beautiful leisurely drive through the Pembrokeshire Coast National Park, and it was particularly interesting to see the Preseli Hills, which, you will remember, was the source of the monoliths for Stonehenge. The rock formations seemed ready-made, Stone-age builders' yards for standing stones.

The seafront has gentle curving bays with a dark beach of shingle and flat, smooth pebbles perfect skimming stones. A popular pastime seems to be building small sculptures with the flat pebbles, similar to tors found on mountain trails, or environmental artists, as we saw in Grizedale Forest in the Lake District.

Elegant, bay-window houses create an impressive seafront façade, all painted in individual colours, pastels to the south changing to the north into bright blues, yellows, lilacs, greens and turquoises. We boarded the cliff funicular railway to the top of Constitution Hill, giving us a spectacular view of Cardigan Bay and a panorama of Aberystwyth, especially from the bar at the top of the hill.

Aberystwyth Castle stands on a promontory between bays, commanding a defensive position of strategic importance since the Welsh competed with the Normans for routes to Ireland. The castle is in a poor state of repair as it was burnt down by Cromwell's Troops in 1649. Aberystwyth was the home of the Royal Mint, and silver coins were minted from local mines. The Royal Mint is still in Wales, in the village of Pantycelyn, not far from Cardiff.

Aberystwyth town flourished with the arrival of the Cambrian Railway in 1864, bringing prosperity from tourists, new businesses and hotels. The grand Gothic-revival Castle Hotel was bought by the University College of Wales in 1872. As to be expected in a University town, Aberystwyth has a wide selection of bars, pubs with character, clubs, restaurants, and bookshops, and it is home to the National Library of Wales. There is an arched stone bridge over the river Mynach, Devil's Bridge Falls and an impressive clock tower in the town centre.

It was time for a pub lunch, and we had a 'close encounter of the (almost) 3rd kind.' We got chatting to a local character who engaged us in a most interesting conversation. He was a member of a UFO group and told us that Aberystwyth is 'Europe's Roswell.' (After the site in Arizona where an Alien spaceship is thought to have crash-landed in 1947). Apparently, a mystery surrounds a similar crash in a field near Aberystwyth in 1983. Despite eyewitness accounts, there was no mention of the incident in any local or national papers, apart from the Sunday Express writing of 'strange debris falling from the sky.' No pilots or crafts were reported missing. There was nothing on radar scanners, and the Ministry of Defence stated that there was nothing in the sky in that area. The site was sealed off, and the RAF did a military clean-up, but one or two mystery pieces have been found.

It was certainly an intriguing encounter with our lunch companion, who was eloquent, intelligent and charismatic, telling his story. He didn't have pointy Spock-like ears, although he did phone home at one point. As we said our goodbyes, he asked what was next on our motorhome odyssey. I couldn't resist it… 'To infinity and beyond.' Anyway, the story must be true because it was told to me by that mythical font of all knowledge, a man in a pub.

The Iron Man

The drive north took us through the sensational Snowdonia national Park and around the coast of Tremadog Bay to a caravan park next to Harlech Castle.

As we have seen in Scotland, King Edward 1st is known as 'The Hammer of the Scots.' Also, I think he could just as easily be known as 'The Hammer of the Welsh.' To subdue continuous Welsh uprisings, he built a castle chain known as 'The Ring of Iron.' There are about eight, all tourist attractions today, so the Welsh Tourist Board can thank the English for building them! They included Conwy, Caernarfon, and Beaumaris and were designed by a genius of castle-building called Master James of St. George, who was brought over from Savoy in France by the King. I'm surprised that he isn't more famous in view of the iconic buildings he has created.

Harlech Castle was built as an impregnable fortification, and it became the most formidable fortress in Europe. It stands on the Harlech Dome, a 200 ft. high rock lapped by the sea. Incidentally, the sea level has since dropped, and the shore has receded about half a mile. The caravan park where we stayed was once the bed of the Irish Sea. (I was under the impression that sea levels were supposed to be rising due to climate change and melting glaciers.)

The Castle, with Snowdonia as a spectacular backdrop, has inspired numerous artists over the years, notably JMW Turner. The round towers reminded me of Citadels I had seen in the Middle East in places like Homs, Aleppo and Damascus in Syria, which was confirmed by information on display. Before he became King, Prince

Edward joined the 8th Crusade to the Holy Lands in 1270 and was inspired by Crusader Castles.

Standing on solid rock meant that Harlech Castle couldn't be undermined to destroy the foundations and bring it down. A blockade to cut-off supplies was futile because the castle could be re-stocked by sea. Steps still exist which led down to a dock. The bombardment was ineffective against 12 ft. thick walls and round towers. The most ingenious innovation was to make the weakest point of a castle, the Portcullis, into its strength. In sports, it is often said that 'the best form of defence is attack.' Combine this with the saying, 'come into my parlour, said the spider to the fly,' and the attackers become the victims. Instead of the twin towers and a portcullis gateway, Harlech has four round towers at the entrance, creating the first trap. As invaders entered, they were sitting ducks as they were bombarded on all sides with boiling oil, arrows and boulders. As they broke through the inside gate, cleverly designed passages funnelled them into restricted areas with 'murder holes' above.

Significant names from history include Prince Llewellyn ap Gruffudd, Prince of Wales, who led uprisings against Edward. I suppose he could be considered Wales's equivalent of Scotland's William Wallace. In the same way that Edward took the Stone of Scone symbolically from Scotland, he dismantled Llewellyn's Royal Hall and reconstructed it inside Harlech Castle's walls. A century later, another Welsh hero, Owain Glyndwr, actually conquered the Castle and made it his seat in 1404. His tactics were simple…he bribed the garrison. A long siege in 1468 inspired the rousing song 'Men of Harlech,' which, if we are to believe the film Zulu, was sung at the 1879 Battle of Rorke's Drift in South Africa. Eleven Victoria Crosses were awarded, but the singing is pure movie fiction. That's a pity because I thought Victor Emmanuel's singing was an inspiration, unlike Michael Caine's tortuous attempt at an officer's posh accent. The displays in the castle were excellent and presented in a medieval style rather than the more usual modern typography and signage. The view of the surrounding area was sensational, and I couldn't help saying, 'I can see our house from here,' as we looked down at the caravan park below. A modern stainless steel sculpture of the Welsh Dragon stood on a plinth at the entrance to the site, a wonderful photo opportunity of the Dragon with the Castle behind.

I'm Not a Number

From Harlech, a short drive along the coast brought us to the unique destination of Portmeirion, a fantasy village which re-creates a part of Italy as if teleported to North Wales.

Quote: *'Cherish the past, adorn the present, construct for the future'.* Clough Williams-Ellis, the architect who conceived and constructed Portmeirion.

Portofino inspired him on the Amalfi Coast of Italy. As students hitchhiking through Italy in the 1970s, we have been to Portofino. Portmeirion feels so authentic that it rekindled memories: pastel shades of blue, ochre and terracotta and seemingly haphazard arches, niches, water features and architectural embellishments. Statues include Hercules and Lord Nelson.

The lawns, gardens, and cypress trees all complemented the ensemble to create a Mediterranean feel. Most of the features are imported from abroad in Italy and throughout Europe as Williams-Ellis sourced dilapidated buildings and reclamation yards for architectural stone features, doors, windows, gates and sculptures. He began work in 1925, intending to develop the site as a tourist attraction while enhancing the area's beauty, surrounded by woodland and standing on a rocky outcrop overlooking the beautiful Trench Bach estuary.

The world fame of Portmeirion was reflected in the different Nationalities: Japanese, Americans, Germans, and Australians. Particularly impressive was a group of Indian ladies dressed in traditional brightly coloured saris. They told me they were staying at the Portmeirion Hotel to attend a wedding.

The fame of Portmeirion was enhanced by the television series The Prisoner, which filmed all 17 episodes there. The actor Patrick McGoohan conceived and wrote the mysterious series, which was first broadcast in 1967 and has developed a cult following. There is even a bronze bust of McGoohan and a Prisoner Shop selling T-shirts, mugs and posters.

The basic premise of The Prisoner is that McGoogan's character has resigned from an unspecified job. He is gassed and wakes up in a mysterious village. No-one has names, and he is number 6. Unlike the rest of the inmates, he rebelled against the system and made escape attempts only to be re-captured by an ominous giant white balloon. Episodes verged on the surreal, with baffling storylines, and the show was not particularly successful.

I had always assumed that the Prisoner was a spin-off from the earlier, highly-rated series called Danger Man, in which Patrick McGoohan played John Drake. However, at no point in The Prisoner is there any reference to Danger Man, even though the inference is there. It's been suggested that this was to avoid any copyright payments. Actually, Danger Man first appeared in 1960, preceding the first James Bond movie, Dr No, by two years, and Patrick McGoohan has been offered the role of James Bond more than once.

In Italy in the 18th Century, a particular genre of art was known as 'Italian Capriccio' in which the artist could move buildings around. I mentioned this in a previous book, giving the example of a painting in the Tate Gallery in London by William Marlow, who moved London's St. Paul's Cathedral to Venice. I think Clough Williams-Ellis has achieved a real-life capriccio at Portmeirion.

Snowdon

The magnificent vista of Snowdonia inspired us to marvel at the view from the 1,085-metre summit of Mount Snowdon, Wales' highest mountain. There is a trail popular with hikers, but we decided to take the train. The Llanberis Mountain Railway opened in 1896 and retains its Victorian charm. The station is painted green and beige and is of the style one sees today, mainly on model railways. The quaint trains look straight out of Thomas the Tank Engine, or, being Wales, perhaps that should be Ivor the Engine.

As the train climbed out of the station, we were surrounded by woodland. Houses on either side didn't have much in the way of privacy as passengers looked out over their gardens. Some upstairs bedrooms were actually at eye level. It must be quite disconcerting if someone had inadvertently forgotten to close the curtains as a train full of gawping passengers glides past. It reminded me of James Stewart in the Hitchcock movie 'Rear Window.' There are several picturesque waterfalls, and gradually, the trees thinned out as the landscape opened up into moorland, with sheep everywhere. As we gained altitude, the views to the horizon were spectacular, and steep cuttings in the rock are a testament to the ingenuity of engineers and workers of the Victorian era. We followed the Llanberis Pass and looked down upon tiny cars on the road below while the continuous lines of hikers looked like columns of ants. At the summit, there is a sign carved in stone: 'The Summit of Snowdon. Here You Are Nearer to Heaven.' Under a clear blue sky, who could argue?

The view was sensational, taking in the mountain range, Menai Straits and the Irish Sea.

Back down at Llanberis station, we had time to browse around. The signage was in the traditional railway station style logo: Station Grill, Station Shop, and Station Buffet. Most lettering was in Welsh, with some helpful English additions. One sign in particular caught my eye. It read: SIOP YR ORSAF.

I said to Norma, "Is it just the way my mind works, or does that sign say 'Shop Your Arse Off ?!'"

"Well, I wouldn't have thought that, but since you've mentioned it, I can't unsee it." Curious, I approached one of the uniformed railway staff and asked what it meant. I was slightly taken aback by his supercilious, rather condescending attitude.

"Do you not speak Welsh, sir?"

"Well, if I did, I wouldn't be asking you. Anyway, I wouldn't mind betting that most people on this platform don't speak Welsh." He softened his tone following my indignant response. "Sorry, sir, I'm a passionate Welsh speaker and member of a society dedicated to spreading the language."

"Good luck with that," I said, intending to be sincere. However, there seems to have been a hint of sarcasm in my tone. It was now his turn to be indignant.

"You know, sir, that Wales isn't the only country where Welsh is spoken. It is a common language in Patagonia, that's a region in Argentina."

"Yes, I know where Patagonia is, and I have heard that story."

Undaunted, he continued his mini-lecture. "That was told to me when I was in Bets y Coed," he said, "Where did you hear it?"

"When I was in Patagonia."

With that, he turned away, held up his flag and blew his whistle. He never did translate SIOP YR ORSAF.

In case you're wondering, I looked it up: It means a Community Centre.

Caernarfon Castle

A World Heritage Centre, Caernarfon Castle, was begun in 1283, and it's horizontally striped walls were modelled after those of Constantinople. It was Longshanks' primary residence in Wales and consequently was adorned with imperial grandeur, such as carved stone eagles and niches for statues. It works as a functional fortified castle while at the same time displaying aesthetic architectural structures and proportions. A novel feature is the carved heads along the battlements to act as a deterrent to potential attackers. From a distance, they appear to be soldiers on permanent lookout. I suppose the modern-day equivalent is cardboard cut-out police cars parked on motorway bridges.

As we entered through the King's Gate, two knights in armour entertained a crowd with a sword-fighting demonstration. Each hexagonal tower had a specialist function: a well for drawing water, one for storing grain, the treasury, a look-out tower, and the Eagle Tower, which housed the Royal apartments. King Edward's Queen Consort, Eleanor of Castille, added her touch to some design features. For example, the Eagle Tower is topped-off with smaller towers, based on the coat of arms of Castille, her home in Spain. The view from the battlements overlooked the River Afon Seiont, which flows into the Menai Strait, and I am running out of superlatives to describe the commanding views of Snowdonia.

Our guide took us through passages within 'curtain walls', which enabled the garrison to move around the castle unseen by attacking armies. He demonstrated how bowmen shot arrows through the narrow vertical slits before quickly moving along the passages to another vantage point. He told us the almost unbelievable story of when just 28 men withstood a siege while massively outnumbered. By coordinating their movements, they created the illusion that hundreds were defending the castle. It's the same idea as in the movie Home Alone when Macaulay Culkin cleverly gave the impression that a party was going on, thereby fooling the inept potential burglars.

Ich Dien and Ostrich Feathers

Caernarfon Castle is synonymous with the title of Prince of Wales, and this dates back to the reign of Edward 1st. After defeating various Welsh kingdoms and principalities, Gwynedd was the last bastion of resistance. As a political gesture to give something to the people, Edward arranged for his pregnant wife to travel from London to Caernarfon so that she could give birth in Wales. His son, the future King Edward II, was born and became the first Prince of Wales, completely disregarding the fact that there had been regional Princes who had claimed the title over centuries. This is why the Prince of Wales Investiture Ceremony is held at Caernarfon Castle. The last was in 1969 when Prince Charles became the 21st, and now his son, Prince William, has succeeded to the title.

Our guide finished the tour by explaining the origin of the three ostrich feathers, the emblem of the Prince of Wales, which often replaces the Dragon in certain contexts, for example, the logo on the red shirts of the Wales rugby team. In the 14th Century, Edward, Prince of Wales, was known as the Black Prince after the distinctive colour of his armour. He famously 'won his spurs' at the Battle of Crecy in France in 1346, and he was so impressed by the bravery of his vanquished opponent John of Bohemia that he took the shield from his dead body and adopted its Ostrich Feathers Coat of Arms as a mark of respect. The inscription ICH DIEN on the shield means 'I serve' in German.

The walled town of Caernarfon has grown around the castle, and it was interesting to wander the cobbled streets with pastel-painted shops and houses. The streets have appropriate names, such as Castle Ditch, Shirehall Street and Castle Street, with plenty of craft shops, pubs, restaurants, and everything to cater for tourists.

Trivia Alert: When Queen Eleanor died, the grief-stricken King honoured her by building large stone crosses as memorials to mark the processional funeral route back to London. The last stop was at the village of Charing, known today as Charing Cross.

Menai Bridge

The Menai Bridge opened in 1826 and was designed by Thomas Telford to link North Wales and the island of Anglesey. The tides from the open sea enter and recede from both the east and the west of the Menai Strait, causing the water to flow in opposite directions at the same time... a Maelstrom. Numerous ships have been wrecked over the centuries. An information board had the heading: 'Bridge Over Troubled Waters', referring to the treacherous tides and currents below. It's well known that Paul Simon wrote the song 'Homeward Bound' at Widnes railway station, not too far away. I wonder if he was on his way to Anglesey and was inspired by the sign.

Beaumaris Castle

Beaumaris Castle on Anglesey is another of Edward Longshanks' 'Ring-of-Iron' castles. It is nowhere near high enough to withstand a siege, and if castles had bungalow versions, this would be it. The architect followed a similar blueprint to Harlech with a double portcullis trap and murder holes. Similarly, it was built adjacent to the coast to be re-supplied from the sea and as a centre for trade.

The castle was located near marshland for enhanced security; the word Beaumaris means beautiful marsh. However, building work was discontinued because the King needed to focus his priorities and march on Scotland to subdue rebellious outbreaks.

Our Ring-of-Iron tour continued along the coast to Conwy Castle, which was King Edward's administrative centre, and James of St. George incorporated many of his signature features: located on the River Conwy, overlooking the Menai Straits, eight towers with distinctive features, a Royal Chapel and Great Hall for lavish entertainment, murder holes and some of the best-preserved machicolations (openings for throwing down stones or boiling oil.)

Conwy is a small market town selling a wide selection of locally caught fish. The streets and quaint buildings follow the same standard description of the other Welsh castle towns.

Trivia Alert... People born within the walls are known as Jackdaws, after the birds that live on the town walls.

An impressive feature of Conwy Castle is a bridge linking it to the town. Thomas Telford designed it, which is in keeping since it evokes images of a medieval drawbridge. An example of a bridge genius collaborating with a castle genius... seven centuries apart.

Lower Gate Street took us to the river and a beautiful view. The harbour wall was strewn with lobster pots, ropes and everything associated with the fishing industry. The Conwy Mussels Company was located at the waterfront, and I was intrigued by a modern sculpture of mussels carved in limestone standing about 10 feet high, with abstract lines and curved shapes. A bright red terraced house advertised itself as the 'Smallest House in GB' and had a lady in traditional Welsh dress selling tickets and posing for photographs. It receives 50,000 visitors a year and is owned by Jan Tyley. Her great-grandfather bought the house in 1891, but unfortunately it was deemed too small for habitation. The house was built in the 16th Century when people were smaller. Ironically, the last person to live in the house was Robert Jones, a 6ft 3inch local fisherman. He probably didn't own a cat. Walking into the town, the narrow streets had an interesting variety of shops selling books, maps and 'Conwy Collectables' and even 'The Knight Shop' with a suit of armour standing at the door.

A 300-year-old coaching inn is now a 4-star hotel, which retains its charm. An interesting building in Castle Street is Aberconway House, dating from the 12th Century. It has an overhanging upper storey and decorative supports. It was a merchant's house and is now owned by the National Trust.

Star

One morning, we were woken up by a tap, tap, tapping on the motorhome. At first, I thought it was rain drips from the leaves above us, but I realized it was much more pronounced in a regular rhythm.

"Sounds like someone knocking at the door," said Norma. She looked out of the window. "It *is* coming from the door," she said with a bemused smile.

I sat up and said, "It sounds like a rent-man's knock, as my dad used to say."

"Not exactly… it's a duck!"

"A duck?!?! I've heard that this is what happens all the time at Centerparks when ducks, geese and swans that live on the lake knock for food," I said, rubbing my eyes.

"Yes, but this particular duck happens to be wearing a black bow-tie around his neck."

I got out of bed while surreptitiously glancing at last night's gin bottle. I looked out of the window, and there he was, bold as brass, standing on the step, pecking away. He noticed us at the window, so he turned around 'as he went with a quack and a waddle and a quack and a very unhappy tear.' Except that this one wasn't ugly. He was the best-dressed duck I've ever seen. He went up the steps of next door's caravan and went inside.

"That's the kind of thing people try to get away from on holiday," I said.

"What is?"

"People knocking on the door with bills."

After breakfast, we decided to visit our neighbours. We knocked on the door and said, "Good morning, we've come to see your duck."

The owner called to the duck, which came to the door. It was accompanied by the most beautiful Border Collie, which *wasn't* wearing a bow tie. That would have been ridiculous. Over a cup of coffee, our neighbours Barrie and Sue told us that Star was a celebrity in demand for children's parties or village fetes. The dog was called Drake, and they also had a fluffy rabbit called Boudicea. Barrie, an Aussie, had written a book about Star, and he managed to sell us a copy. Star was an Indian Runner Duck bred to protect paddy fields in India from parasites.

Llandudno

We went on a day trip to Llandudno, the largest seaside resort in Wales and known as 'The Queen of Welsh Resorts.' The town dates back to the 13th Century, taking its name from the Patron Saint, St. Tondo. The Georgian and Victorian buildings lining the promenade Gloddaeth Crescent are as elegant as any we have seen. They are all about four storeys in similar architectural style. The first was the four-star St. George's Hotel, which opened in 1854, and owners along the crescent were required to choose colours from a pastel chart. The only concession to modernism is the North Wales Theatre, which opened in 1994, a glass building incorporating a Conference Centre. There is a wide promenade, and an Egyptian-style obelisk on St. Edward's Square is the Llandudno Cenotaph, with a large model of a red poppy displayed in an adjacent garden.

The resort's main feature is the Great Orme, a rugged rock promontory jutting out into the Irish Sea. We strolled along the beach, which consists of large smooth stones leading to a stretch of sand. A bandstand and a Punch and Judy Show keep alive the traditions of a seaside resort.

Llandudno pier was opened in 1878 and is the longest in Wales. It is now a grade II-listed building with the usual gift shops and arcades. The Ocean Café and Bar has impressive stained glass windows.

Overlooking the pier is the Grand Hotel, ideally situated with a view of the town and the bay. It must have been truly grand at one time, but unfortunately, it looks a little tired and in need of some TLC to restore it to its former glory.

The options for ascending the Great Orme include car, walking, driving, tramway cable car or The Great Orme Tour Bus. This is an immaculately refurbished 1950s coach, the style I remember as a child. They were called Charabancs, or 'Sharries' back in the day. We decided on the Tramway and walked up to the station via Happy Valley Park with its traditional, circular, wrought-iron Victorian Bandstand. As the tram gradually climbed higher, we gasped at ever-improving panoramas all around, culminating in the sensational experience from the summit of the Great Orme. I suppose the only 'blot on the landscape' (or should that be 'seascape'?) was the sight of a windfarm on the horizon; A forest of 160 wind turbines 10 miles off-shore provides power for 400,000 homes, and sustainable, cleaner energy is the future. At least out to sea is preferable to on land.

We had decided earlier to have a meal at an interesting-looking Wetherspoons in the town centre. It was formerly a Picture House dating back to the 1930s, and we were fascinated by the Art Deco and some Egyptian embellishments. It must have been popular in the days when every town had several cinemas.

We walked back along the Prom and stopped at a statue of The Mad Hatter from Alice In Wonderland by Lewis Carrol, whose real name was Charles Dodgson. He was born in Daresbury in Cheshire in 1832 and often stayed in Llandudno, where he wrote some of the book.

Trivia Alert… Incidentally, the term 'mad as a hatter' originates from the millinery trade, where mercury was used to make felt for hats. This was found to induce insanity.

We continued along the North Wales coast via the holiday resorts of Colwyn Bay, Rhyl and Prestatyn and stopped at Flint on the estuary of the River Dee.

When we first entered Wales, I promised that we wouldn't be overdoing the castles, but just as we were about to leave North Wales, there is one more ruined castle to explore briefly. Flint Castle is another of Edward's Ring of Iron, constructed as a foothold for his conquest of Wales. On a rocky outcrop protected by a moat and the river, it is located one day's military march from Chester with the intent of bringing in English settlers.

An information board stated, 'Castle for a King as Hard as Flint'. Today, it is in a state of disrepair, more than the other Ring of Iron castles, due to Welsh uprisings over the centuries and during the Civil War when both Royalists and Parliamentarians held it. In 1647, Oliver Cromwell destroyed it to prevent the opposition military from using it. It was abandoned for many years, and stone was plundered for local buildings. We picked up the M56 Motorway and drove once again to our regular base in St. Helens.

Our journey's fourth and final leg was next: The Island of Ireland.

Phase Four: EIRE and NORTHERN IRELAND

Dublin Fair City

The ferry from Liverpool to Dublin was smooth, and we had plenty of time to relax and stroll around. I had a closer look at the wind turbines visible from North Wales in endless rows of perfectly straight lines. On arrival in Dublin, we drove to our caravan site. We have stayed at dozens of sites on our travels so far, but I noticed one significant difference at our first Ireland site. Kids weren't kicking footballs or passing rugby balls but were hitting hard, white balls with strange wooden sticks, our first introduction to the Irish sport of hurling. The main focus for target practice was a sign which stated, 'No ball games.'

The site was very spacious, with a central grassy area and next to a large public park. We spent the rest of the day settling in and went for a walk to a nearby pub for a meal and the inevitable pint of Guinness, our first in Ireland.

The bus stop was conveniently at the site entrance, and we went into the city on our first morning.

Trivia Alert... Let's start with a quiz question: Apart from facing each other across the Irish Sea, what links Dublin and Blackpool?... In Gaelic, Dublin means... Blackpool. It derives from streams flowing through dark peat bogs, creating black pools.

We started at the Dublin Museum to give us an overview of the history of Ireland and many of the places we will be visiting. The Romans *never* conquered Ireland or even attempted to. They couldn't see the point since it was an island at the outer limits of the known world with no strategic value. Furthermore, the climate wasn't inviting, and Julius Caesar named the island Hibernia, the Land of Winter, as in 'to hibernate.' However, there is evidence that the Romans traded across the sea from Britannia since Roman coins have been discovered in

Ireland. Local tribes were allowed to develop independently, and there was a trade in slaves. In fact, it was the slave trade that initially transported St. Patrick to Ireland. After the fall of Rome, Celtic Gaels raided Britannia from Ireland and captured a 16-year-old shepherd, Patrick, from what is now Wales. He was enslaved for several years before escaping back to Britannia, where he worked for the Church. Later, the Pope sent him back to Ireland to preach Christianity. So there we have it; St. Patrick, the Patron Saint of Ireland, was Welsh. Later, Irish monks travelled abroad to spread the Gospel, including Columba, who, let's not forget, first spotted the Loch Ness Monster.

Many small Kingdoms throughout Ireland resulted in numerous internal wars over centuries. The Celts introduced some order by dividing the country into the distinct districts of Munster, Ulster, Leinster and Connacht, which exist to this day. Eventually, in the 10th Century, Brian Boru, described as a 'born warrior', became the 'High King' of all the land.

Trivial Alert... He was famous for playing the harp, which is why the harp became the national emblem of Ireland. Ireland is the only country with a musical instrument as its national emblem. The harp is based on the ancient Lyre when Irish Kings employed harpists to entertain at Court. A prestigious appointment in Gaelic society.

The Vikings played a significant role in Irish history. In 795 AD, Norwegian Vikings sailed around northern Scotland and invaded ferociously against undefended Monasteries and villages. Utilizing their naval prowess, the Vikings were able to set up bases along the coast at Dublin, Cork, Waterford, Wexford and Limerick.

Dublin is divided by the River Liffey, spanned by several bridges, including Millennium, Samuel Beckett, O'Connell and the most famous, The Ha'Penny Bridge, which takes its name from the days when a toll was charged. There is a bronze statue of Molly Malone, wheeling her wheelbarrow (through streets broad and narrow, selling cockles and mussels, alive, alive oh.) There are numerous examples around the world of statues with shiny hands or feet where the public has rubbed the bronze for good luck. The statue of Molly Malone in Dublin is wearing a low-cut dress, so no prizes for guessing which parts of her anatomy have been well-stroked and are gleaming in the sunlight. By coincidence, at the time of writing, a hilarious bronze statue made news around the world. It was of a South American

Football manager called Marcello Gelado (no, I'd never heard of him either). He is smiling while holding aloft a trophy won by his club, River Plate. The sculptor has been rather generous and flattered the manager with an overly bulging, euphemistically termed 'lunch box'. It's started to shine already. I'm not sure if it grows bigger, but his smile seems to be broader. If it gets too shiny, it'll look as though he's had a vajazzle.

Dublin is a lively city, full of character and vibrancy, with Graeco-Roman buildings mixed with the modern. There are over 700 pubs and clubs, including the oldest, The Brazen Head, dating from 1198, and the most famous, The Temple Bar, painted red and festooned with floral displays. There is a warm, convivial atmosphere, with pictures taking up every inch of wall space, but it was a little crowded, perhaps a victim of its own fame. We went for a Guinness at the Quays Bar, where an Irish band was performing with guitar, uilleann pipes (Irish bagpipes), concertina, tin whistle, flute and a bodrhan, which we were told is a traditional Irish drum, wooden, hand-held and hit with a small double ended drumstick called a tipper.

Trinity College 'doubled' as Liverpool University in the movie 'Educating Rita', starring Michael Caine and Julie Walters. The Book of Kells, the 9th Century manuscript that documents the Gospels, is on display in the library at Trinity and is one of the World's most famous cultural treasures. The Long Room is an attraction in its own right, with over 200,000 books on shelves from the floor to a vaulted wooden ceiling. There are numerous marble busts of famous writers, but none of the busts outshines Molly Malone's.

Trivia Alert... The phrase 'beyond the pale' when describing someone different from 'mainstream' is thought to derive from Dublin. The Pale was a strip of land around the city fenced by the English to exert control. Palus is Latin for stake.

The St. James's Gate Guinness Brewery is situated at the side of the River Liffey, but contrary to popular perception, the water of the Liffey has *never* been used in the brewing of Guinness. The water used is from the Wicklow Mountains. Today, part of the Diageo Group, the Guinness Brewery was founded in 1759 by Arthur Guinness when he signed a lease that included the rights to import Wicklow water.

The black wooden gates with the Guinness name and famous harp logo must be amongst the most photographed in the world, alongside Graceland or The Palace of Versailles. Entering the Storehouse is more like going into a cinema foyer with a roped-off reception, ticket booths, illuminated signs, subtle lighting and a wall of historic photos. A guided tour is an option, but the layout and information are excellent and self-explanatory. A grand atrium of exposed steelwork is open and dramatic with seven floors. The one-way system takes visitors through all the stages of brewing, backed up by television, illustrations and installations. A large wall sign informs us that the word 'beer' comes from the Anglo-Saxon 'baere', meaning barley. The iconic colour and flavour of Guinness derives from the roasting. A large wall clock indicates when the tasters will be testing the next brew, and underneath is written, 'Well, someone's got to do it.' Indeed, tasters are employed to travel the world as quality controllers at Guinness Breweries. I inquired, but they had run out of application forms.

There was a display of historic posters and advertising slogans such as the Toucan, 'Guinness for Strength', 'Guinness Time', and 'My Goodness, My Guinness'. Also on display were hundreds of historic bottles and cans.

A movie showed coopers making the casks, a display of barrels, which was a work of art, historic tools and the Cooperage Café. Higher up, there is Arthur's Bar and the Gravity Bar, where we exchanged our entrance voucher for a pint of Guinness while enjoying a 360-degree view of Dublin.

Grafton Street is a music hub with a bustling, entertaining feel, and it was great fun to stroll and browse. Gallagher's Boxty House is renowned for its authentic Irish cuisine with a wide range of potato mash and unique combinations of fillings. I plumped for dumplings in chilli sauce and plump is how I felt when leaving. Delicious.

Dublin Castle, with its distinctive round tower, is built on the Viking settlement site, where Presidents of Ireland are inaugurated. The city has many churches, the most famous being St. Patrick's Cathedral, while Christ Church Cathedral is even bigger. As you know, I'm obliged to visit every gallery, so we briefly visited the National Gallery of Ireland, which has familiar artists, including Picasso, Van Gogh and Monet.

We can't leave Dublin without acknowledging its rich literary heritage, which includes an astounding number of poets, playwrights, and authors. There must be something poetic in the Irish psyche (or could it be the Guinness?) which can produce such creative minds as James Joyce, WB Yeats, George Bernard Shaw and Samuel Beckett, to name just a few. James Joyce, born in 1882, wrote Finnegan's Wake and Ulysses, his masterpiece, which is about a day in the life of a character called Leopold Bloom, and visitors can walk in his steps around Dublin. In a large family with a drunken father, Joyce lived in a grim, down-at-heel Dublin. They were poor and had to move house many times, and in his book, The Dubliners, Joyce doesn't hold back with his descriptions. He used real place names and pub names, and consequently, it took him ten years to find a publisher. By contrast, in more recent times, Maeve Binchy, who was born in 1939, has sold over 40 million books, specializing in anecdotal stories, often based on eavesdropped conversations in coffee shops, pubs and markets in Dublin. Surprisingly, Oscar Wilde wrote only one novel, The Picture of Dorian Gray, whose portrait grows older while he remains ageless. Wilde is better known for his plays, notably The Importance of Being Earnest, which was described on a theatre poster as a 'Trivial comedy for serious people.' Oscar Wilde was a controversial, flamboyant, Victorian celebrity famous for his wit and one-liners; my favourites being, 'I can resist everything except temptation,' and, 'I'm not young enough to know everything.'

We first encountered Dublin-born Bram Stoker and Dracula when we were in Whitby, and the coveted Horror Writers' Award is in his name. At the same time, Samuel Beckett, who wrote Waiting For Godot, has a bridge over the Liffey named after him. George Bernard Shaw won the Nobel Prize for Literature in 1925, and one of his most famous works, Pygmalion, was made into the movie My Fair Lady starring Rex Harrison and Audrey Hepburn. Like most writers, Shaw had a talent for coining life-affirming phrases, such as 'We don't stop playing because we grow old, we grow old because we stop playing,' and 'Youth is wasted on the young.'

CS Lewis (that's Clive Staples for any quiz buffs) wrote the Chronicles of Narnia series, the best-known being The Lion, The Witch and The Wardrobe, and he was right on target when he said, 'Someday you'll be old enough to start reading fairy tales again.'

Brendan Behan, born 1923, was a former member of the Irish Republican Army (IRA) who spent time in prison and wrote Confessions of an Irish Rebel. In terms of lifestyle, he reminds me of Dylan Thomas as a hard-drinking raconteur who enjoyed telling anecdotal stories in the pub. Brenden Behan wasn't overly fond of critics, whom he dismissed with the following words; 'Critics are like eunuchs in a harem, they know how it's done, they've seen it done every day, but they're unable to do it themselves.

Dublin was a fantastic introduction to Ireland. We headed south on the M11 to Bray, along the beautiful promenade lined with restaurants, cafes and pubs. We detoured inland for a taste of the Wicklow Mountains, the source of Guinness. I felt like a pint every time I saw a waterfall.

Like in Scotland, Irish surnames follow the patronymic tradition in which the prefix O or Mac indicate a father's name. They are interchangeable although it was thought at one time that the O was elitist and titled while Mac was an off-shoot. The tradition began in the 11th Century under the reign of Brian Boru, to identify each tribe. For prestige, some names go back through ancestry to relate to a distinguished family member rather than father or grandfather. Even today throughout Ireland, certain names gather in clusters in various counties.

We had been this way before, many years go, and as we drove through a village, we both had a feeling of Deja-vu. Memories gradually came back as we laughed about a story which couldn't happen in today's internet, Wi-Fi age… We had been on holiday with Norma's brother Alan and his wife Hilary, touring by car. We stayed at a farm, which a colleague had highly recommended, with the words 'as wide a range of breakfast menu as you would find on a five-star cruise ship, only better.'

Following a substantial breakfast one morning, I asked our hostess, the farmer's wife, if English newspapers were available locally.

"Yes, the post office in the village sells them. It's only about fifteen minutes walk."

"Just what I need," I said, patting my stomach.

The small post-office had a bay window of small panes of glass like a Dickensian Old Curiosity Shop. An old-fashioned doorbell announced my arrival as I pushed open the door.

"Good morning, sir," said the postmaster cheerily, "I haven't seen you in here before."

"Good morning to you. I'm on holiday, staying at the farm up the road.

"So you'll have had the world-famous breakfast," he said while pulling what looked like a beer pump on the counter.

"You'll be having a Guinness?" he asked matter-of-factly.

"Er, mmm," I muttered while looking at my watch.

"Don't worry, sir, the sun is over the yardarm somewhere."

"In that case, thank you very much."

We sat down to enjoy a pint together (remember, this is in a post office), and eventually, he asked, "So how may I help you?"

"I believe you sell English newspapers," I said, wiping away a white froth moustache.

"Indeed, I do, sir. Do you want todays or yesterdays?"

"Today's, please."

"In that case, you'll have to come back tomorrow."

Welcome to Ireland.

Back to the Future, we continued through Roundwood through the 'Glen of Two Lakes' and stopped at Glendalough, the site of a Monastic settlement founded by St. Kevin in the 6th Century. The stone ruins are dominated by a tall round tower, which was a belfry and a beacon for pilgrims. It also provided a refuge for monks against invading Vikings. Today, there is St. Kevin's Way, a route for pilgrims to follow: The Celtic Camino. After lunch and photos, we set off for the next motorhome site at Redcross, a tiny hamlet outside Wicklow.

We set up our pitch and went for a walk. It didn't take long, and it was a street 100 yards long with two pubs and the Wicklow Brewery. The following day, we walked along Flanagan's Trail through the countryside with fields of deer, keeping company with South American Alpacas. We had a picnic lunch followed by a drink at Mickey Finn's pub. A relaxing day before going into Wicklow town tomorrow.

Wicklow is a working harbour founded by the Vikings at the mouth of the Wicklow River. This was the invaders' usual strategy enabling them to sail inland. The town is tidy and compact with a busy road through the centre with shops and pubs on either side.

The motorway down the coast was an easy drive to Wexford, but we made a detour on the way.

D-Day

We stopped at the coastal village of Curracloe for one reason: the beach and local area were locations for the D-Day Normandy landings in the movie Saving Private Ryan. Having been to the actual beaches in Normandy, where the allies landed on June 6th, 1944, and being a keen film fan, I was interested to see how authentic the beach at Curracloe was. Apparently, Steven Spielberg wanted to film in Normandy but was not granted permission, so his location scouts needed to find an alternative. Curracloe Beach is one of the finest in Europe, with sand of Caribbean quality, but it *isn't* where the movie sequence was shot. I couldn't recognize any similarity to Omaha Beach, but we were told that the landing was filmed at adjacent Ballinesker Beach. The location manager made a good choice.

To recreate the biggest amphibious landing in history must have been a daunting task, but Steven Spielberg triumphed to create an Oscar-winning masterpiece. He used 1000 real rifles, plus 500 imitation rifles, the Irish Army Reserve, 1500 extras including actual amputees, 40 gallons of fake blood, false bodies and thousands of false limbs, which must have cost an arm and a leg. A huge amount of money was pumped into the local economy, but, would you believe, some locals complained about 'bombs going off in the morning.'

Ballinesker Beach and the Omaha beach Restaurant in Curracloe attracts tourists, including Americans who pay their respects by proxy, as it were. Spielberg offered to donate to Wexford County Council all the sets and props when filming was completed. They turned him down. A missed opportunity which must have cost the Wexford tourism economy millions of Euros over the years.

Wexford

Arriving in Wexford, our caravan site was handily situated just over the road bridge which spans the River Slaney, which opens to the Irish Sea. The waterfront buildings are individual and unchanged, and dozens of fishing trawlers were moored along the river. Not surprisingly, there was no shortage of fish and chip shops and restaurants, and we decided to try Sharkey's because it boasted 'the best fish and chips in Ireland.'

The Vikings founded Wexford in 800 AD, who ruled until being overthrown by the King of Leinster. The town suffered severely during Oliver Cromwell's Irish Conquest, and in 1649, was burned down. In 1798, Wexford became the main centre of anti-British rebellions, and in the town centre, there is a sculpture of an anonymous Pikeman to commemorate Irish heroes of that period. Near to the waterfront is a commanding statue of a man wearing a tricorn hat and 18th Century frock coat. The plaque informed us that it was John Barry, but his clothing told us that somehow it couldn't be the musician famous for 'The James Bond theme.' This John Barry was in fact, a Wexford man and founder of the American Navy who captured the first British ship during the American War of Independence. Bringing us up to date is a life-size action statue of Nicky Rackard, a local man who was one of the sport of hurling's greatest players.

The compact town centre is mainly pedestrianised along North and South Street. There are many individual shop fronts in various colours, and not surprisingly, a few selling fishing tackle.

We came across a particularly interesting bookshop, called imaginatively, 'The Bookshop', which advertised new, used and antiquarian books. It was packed from floor to ceiling with creaking, bending shelves, piles of books on the floor, and a Dickensian labyrinth of chaotic alcoves. It was fascinating, and I could have spent the day there. However, as the old advertising slogan used to say, 'It's Guinness time.' We found a fantastic Irish pub called The Centenary Store and noticed on the television news that storm Hannah was approaching from the South, and storm warnings were announced. We walked back over the bridge and were alarmed to see that people on the campsite were 'battening down the hatches.' Tents and awnings were taken up, and owners were stretching protective storm tapes over the caravans and pegging them down on either side. We felt a little safer in a more stable, heavier motorhome.

Trying to sleep during the night was almost impossible, with the sound of the wind and the sea crashing on the rocks below us. It felt as though we were hurtling along on an overnight train as windblown objects flew past.

The following morning, the weather had calmed down. Tentatively, I looked out to see a collection of plastic objects scattered randomly, including our doorsteps, which had gone on a walkabout.

"What's it like outside?" asked Norma.

"Toto, I don't think we're in Kansas anymore."

Waterford

We followed the N25 to Waterford via New Ross from Wexford and continued to our caravan site at Newtown Cove near Tramore. This is located on the Copper Coast, a UNESCO Geopark, where stone remnants of mines are dotted along the cliffs. There is a pleasant beach popular with surfers, where we relaxed for the afternoon. The following morning, we caught the bus to Waterford.

On the bus, Norma said, "You haven't forgotten that it's my birthday this week."

"Of course not, I've already booked us a table... I hope you like snooker."

The Vikings founded Waterford, Ireland's oldest city, in 850 AD. As we discovered in Wexford, the Vikings preferred to settle at a river estuary, and in Waterford on the River Suir, they could sail inland about 50 miles for easy pickings at rural settlements, churches and monasteries.

The Waterford Viking Triangle consists of several museums and heritage centres, such as the Medieval Museum, Viking Longboat, and King of the Vikings Centre. Reginald's Tower, named after the first leader, is a round, stone-built structure which was originally the corner of the city walls.

The city centre is modern, largely pedestrianized, with many street musicians. Bringing us right up to date is the city Square Shopping Centre, a shopping mall with the usual array of stores.

Waterford Crystal

The famous Waterford Crystal factory is close to the town centre. Founded by two Quaker brothers, George and William Penrose, the factory opened in 1783. We booked a guided tour, and l was surprised to learn that most of Waterford Crystal found abroad is made in Slovenia, The Czech Republic, Hungary, and Germany. In Waterford, they make ranges of glassware, decanters, and trophies for sports, including cricket, motor racing, and golf, such as the Solheim Cup and the Irish Open. In addition, there are commissioned pieces: A grandfather clock, HMV record player, piano, astronaut, and Cinderella's carriage, to name just a few examples on display.

As we progressed through the factory, it was apparent that tradition underpins the skill and dedication of the highly trained craftsmen and women. Indeed, an apprentice trains for five years, culminating in an apprentice bowl which incorporates every technique. On graduation, they are allowed to keep the bowl.

We watched every stage, from blowing molten glass to cutting and engraving. Anything less than perfect is thrown into the cullet (broken glass) skip and re-used. 'There are no seconds at Waterford Crystal,' the guide announced proudly. Some pattern books have survived since the 18th Century, and a Waterford characteristic is the style and taste of the period.

The store displayed a range of products, and I wanted to buy Norma a birthday present of emerald earrings and a ring. "Her birthstone is emerald," I said to the salesman. "Where better to buy than the Emerald Isle," he replied. Got to be the salesman of the year.

We followed the N25 coastal route from Waterford to County Cork and our next stop at Blarney Caravan Park, close to the castle.

What a Load of Blarney

As castles go, the ruins of Blarney Castle cannot be compared to more imposing Castles such as Edinburgh, Alnwick or Carnarvon. Yet, it is arguably better known than any of them because it is home to the world-famous Blarney Stone. A quarter of a million visitors a year bend over backwards to kiss the stone, including that great orator Winston Churchill, so it seems to work. To give it its alternative name, the Stone of Eloquence conveys the gift of the gab and like all myths, there are several versions as to the origin. It is at the top of the 90-foot tower, accessed by stone steps and, like Disney theme parks, there are signs to inform visitors how long to go from specific points; for example, The queue from here is 30 minutes.

"That's a strange word, isn't it," I said to Norma.

"What is?"

"Queue."

"Why?"

"Well, it's just a letter Q with four silent letters standing in line behind it."

Attendants helped people of all shapes and sizes to get into positions.

"It could hardly be called the Stone of Elegance," I whispered.

I managed to scrape my forehead on the wall as l struggled to get up, like a turtle on its back.

"It felt more like a Glasgow kiss," I said, rubbing my head.

Back on terra firma, she asked, "So what do you think of that?"

"Difficult to put into words," l replied.

"So it didn't work for you then?"

"Don't think so… it's given me irritable vowel syndrome."

Built on a rocky outcrop to provide commanding views of the surrounding landscape, the first stone castle was built in the 13th Century. It became the seat of power for the Kings of Munster, the McCarthy clan. One story is that a King had to present a case at a meeting and asked a Goddess, The Queen of the Banshees, for advice. She told him to kiss the first rock he sees, and it will give him powers of persuasion. He won his argument and had the bluestone rock cut to shape and set into the wall of his castle. Another theory is that Dermot McCarthy saved an older woman from drowning, and she showed her gratitude by revealing to him the magic secret. Some believe that the Blarney Stone is part of the Scottish Stone of Scone, and it was given by King Robert the Bruce in return for support at the Battle of Bannockburn in 1314 when the English King Edward II was defeated. Queen Elizabeth I had dealings with Cormac McCarthy, making lots of demands. Every time Cormac was summoned, he used flattery to prevaricate until another day. Exasperated, the Virgin Queen said, "What a load of Blarney." I hope that was what she said because Bollocks Castle just wouldn't have the same ring to it, and who would queue to kiss the Bollocks Stone? On second thoughts, don't answer that.

The surrounding gardens are beautiful and include magical wishing steps, a hermit's cave and, bizarrely, a poison garden. We visited the gift shop, and in keeping with our foodie theme, we bought a Blarney Stone, a slab of cake incorporating vanilla and crushed peanut coating.

While on the subject of myths and folklore, we can't leave out Leprechauns.

Ireland has been famous for its leprechauns since medieval Irish folklore. The ancient origins of the myth are illustrated in place names: Knocknalooricaun in Count Waterford derives its name from 'hill of the leprechauns' and Poulaluppercadaun in County Kerry means 'pool of the leprechaun.'

They are small, mischievous, and illusive while protecting a pot of gold. They are usually depicted with a red beard and a green hat, a popular St. Patrick's Day outfit.

Cork

The bus journey from Blarney to Cork took about 25 minutes. The city was founded by the Vikings on the River Lee, following the invaders' usual strategy of establishing settlements at the mouths of rivers along the Irish coast.

Cork regards itself as Ireland's 'real' capital and takes pride in its 29 bridges, beating Dublin's total. Cork also calls itself 'The Food capital of Ireland' and even has a Butter Museum to spread the word. The 18th Century English Market is a tourist attraction in itself. Its name derives from the time when only Protestants, known as the English, were allowed to own stalls. It is a huge space over two floors which sells every type of food. Stallholders exude Irish friendliness, and the general ambience attracts locals and visitors often as a place to meet and soak up the atmosphere.

The same description can be applied to Cork in general, a student city full of great pubs, many with live music and dancers. The centre is clean and pedestrian-friendly, with historic buildings and top-quality stores. The street lighting is modern and unusual. Rather than traditional lampposts, they comprise poles which project at an angle over the road, supporting rows of floodlights. The kind of arrangement you would expect at a sports event or stage lighting at a concert, but they fit in well.

St. Fin Barre established a monastery in the 7th Century, and the Cathedral is named after him. There is also the 18th Century St. Ann's Church, which is also known as Shandon Church, with its distinctive square towers reminiscent of Middle Eastern minarets. A novelty is that visitors are invited to ring the Shandon Bells. The ropes are numbered, and a booklet outlines the order of pulling for the various peels. An ideal introduction for aspiring campanologists.

Cobh

We took the local train from Cork for a day trip to Cobh (pronounced Cove). It is a beautiful town with a perfect natural harbour, one of the largest in the world, an ideal setting for the rows of pastel-washed harbour-front houses overlooked by the dominant cathedral at the top of a steep hill.

The promenade is landscaped with gardens and has a Victorian wrought-iron bandstand. In a prominent position is a bronze statue of Annie Moore. Who?

Trivia Alert… She sailed from Cobh in 1891 and was the first person to be granted entry to the USA via the newly-opened Immigration Centre on Ellis Island in New York, a tourist attraction and museum today.

Queen Victoria visited Cobh in 1849, and the town was re-named Queenstown in her honour. Following Ireland's independence from England in 1922, it reverted back to its original name. It's well known that Queenstown was the final port of call for the Titanic before its ill-fated Atlantic voyage in 1912, and there is a Titanic Experience Museum. The original White Star Line booking office is unchanged next to the wooden remnants of Heartbreak Pier; so called because it's where Irish Emigrants said goodbye to family and friends, probably for the last time, as they went in search of a better life in America. Adjacent is the John F. Kennedy Memorial Park, which the President visited in 1963, the year he was assassinated. There is also a memorial to the Lusitania, a Cunard Passenger Liner torpedoed by a German U-Boat outside Cobh harbour in 1915. Just to continue for a moment on this rather gloomy theme, Spike Island in the harbour was once a Monastery, a Fort and a prison. It's abandoned and overgrown but attracts tourists on boat trips. It's known as Ireland's Alcatraz. We declined the tour, having been to Alcatraz in San Francisco and in enough castle dungeons to last a life sentence.

We climbed the steep streets and steps up to St. Colman's Cathedral, named after an Irish Saint. The views were panoramic, and on the way down, a famous shot is of a row of colourful houses on a street called West View, with the Cathedral as a backdrop.

Back in town, we were ready for a pint and went into a pub intriguingly called The Roaring Donkey. We were told the name dates from when the Cathedral was being built, and donkeys were used to transport stones and bricks up the steep hills. We were given the usual friendly Irish welcome, and a few were sitting around a table playing guitars. I asked if I could join in and even got a free Guinness. A great craic!

Today, Cobh welcomes 100 cruise ships per year, which is a tremendous boost to the economy, and it is a major port for container ships. A sad period in its history was when it was the main port of embarkation for desperate people trying to survive the potato famine, which I think is worth mentioning at this point.

Irish Potato Famine

The 19th Century famine in Ireland was caused by potato blight. This fungus infection (phytophthora infestans) invaded the potato crops, turning them into a rotten, black, slimy pulp. The potato, originally brought from the Americas to Europe by the Spanish in the 16th Century, was easy to grow in Ireland and consequently became the main food source. A series of crop failures from 1845 led to starvation and diseases such as scurvy, dysentery, typhus, cholera, and smallpox. This hell on earth resulted in one million deaths, while two million people were forced to emigrate. The ships that sailed from Cobh to America, Canada or Australia became known as 'Coffin Ships' due to the 50% death rate during the voyages. The absolutely destitute poorest people couldn't afford to pay for an ocean crossing and went to Britain, Liverpool in particular.

The British Government exacerbated the tragedy when it could have alleviated much of the suffering. Countries in Europe, Belgium in particular, banned exports of grain in order to feed their own inhabitants. However, under Prime Minister John Russell, the British Government continued to export grain and animals from Ireland while the rural Irish poor were starving. Furthermore, Irish landlords were informed that they were obliged to pay tax on any land occupied by tenants. To avoid payment, the landlords evicted occupiers of small holdings, and even whole villages were cleared. It was an appalling, inhumane attitude, and some Government officials even regarded the whole episode as divine intervention, an act of God. Having learned more, I think that it was not only a blight on the potato, it's a blight on British history.

The Angel's Share

Jameson is probably the most famous brand of Irish whiskey, and a visit to the nearby distillery was definitely on our bucket list. John Jameson founded the original distillery in Bow Street in Dublin in 1780, and today, this original site is a Jameson Heritage and Visitor Centre. The Jameson Distillery moved to Midleton, County Cork. We took the private bus service from St. Patrick's Quay in Cork to Midleton and were able to buy tour tickets on the bus. One stark stone building looked like a Dickensian Prison, but we found it was once a woollen mill, then a flour mill. The tour was interesting and entertaining as we were escorted through all the stages 'from grain to glass.' There is also a Micro Distillery, which experiments and innovates with recipes and blends. In the barrel-making department a, Cooper explained that they try different types of wood, such as chestnut. The work force is family-orientated, and there is a convivial camaraderie. However, specific strict rules had to be followed, the main one being, quote: '*Don't* blow up the Distillery!'

The art of blending was explained to us. The Scotch model of blending is that different distilleries can pool their products, whereas technically, Jameson can be called a single blend, all in-house, of different types and batches. As whiskey matures over 3, 6, or 12 years, the colour and taste change; at 18 years, it is a deep amber. Irish is triple stilled, which gives it smoothness. The loss of volume over these years is known as the 'Angel's Share', and on the ceiling are a pair of wooden carved Angel's Wings. A few too many sniffs, and it would be more like the song by the Irish Group Westlife... 'Flying without wings.' I asked our guide why Irish Whiskey is spelt with an 'e' as opposed to Scotch Whisky. He explained that it is merely a difference in spelling from the Scottish and Irish Gaelic word for 'water of life': Uisce Breatha.

The Wild Atlantic Way

Leaving Blarney site, hopefully, blessed with the 'gift of the gab', we picked up the N71 south of Cork and drove through Bandon to Clonakilty, our starting point on the 'Wild Atlantic Way', a coastal route from County Cork passing through nine Counties to County Donegal, the most northerly point in Ireland. The Wild Atlantic Way is a similar concept to Scotland's North Coast 500, a designated route for travellers to follow. Whereas the NC 500 is marketed and signposted with a shield logo, the Wild Atlantic Way has a simple logo of a horizontal zig-zag. I assume this is a representation of the letters WAW, linked to also evoke images of crashing Atlantic waves. The route will take us to the jagged peninsulas in the south west around Bantry Bay and Dingle Bay, like a hand of sharp fingers thrusting into the Atlantic. We will be skirting famous bays along the west coast, such as Galway Bay, Sligo Bay and Donegal Bay, and stopping at sites of dramatic, geological grandeur and places of cultural and historical significance.

The Cruel Reason Why I Left Skibbereen

From Clonakilty, we continued along the coast through Skibbereen, which means 'little boat' in Irish Gaelic and is located close to the most southerly point of mainland Ireland. It's an attractive town, but its pleasant ambience belies a tragic period in its history. As we found out in Cobh, the potato blight resulted in devastation throughout the land, and Skibbereen has been described as 'the epicentre of horror.' The ruins of a dreaded workhouse stood as a grim reminder of the past when thousands of bodies of adults and children were tossed into mass burial pits. A song called 'Skibbereen' about the Great Famine contains some of the saddest verses ever written. There is a verse about landlords and bailiffs setting a roof on fire to drive-out a tenant farmer's family. One line is, 'the taxes and the rents to pay, I could not redeem, and that's the cruel reason why I left old Skibbereen.

On Bantry Bay, our caravan site was at Ballylickey, near to Bantry Town. Our pitch was right on the rocky shore, giving us yet another great view.

The next day, we decided that the best way to fully appreciate the poetic beauty of the bay was to walk into the town of Bantry. It took us about two hours, including numerous photo stops. As we got to town along the now customary pastel terraced rows, we couldn't resist a shop advertising hand-made chocolate. In front of the church, the town centre is a plain, functional, open square that hosts a weekly market. It is dominated by a bronze statue of Theobold Wolfe Tone, who, according to the inscription, went to America and united Irish communities in the 18th Century. There is also a ship's anchor displayed like a modern sculpture. Again, the streets are pastel-shaded and have craft shops, book shops and typical Irish pubs such as The Anchor Tavern and the most famous, Ma Murphy's Bar, which first opened in 1840. We went for a well-earned drink in The Bantry Bay, followed by the inevitable fish and chips. At the end of the main road is a picturesque waterwheel, a remnant of the past. We could have caught a bus back to the campsite at Eagle Point, but we were feeling energetic and needed to walk off the calories, taking even more photos along the way.

Ring of Kerry

From Bantry Bay, our next section of the Wild Atlantic Way was Kenmare and The Ring of Kerry. We continued on the N71 along the designated scenic route to Glengarriff on the north shore and then a switchback section of the road around the intriguingly-named Knockboy Mountain (possibly associated with leprechauns) to Kenmare, which is yet another place that is regularly short-listed as Ireland's most beautiful village.

The town has the customary pastel-washed range of tones, with streets lined with pubs and restaurants. O'Donnabhain's Irish Bar on O'Henry Street has banknotes pinned to the ceiling as a mark of tourist appreciation. The bar sells its own locally crafted beer, Kenmore Stout, a lovely pint that went on to my foodie list.

Within an easy walk of the town centre, we stepped back in time thousands of years to view a Bronze Age Stone Circle. Adjacent is the Hawthorn Fairy Tree, and following ancient Celtic tradition, we left a wish on a card for the Fairies to read.

Part of the Wild Atlantic Way, The Ring of Kerry is a route around the Iveragh Peninsula. We drove through the small villages of Tahilla and Parknasilla along the northern shore of the Kenmore River. It almost goes without saying that they were gorgeous in the now-familiar Irish 'decor' of pastel shades. We stopped for a break in Sneem, which stood out because it displays a brighter palette of colours, notably Bar D.O' Shea, which must have acquired tins of shocking pink paint at a knockdown price.

We continued towards Waterville, and en route, we parked at a point called Com an Chiste, identified by the Wild Atlantic Way sign marking an outstanding viewing place as we looked over O'Carrol's Cove and the rugged landscape. It's a popular place for surfers, wearing wetsuits even though it was summer. We were told that seals and dolphins can often be seen, and surprisingly tropical fish due to the Gulf Stream flowing across the Atlantic from the Caribbean. It's what warms the British Isles, which sounds a ridiculous statement in view of the climate. It's worth remembering that Britain and Ireland are on the same latitude as Hudson Bay in Canada... where polar bears often stroll into Churchill in search of food, human or otherwise. If ever the Gulf Stream got cut off, the Emerald Isle would become the White Isles. I digress.

Waterville fits the same uniform pastel description as many other Irish villages. Mick O'Dwyer was a famous Gaelic footballer with a pub and a bronze statue in his name. Also, there is a statue of Charlie Chaplin by sculptor Alan Ryan Hall. Chaplin spent regular family holidays in Waterville, and the village hosts an annual Charlie Chaplin Comedy Festival, which attracts thousands of fans. His shiny bowler hat has been well-rubbed for good luck. Opposite the statue is the Bayview Hotel, famous for its lobster cuisine. It lived up to its reputation.

Before arriving at our next Campervan site at Cahersiveen, we took a detour off the main road to Portmagee, a colourful, working fishing village at the tip of the peninsula. The fish and chips in the Fisherman's Bar were as fresh as any we have found. We had fabulous views of cliffs along the Skellig Coast, particularly Skellig Island, featured in a Star Wars Movie. Apparently, many of the cast enjoyed the craic in The Fisherman's Bar. Another movie, The Spirit of St. Louis, starring James Stewart, was filmed in Portmagee in 1956. It was the first sighting of land by Charles Linberg on his historic solo flight across the Atlantic on his way to Paris.

Trivia Alert... the first Trans-Atlantic Cable started from this area in 1858.

Monks thought the Skellig Coast was 'Heaven on Earth' one thousand-five hundred years ago. Who could argue? Our next motorhome booking was at Cahersiveen.

The Liberator

The caravan site at Cahersiveen was just off the main Ring of Kerry Route, right on the shore of an inlet at the mouth of Dingle Bay. We walked into town and along the main street. Similar in character to numerous others, we had driven through solid terraces painted in a range of colours from pastel to bright. The Skellig Six 18 Whiskey Distillery is on the main road, but we gave it a miss on this occasion. Standing by a bridge over the river is a white castle-like structure called The Old Barracks, with Baronial turreted round towers topped off with a cone roof. It reminded me more of the Bavarian Castles along the Rhine. Close by, a foreboding ruin of a Dickensian workhouse stands derelict and overgrown, one of many built as a consequence of the great famine.

The name Cahersiveen derives from Irish Gaelic, meaning round stone fort, and we went to see the nearby Leacanabuaile Fort, one of many ringforts built for local Chieftains. Also, we visited the ruins of the 16th Century Ballycarbery Castle, a solid, square edifice partly covered theatrically in moss. It was owned by a branch of the McCarthy family, which I assume is the same dynasty as the owners of Blarney Castle.

One person who *must* have kissed the Blarney Stone was the great orator and politician Daniel O'Connell, who was born in Cahersiveen in 1775. He came from a poor family and grew up to be known as 'The Liberator'. The Act of Union in 1801 meant that Parliament ruled Ireland in London, and the Irish Catholics were not allowed to hold any offices of state. O'Connell was opposed to any form of violence as he believed in the power of persuasion. His passion was repealing the Union Act, and he mobilised Catholic and organised Churches to hold collections. He addressed mass meetings and mesmerized thousands with his speeches. He was vain, with a huge ego, and he had actually trained to project his voice by studying actors at the theatre. He challenged the law, and in 1828, he became the first Irish Catholic in a hundred years to stand for Parliament. He won a by-election in County Clare and brought in the Catholic Emancipation Act in 1829. He championed women's rights and was instrumental in abolishing slavery. He died in Italy in 1847 on a pilgrimage to meet the Pope. His recorded last words were 'My body to Ireland, my heart to Rome, my soul to heaven'. A great Irishman indeed.

From Cahersiveen, we continued along the scenic route of the Ring of Kerry, hugging the southern coast of Dingle Bay. We stopped for a break at Glenbeigh Village. From Ross Bay beach, we enjoyed sensational views across the blue waters of the rolling waves in the bay to the blues, lilacs and magentas of the Dingle Peninsula, nature's version of the colour scheme of Irish villages.

Killorglin marked the end of the King Puck Ring of Kerry route, and we stopped for lunch in this interesting town of solid, colourful buildings with a rich heritage, culture and folklore myths. A surreal sculpture of a goat wearing a crown stands on a rocky plinth next to an arched stone bridge over the River Laune. Here's where we must remember Coleridge's 'suspension of disbelief.' The story goes that in the 17th Century, Oliver Cromwell's troops were advancing towards Killorglin, and a wild mountain goat must have thought, 'let's get the flock outta here.' It went into the town to warn the inhabitants of impending doom. This gave them time to strengthen their defences, and the event is commemorated with the annual Puck Fair. A wild goat is brought down, crowned and treated like Royalty. The plaque on the plinth of the sculpture reads, 'Kings may come, and Kings may go, but King Puck goes on forever.' After lunch, at a well-known pub called The Old Forge, we took a detour inland to Killarney National Park and the city of Killarney on Lough Leane.

We stayed at a caravan site near Killarney, a charming town with a distinctive rural character exemplified by the horse-drawn carriages called 'Jaunting Cars.' We decided this would be an ideal mode of transport to explore the town and surrounding attractions. The 19th Century St. Mary's Church of Ireland is popularly known as the

Church of Sloeberry, which is what Killarney means in Gaelic Irish, Cill Airne. The Vikings have left their mark in the area, and our driver/guide came out with a good line when he said they brought 'ship-building skills, red hair and freckles.' I suppose that was his version of Monty Python's, 'what have the Romans ever done for us.' Colourful shops and pubs showcase Ireland's culture and musical traditions.

Ross Castle was seized by Cromwell's troops in 1652, and another stark landmark is Muckross Abbey, a ruined 15th Century Franciscan Friary. A huge 500-year-old Yew tree grows up from the courtyard, framed by arched cloisters, providing a surreal subject-matter for artists and photographers. Another visually inspiring place is the Torc Waterfall (Easach Toirc), a sensational white water cascade coming off Torc Mountain over boulders and surrounded by lush greenery.

A major attraction is Muckross House, a Victorian mansion once owned by Henry Herbert, a Member of Parliament. It was built in the Tudor style and has 65 rooms, all beautifully maintained with 19th Century furniture and the traditional rows of family portraits and stag heads mounted on the walls. Queen Victoria visited in 1862, and the house was donated to the nation in 1932, along with the 11,000-acre estate which formed the basis of the first National Park in Ireland. Today, there are landscaped gardens, a traditional farm, workshops, a pottery studio and a gift shop.

The Rose of Tralee

After a few tranquil days in beautiful Killareny National Park, we drove back to the coast along the major N22 to Tralee, where we stopped for a break near the wide Banna Beach on Tralee Bay. The town adheres to the familiar 'Irish' footprint: solid, square, bright buildings and a church with an impressive spire. There are several statues located around the many open spaces and parklands. These range from the modern to the traditional, and a poignant one was of a poor family in desperate times. Not one to rub for good luck since luck had obviously deserted them.

A 19th Century song called 'The Rose of Tralee' is about a lost love, and today there is an annual rose festival in the town. It's a cross between a beauty pageant and The X Factor, in which ladies representing town's worldwide travel to Tralee to attend various shows, functions, and dance performances.

Irish dancing is an important part of the heritage and culture of Ireland, and there was a huge revival following the world-wide success of Riverdance. The roots are from pre-Christian Celts and Druids, whose rituals involved dancing, often around sacred trees. The Hill of Tara, the seat of the High King of Ireland, was the centre of Celtic life, and annual festivals have been held for over 1000 years. Dancing evolved with many routines with little upper body movement and precise, quick foot movement. Festivals were crowded, and there was little room for arm movement. Having tried to get to the bar in a crowded Dublin pub, I can understand how the dance evolved.

The town's Rose Garden has 35 varieties, and there is a bronze statue of Mary O'Connor, the first Rose of Tralee, and the glass rose wall is engraved with the names of all the previous winners. I know what you're thinking, and the answer is yes... Mary has been well rubbed for good luck!

We continued via Listowel to our next stopover near Limerick.

There Was a Young Man From...

From our motorhome site, it was a pleasant walk to Limerick along the banks of the River Shannon. Limerick was founded by the Vikings in 922 AD, and a thriving city has grown on either side of the river. The 13th Century King John's Castle stands by the river next to a multi-arched stone bridge. The constant sound of the fast-flowing Shannon, the largest river in the British Isles at 240 miles, echoes through the arches.

The impressive St. Mary's Cathedral dates from the Norman period, and nearby is the Treaty Stone, displayed on a plinth. The information plaque explained that this was used in 1691 to sign a treaty granting freedom to Catholics. A timeline informs visitors of the War of Two Kings, James II and William III of Orange; The Battle of the Boyne and Sieges of Limerick. The Milk Market is a popular attraction, a bustling market selling locally produced food, cheeses, homemade cakes, takeaway food, and vintage objects. Lucky Lane on Catherine Street is an indoor centre of quirky shops selling art, artefacts, and collectables.

On the other hand, Arthur's Quay is a modern shopping precinct, light, pleasant and functional, like thousands worldwide. The Hunt Museum is located in a grey building with a traditional portico and columns. Incongruously, standing in front are life-size models of two psychedelic horses touching noses. They are painted in a Pop Art style of bright primary colours, like the Superlambananas in Liverpool.

Trivia Alert... Irish coffee was invented at the Little Foynes Airport, near Limerick. The chef, Joe Sheridan, created the drink in 1943 for passengers delayed by the weather. He added Irish whiskey to warm them up.

Following the obligatory Guinness in a typical Irish pub, we set off home. Now, I defy anyone to go to Limerick and not have a go at making up a Limerick, the world-famous 5-line rhyme. As we walked along the footpath, after a few dismal attempts, we decided that it should have an Irish theme combined with our motorhome tour.

Since this book is dedicated to our Satnav, this is the Limerick we eventually came up with:
Our new U2 Satnav bought at the store,
Had Bono and The Edge, Irish to the core,
But the streets had no name,
It drove us insane,
And I still haven't found what I'm looking for.

Bunratty

Leaving Limerick, we drove to Bunratty Castle to spend a couple of hours at the folk park with re-creations of different periods in Irish History.

We parked BBKing and went through reception, emerging as if through a time-warp to days gone by. We started at the 13th Century Bunratty Castle. Bun in ancient Irish Gaelic means 'at the end of a great river.' The Ratty River doesn't sound too inviting unless accompanied by Mole and Badger. Having been on the road for months by now, we were beginning to become 'castled out', but it was impressive with tapestries, heavy furniture and architectural features.

An interesting photographic exhibition illustrated the on-going restoration projects which have been taking place since the 1950s.

The site was originally a Viking trading camp, and a re-creation reminded us of our visit to the Jorvik Centre in York, while a 19th Century village street reminded us of the Beamish Museum in Northumberland. There is an 1835 school, post office, church, a working water mill, a couple of Irish wolfhounds, and, of course, a gift shop.

The most popular photo attraction seemed to be the local village policeman who wore a slightly ill-fitting 1930s uniform; he seemed more like one of Mack Sennet's Keystone Cops.

Wheel Meet Again

From Bunratty, we drove to Shannon Airport, where we had arranged to meet our good friends Steve and Mandy, who were coming over to Ireland from their home in Stoke-on-Trent for a holiday visiting Steve's aunt and uncle. We went to the arrivals hall, looking forward to seeing them again. Their relatives had asked Steve and Mandy to invite us to stay a couple of days to enjoy an Irish craic.

As passengers began to emerge from the baggage carousel area, we spotted Steve first but couldn't see Mandy. Imagine our surprise and horror when she finally came into view. She was in a wheelchair being pushed by a uniformed airport official.

Mandy had a serious expression, unlike her usual beaming smile. After a brief handshake with Steve, we brushed past him straight towards her. Her leg was elevated and wrapped in thick bandages. Norma and I were very concerned as we leaned down to Mandy and asked,

"What has happened?"

"Shut up," she replied quietly through pursed lips, like a ventriloquist.

I thought she must have been in shock. I glanced at Steve questioningly, but he just raised his eyebrows and shrugged his shoulders.

"We can take her from here," offered Steve to the airport officer.

"Thank you, sir, but I'm obliged to see the lady safely into the vehicle."

I almost imperceptibly sensed serupticions glances between Steve and Mandy as we walked to the car park. I thought I would have to drive her to the hospital because I felt it could be more serious than they were letting on.

I opened the side door of the motorhome, and Steve and the airport man helped Mandy to her feet. She hopped and groaned as they helped her up the steps and made her comfortable. Steve thanked the attendant.

"No problem, sir. I hope she will be okay and have a safe journey."

I expected him to take the wheelchair back to the airport, but it was Steve who folded it and started to put it into the motorhome.

"So, it's Mandy's *own* wheelchair?" asked Norma, becoming increasingly anxious.

"Steve, what on earth has happened?" I asked a little more forcibly.

He glanced briefly towards the departing airport official before saying from the side of his mouth, "Shut up."

We both felt we were encroaching on a taboo subject they didn't want to discuss. When the four of us were inside, Steve closed the door and looked out of the window. Norma and I sat there expecting grave news, but Steve and Mandy smiled at each other and gave out a simultaneous 'phew' of relief.

"Has he gone?"

"Yes," said Steve.

"Good," said Mandy as she started to unravel her bandages, "My leg is killing me."

"Is that wise?" suggested Norma, but Mandy continued unperturbed until her leg was bare, showing an elastic bandage's imprint pattern on her skin.

"That's a relief… in more ways than one," she said as they started to howl laughing.

"Are you going to tell us what's happened?" I asked with a slight air of exasperation.

"Nothing."

Norma and I looked at each other in disbelief. We had run out of questions. Finally, following a brief pause for dramatic effect, Steve asked rhetorically,

"Do you know how much it costs to send a wheelchair as cargo?"

I shook my head.

"A fortune." He continued with, "And how much for a wheelchair-bound passenger?" He looked at Mandy, who answered.

"Nothing."

We listened open-mouthed.

"The wheelchair is for Steve's uncle, and I volunteered to act the part. I've never had such care and attention, pampered VIP service and queue-jumping in my life."

Norma and I joined in the triumphant laughter, relieved she was fit and healthy but stunned by their audacity.

"Wow!" I said in a tone which can only be described as appalled admiration, "And it certainly looks like a state-of-the-art machine."

"If it were a car, it would be a Ferrari," said Steve proudly, "And it's got an electric pack and joy stick. I bought it on mates-rates from a contact at home."

We arrived at their relatives' house in a village close to Lough Derg; needless to say, Steve's uncle was overjoyed. Its transit from England to Ireland remains a closely guarded secret. That is, of course, unless he reads this book.

Following a few great days with friends, we headed back to the coast to pick up the Wild Atlantic Way. En route, we stayed in Ennis, the County Town of Clare, standing on the River Fergus, which flows through the middle of town to the Shannon Estuary. A statue of Daniel O'Connell stands on a memorial column in the town centre. The narrow streets, alleyways and countless pubs seem to have music in its DNA. Ennis is home to several music festivals, and there are street musicians and street dancers, from children to pensioners. A town oozing Irish character!

Trivia Alert... Ennis was the birthplace of the great, great grandfather of Muhammad Ali. He emigrated to Kentucky in 1860 and married an African-American woman. Ali himself visited Ennis in 2009 and was made a freeman of the town. Although suffering from Parkinson's, he managed to acknowledge a huge crowd, and his visit attracted worldwide media attention.

After a pub lunch at Paddy Quinn's Bar, we drove through Ennistymon, another beautiful village, to our next camping site at Doolin.

Home of Irish Music

Beside a stone bridge is a row of pastel co-ordinated shops, thatched cottages and a pub. As we continued to the Nagles Caravan site, the views became even more awe-inspiring with the magnificent towering Cliffs of Moher. The 16th Century Tower of Doonagore Castle on Doolin Point is the inspiration for the village logo.

The following day, we went for a walk along the footpath at the top of the Cliffs of Moher, and it's easy to understand why this is Ireland's number one natural attraction. They were formed 350 million years ago and stand 702 feet at the highest point. The cliff face plunges vertically, and the view over the edge of the wild Atlantic waves crashing against the rocks is exhilarating. There are no safety rails, and signs warn hikers to be vigilant. The horizontal strata of sedimentary rock are a natural work of art, a timeline of geological history.

Doolin is regarded as the 'Home of Irish Traditional Music', and music is a way of life, with live performances in every pub, the most famous being Gus O'Connor's Pub.

"Are you staying for the hoolie?" a musician asked me.

"What's a hoolie?"

"It's a party, a sort of cross between a hoedown, a shindig, and a hootenanny."

"Thank you for clearing that up for me."

Another great craic.

Father Ted

Our caravan site was adjacent to the ferry terminal, and we booked a trip over to Inis Oirr (pronounced Inisheer), the smallest of the three Isles of Aran. It is just 3km x 2km in area with a population of 250. The island is a patchwork of green fields bordered by grey drystone walls and a maze of narrow lanes. We went for a walk, stepping aside occasionally for a local pony and trap or a horse-drawn tourist buggy. We went to see the rusting wreck of the MS Plassy, famous for the opening sequence of the Irish comedy series Father Ted. So, in effect, we were on Craggy Island. The shipwreck has been there since 1960 and is a popular attraction, particularly for photographers. I tried to be creative with abstract shapes and close-ups of the patterns and colours of rust. One day, I'll turn them into a painting.

We stopped at the 15th Century O'Brien's Castle ruins, which overlooks the harbour. Another interesting place is the hillside graveyard of St. Teampall Chaomhain, overlooking the sea and the sunken ruins of a 10th Century church. It was like a scene from a Bram Stoker novel. I quoted Father Jack (a character in Father Ted) by shouting, 'Drink!' so we had lunch at a harbour pub while waiting for the ferry to Doolin. From the ferry, we had the most magnificent view of the Cliffs of Moher, and from sea level, the height and rocky formations were majestic and overwhelming. Most passengers had inside seats, but we braved the sea spray to take photographs but decided against re-enacting the scene from Titanic.

Matchmaker... Make Me a Match

Back on the road after a magical stay in Doolin, Lisdoonvarna was only a few miles away, but we made an early stop out of curiosity. The name derives from the Gaelic Lios Dun Bhearna, meaning Small Town. We were by now familiar with the pastel Irish villages, but this one went to the opposite extreme with walls decorated with brightly coloured paintings, all *demanding* to be photographed. We had been told that Lisdoonvarna was famous for its annual 'Matchmaker' Festival, an old Irish tradition called 'babhdoir', which had an appointed 'Matchmaker.' An early version of a modern-day online dating site. Over 60,000 of all age-groups attend to dance and enjoy the music in many bars during the festival. England has a similar ritual; it's called 'Grab a Granny Night'. One pub in particular, the extravagantly painted 'Matchmaker,' has a sign which reads, 'Marriages are made in heaven, but most people meet in The 'Matchmaker Bar.' The owner and official matchmaker is called (I'm not making this up)... Willie Daly.

Leaving one of the highlights of the Atlantic Way, we followed the southern edge of Galway Bay, skirting the Burren National Park and its dramatic 'limestone pavement' natural formations, passed 'the fields of Athenry' to our next stop, the holiday resort of Salthill, south of Galway City.

Galway Shawl

The caravan site at Salthill in County Galway was on the seafront, and after we had pitched up, we strolled into town. Salthill is one of Ireland's most popular seaside holiday resorts, whose heyday was in the 1950s and 60s, but it has retained the charm of that era, and the sandy beach on Galway Bay was crowded. An interesting structure is a short pier leading to concrete steps and diving boards. There was a queue of bathers of all ages. Watching a demonstration of dives, acrobatic jumps, and dive-bombs was interesting. The cold Wild Atlantic didn't tempt me. Apparently, it is used all year round by the local hardy souls. The wild nature of the Atlantic is emphasized by the barrier of massive rocks to protect the seafront. Along the prom was a traditional, old-fashioned fairground called Fun Park with a big wheel and dodgems. An open grass area is landscaped with flower beds and trees, and the seafront has rows of good-quality hotels and guest houses. It reminded me very much of Southport's style and character near where I grew up.

The next day, we caught the bus to Galway. An interesting route through well-kept housing estates. Taylor's Hill has big, detached houses overlooking Galway Golf Course and Galway Bay. We were dropped off at Eyre Square in Galway. It is an ancient city dating from the 12th Century and was once an important trading port, particularly with France and Spain, but declined during the Irish Famine. Eyre Square has a sculpture dedicated to Galway Hookers. Don't get the wrong idea. It has nothing to do with a Red Light District. They were fishing ships, and the modern sculpture represents sails. You can go into a pub and ask for a Galway Hooker, an Irish Pale Ale, so I added it to my foodie list. The town has a vibrant, friendly atmosphere, and there are separate areas, each with its own distinctive character.

The Latin Quarter is thought to derive from the influence of Spanish sailors and merchants, and a popular attraction is the Spanish Arches in the original city walls by the River Corrib, through which Spanish wine and goods were imported. Part of the wall is actually preserved and incorporated inside a modern shopping mall, similar to what we saw in Chester.

An interesting section of the wall has Lynch's Window dating from 1493. The Lynch family were one of several families that ruled Galway for centuries. They produced a succession of mayors and magistrates, and on one occasion, James Lynch found his own son guilty of killing a Spanish merchant. He sentenced him to be hanged from the window.

Trivia Alert... This is thought to be the origin of the term to lynch and lynch mob.

The town is full of brightly coloured buildings and countless pubs, especially along Quay Street in the Latin Quarter. A pub in this area is called The King's Head, and a tavern has stood on this site for 800 years. In the 17th Century, Oliver Cromwell's troops commandeered the pub, and Colonel Peter Stubbers took it over.

Trivia Alert... Stubbers was the executioner who decapitated King Charles 1st hence the pub's name.

A bronze statue of Oscar Wilde sits on a bench where visitors regularly accompany him for a photo opportunity. He has shiny knees, in case you were wondering.

The Church of St. Nicholas dates from 1320. He is the Patron Saint of Children and Mariners, which is probably why Christopher Columbus once worshipped there in the 15th Century before setting off on his voyages of discovery to the New World. St. Nicholas is more familiar to us as Santa Claus, Father Christmas himself.

One street is called, helpfully, Shop Street, which I suppose is named to help people like me who go somewhere and forget why! Galway has the largest population of Irish speakers in Ireland, it is regarded as the Cultural Capital, and it has been voted Europe's friendliest city.

From our campsite at Salthill, we followed the N59 to Oughterard on the beautiful Lough Corrib. To the north is Lough Mask, and between the two is the village of Cong. This is where the classic movie 'The Quiet Man', starring John Wayne, was filmed. I mention this in the context of Irish pubs. Is there one, anywhere in the world, that *doesn't* have a framed cinema poster? Here's a point to ponder: Before the Viking invasions, Ireland was a patchwork of independent kingdoms. I wonder if there was ever a King Cong.

Yesterday, We Were in America

We stopped briefly at Clifden on the west coast. This is where British pilots Alcock and Brown landed after the first transatlantic flight in 1919. I've read a book about them called; 'Yesterday We Were in America', by Irishman Brendan Lynch. This was their reply when asked where they had come from. The Daily Mail had offered a prize of £10,000 (a million pounds today) for the first to fly across the Atlantic Ocean. With the aid of just a spirit level, a compass and a sextant, Alcock and Brown battled against freezing conditions, fog, rain, clouds and the dark. They went into a spiral at one point but managed to pull out just before hitting the water. They said that they could actually *smell* the ocean. They were following a similar course as the Titanic 7 years earlier and could have quite easily hit an iceberg themselves. They landed in a boggy field in Clifden, and today, a monument marks the spot. What incredibly brave pioneers they were.

Alcock and Brown were given a hero's welcome in Galway and mobbed in London, where they were presented with a cheque by Winston Churchill.

Trivia Alert... It's a common misconception that American Charles Lindberg was the first to achieve this feat in 1927. He wasn't. Not even the 2nd or 3rd. He was the 92nd person to fly across the Atlantic! But he was the first to fly *solo*.

Trivia Alert... As a metaphor to illustrate the exponential advancement of technology, here is a startling fact. Orville Wright and Neil Armstrong lived lives that overlapped by about ten years. The first man to fly and the first man on the moon could have actually met each other and shaken hands. They didn't, but the fact they *could* have is amazing.

The same phenomenal rate of advancement is happening today to such an extent that scientists are warning of the threat to humanity from artificial intelligence. Science fiction is becoming fact.

As we drove through Clifden, a horse fair was taking place, and the roads were lined with horse boxes and horses crossing on the zebra crossings. How confusing.

The Pirate Queen

Our caravan site was on the grounds of Westport House, a stately home dating back 400 years. The interior is impressive, with beautiful rooms, a huge chandelier and a grand marble staircase. It stands on the site of a house once owned by the famous 16th Century 'Pirate Queen', Grace O'Malley, who once ruled the area. Grace O'Malley, or Grainne Ni Mhaille in Irish Gaelic, was born in County Mayo in 1530. Her father was the Chief of The Clan O'Malley and was regularly at sea. Grace shaved her head to board his ship incognito and earned the nickname bald Grace. She was brought up at sea and learned 'the ropes' such as navigation, rigging and fighting. Her hair grew back, long, red and luxuriant. In 1553, Grace inherited her father's title, lands, fleet of ships and castles around Clew Bay. The new Queen continued to lead raids against English rulers and plundered passing ships. In London, she met Queen Elizabeth 1st, another strong woman, and negotiated significant agreements. They both died in the same year, 1603.

There is a giant bronze statue of Grace O'Malley by sculptor Michael Cooper next to the bridge in the grounds. Unlike Molly Malone in Dublin, Grace's breasts are out of reach to rub for good luck, but she does have shiny shoes.

The town was a short walk away along the river through a sun-dappled woodland path and through the grand gates of the estate into Westport. We stopped for a customary Guinness at the appropriately named Gracie's Bar. A band played outside, including the familiar repertoire of The Fields of Athenry and Galway Shawl. They also played a couple of cheery numbers about prison ships to Botany Bay and Van Diemen's Land. The town centre is very pleasant despite the steady flow of traffic. An attractive triple-arched stone bridge is enhanced by hanging baskets of flowers over the Carrowbeg River. This flower theme carries on through the town of brightly coloured buildings and many pubs, such as Matt Molloy's and The Blue Thunder Bar, all close to a Clock Tower, which acts as a roundabout.

Sligo

From Westport, we continued on the Wild Atlantic Way with fantastic views across Clew Bay to Clare Island and passed a couple of Grace O'Malley's castles dotted around the bay. We passed Lough Feeagh and circled the Ballycroy National Park and the Nephin Beg Range through Bangor Erris and Crossmolina on Lough Conn.

Continuing on the N59 through Bellina, we arrived in Sligo and on to our campsite at Rosses Point on a promontory overlooking Sligo Bay. We've stayed at some beautiful locations, and this setting next to Sligo Golf Course is right up there with the rest. We walked to Sligo Yacht Club to take photos and had a drink outside the WB Yeats Country Club Hotel. A walking trail is dedicated to the Irish poet WB Yeats, who is buried in Sligo.

We caught the bus into Sligo, where we had lunch in O'Brien's Cafe, toasted cheese sandwiches, coffee and death by chocolate. Sligo Abbey was an inspiration for Bram Stoker's Dracula. We went into The Thomas Connolly, a heritage pub dating from 1780, which proudly displays an extensive collection of brands of premium Irish Whiskey. There are bars, restaurants and cafes in the town centre along the river. We found a pub called Shoot the Crows, where we enjoyed the Guinness, and I again joined in with a live band.

The Benbulben Mountain overlooks Sligo. It is dramatic, with vertical faces that slope away into a skirt carved with spectacular gulleys and the Devil's Chimney Waterfall.

From Sligo, we followed the N15 through small villages Grange and Cliffony and larger towns Bunndoran and Ballyhannon, skirting the south shore of Donegal Bay. Everywhere, the Wild Atlantic Way logo marked the route. From Donegal, we turned west along the bay's north shore and looped around the coast of county Donegal on the North West tip of Ireland. The N56 took us to Killybegs, a pretty fishing village, where the Sea Food Shack on the harbour sells 'from sea to pan.' The catches couldn't be any fresher. We deviated from the major N56 route specifically to see one of the most spectacular views along the whole of the Wild Atlantic Way, and that's saying something.

Mountain of Stone Pillars

The Sieve League Cliffs are the highest in Ireland and amongst the highest sea cliffs in Europe. The name derives from Gaelic Irish, meaning Mountain of Stone Pillars, the edge of the World at one time. We drove to a parking place and walked to a vantage point. The word 'breathtaking' is perhaps over-used, but in this case it *really* was. The majestic Cliffs are almost three times higher than the more famous Cliffs of Moher, but they have different qualities and aesthetic appeal. Moher are *vertical* cliffs with distinct horizontal strata, whereas The Sieve League Cliffs are very steep slopes tumbling down to the Wild Atlantic, which is carving back a vertical cliff at the base. However, the natural stone-washed splashes of yellow, greens and rusty browns blend and swirl to create nature's work of art beyond human talent. After taking in the grandeur of a monumental spectacle, we headed back to Killybeg and continued north around the north west coast of County Donegal.

We arrived at our campsite in the small village of Creeslough, close to the most northerly point of Ireland. Our feeling of isolation was intensified when we realized that we were the only residents booked onto the site. We set up the motorhome and walked 200 yards down one side of one street and back again along the other. Thankfully, there was a pub, Rosie's Bar, which was packed. Where had everyone come from?

The decor was typically Irish, with the luxury of leather chesterfield chairs. We had a few drinks and a meal in the basement restaurant. After a restful couple of nights at Creeslough, we drove through Letterkenny at the southern tip of Lough Swilly and on to Northern Ireland. The sudden change from kilometres to miles per hour took us by surprise. BBKing had a mph speedometer, and we had used a handy conversion sheet to keep an eye on speed. Paying attention to road signs, I slowed down to what seemed like a crawl. It was only vehicles over-taking and beeps from behind, as it were, that made me speed up. I think this must be a regular occurrence because there were 'reminder' signs up ahead. We followed the enchanting north coast to our next stop-over at Bushmills.

Bushmills

Our campsite in Bushmills in County Antrim was conveniently located on the same road as the famous Whiskey distillery, so we booked a guided tour. Founded in 1784, Bushmills was established by Hugh Anderson and is the oldest distillery in Ireland. The different colours and flavours of the Bushmills range, for example, Blackbush and Redbush, depend on the casks previously used for port, sherry or bourbon and the number of years taken to mature. Also, there are different blends of grain whiskey with single malt. I've just thought of an ideal name for a blend. What about Blackbush Vajazzle? Perhaps not! Bushmills is officially twinned with Kentucky... a blend made in heaven.

Game of Thrones

In the village, there are lots of Game of Thrones mini-bus tours to the spectacular cliff-top locations. Each bus in itself is a work of air-brush art displaying photo-realistic fantasy images of the television series. The most dramatic place on the tour was the Carrick-a -Rede rope bridge. A bridge has been strung across to Carrick Island for 350 years by fishermen for access to catch migrating Atlantic salmon. The current bridge is probably more substantial than previous ones, but it was still vertigo-inducing as we crossed with trepidation. Only eight people were allowed to cross at a time, like traffic lights at road works. The views were breathtaking as we watched guillemots and kittiwakes nesting on the cliffs.

Giant's Causeway

The following day, we took the bus to The Giant's Causeway, Northern Ireland's most visited tourist attraction and only World Heritage Site. It comprises 40,000 basalt columns, created 60 million years ago when volcanic lava extruded from the sea floor, causing it to cool rapidly. This resulted in hexagonal interlocking columns, some as high as 35 feet. It created an undersea causeway which resurfaced at Fingal's Cave (as in Mendelson's Overture) on the island of Staffa in Scotland.

As we approached the site, it looked almost like a man-made sculptural installation with tourists scampering all over like multi-coloured ants. Several formations have been given names: The Giant's Boot, Giant's Gate, Chimney Stacks and the Giant's Organ; the musical version I should emphasise, although I have seen the same name given to several stalagmites floodlit in caverns. We followed the trail along the cliff face, providing dramatic photographs. No wonder it is often referred to as a natural wonder of the world. This is the scientists' explanation, but another much more interesting version of events exists.

An Irish giant called Finn McCool, who was a benevolent friend of the people (the original Big Friendly Giant?), was constantly at loggerheads with a rival giant across the sea in Scotland. His name was Benandonner, which means 'Mountain of Thunder,' and Finn could hear him constantly bellowing and threatening even though they couldn't see each other. The abuse continued both ways, and it became clear that Ben wanted to take over Finn's territory. They challenged each other to a fight, and Finn built the causeway to cross over to Scotland. When he first saw Ben from a distance, he was horrified; Ben was *twice* his size. He turned and ran back, losing his boot on the way, and told his wife. She disguised him as a baby and gave him a sleeping pill. Ben followed, and she welcomed him in, asking him not to disturb the baby while waiting for Finn to come home. Ben looked at this *huge* baby and became terrified. "If this is the size of the baby, how big must the father be?" He turned and ran back across the causeway, breaking it up as he went. When big baby Finn woke up, he was so annoyed at missing the battle with Ben (oh yeah!) that he picked up a huge sod of earth and threw it towards Ben's domain. However, he must have still been drowsy because it landed in the sea, way off course. Today, the hole left by the sod is called Loch Neagh, the largest lake in the Britain and Ireland, and the island it created is now called the Isle of Man. Having been there on this tour, that's one hell of a big sod, which is probably what Finn thought when he first saw Ben. To quote Coleridge, let's 'suspend our disbelief' and conclude that this is a much more interesting explanation than that proposed by science.

Back in town, we called off for a drink at a pub on the main street called, wait for it, 'The Finn McCool.' It was painted yellow with a full-length painting of Finn. In view of the story, I think they should have called it 'The Big Baby.'

Belfast

Leaving Bushmills, we continued along the spectacular coast through Ballycastle and Cushendall to Larne, where we turned inland towards our following site in Belfast.

Close to the campsite was a great pub, a good craic full of characters. We went to watch a football match on the telly, and the place was heaving. The locals had lots of friendly banter, and we seemed to be the only non-Irish customers. We stood near the crowded bar, trying to find a vantage point to see the television, when one of the locals came over and asked us to join their table. We edged our way through the crowd and sat down. Our new friend introduced himself as Pat and his wife, Samantha. Their friends were Eileen and Michael; we were all about the same age. We got on famously as the drinks flowed. I can't remember much of the football.

During the conversation, they became interested in our motorhome tour, which was sadly nearing the end, and we exchanged stories and jokes. I mentioned that I had played the guitar and sang at a few campsites and pubs in Scotland, Cornwall, and Ireland: open mic, local folk nights, plus, of course, karaoke.

"A few of us occasionally play and sing here," said Patrick, "We call ourselves The Elderly Brothers, why don't you join us later."

"I'd love to. I'll get my guitar from the motorhome."

"Have you been playing long?"

"Quite a few years," I replied. "In fact, I've played in front of the Princess Royal, the Prince of Wales, the Duke of Cambridge… and other pubs in the Wigan area."

"Ha, ha, the old ones are the best."

A corner of the pub had a small stage with microphones and music stands. Patrick introduced me to his musical friends, and we had a quick chat about our repertoire.

"We do lots of Irish songs, so just follow us. It won't be hard because we play *everything* in G, C and D."

"I think I can manage that."

"What songs do you do?" they asked me.

"Wide range: Elvis, Beatles and all the usual favourites."

The Elderly Brothers comprised Patrick and me on guitars, Sean O'Reilly on bass, while percussion was by the landlady Anne, who was renowned for her virtuoso performance playing her favourite instrument… the spoons. It was great fun playing the Irish songs I knew, such as Black Velvet Band, Irish Rover, and Galway Shawl. Patrick asked me to do a song and speak to the audience.

"Since we're called The Elderly Brothers, this is my wife's favourite song; 'All I Have to Do Is Dream,' by the Everly Brothers.

Michael joined in to sing his favourite Elvis song, 'Can't Help Falling in Love.' He performed beautifully.

There is a famous song by the Dubliners called '7 Drunken Nights'. The one with the chorus 'You're drunk, you're drunk, you silly old fool'. We didn't sing it but went one better; we *lived* it! As the evening progressed, everyone got merrier. However, Samantha was the first to become paralytic.

"I can tell when she's drunk," said Patrick ruefully, "She starts to sing in tune."

Patrick managed to get Samantha to the front door, but there was no way she could put one foot in front of the other.

"Will you keep her propped upright?" he asked a few of us, and off he went down the road. I thought he had abandoned her in our care. After a few minutes, I heard a 'squeak, squeak, rattle, rattle' noise approaching and thought someone's car was definitely due for a service. Round the corner, silhouetted by the streetlights, came Patrick, pushing an empty supermarket trolley. The flip-up section became a giant cat-flap as he bundled Samantha into it. He then set off home to the sound of 'squeak, squeak, rattle, rattle, snore, snore.' He seemed quite adept at manoeuvring the trolley, which, the same the world over, had a mind of its own. With my guitar on my shoulder and Norma on my arm propping me up, we strolled back to the motorhome, laughing all the way.

"That's the first time I've seen an Irish rickshaw," I slurred.

The next evening, we went back to the pub. We were welcomed warmly and had no sooner sat down when Samantha and Patrick came in. They received a ripple of applause to which Patrick responded with a theatrical deep bow while Samantha looked bemused, wondering what was happening.

"D'ye get home alright last night?" asked Sean.

"Yes, but as I was walking along the road, minding my own business pushing a trolley containing a body, a police car came alongside and slowed to my pace. One of the officers wound down his window but never said a word."

"There's a law against kerb-crawling," I joked.

"Fortunately, Samantha moved, which confirmed that I *wasn't* on my way to dispose of a dead body. I kept going determinedly. Both officers shook their heads and drove off."

"Did you manage to get Samantha off her trolley?" asked Anne.

"She's been off her trolley for years," quipped Patrick.

I wonder what the Garda officers wrote in their reports at the end of the shift. Probably something like, 'Local man wins woman as a prize in a supermarket dash competition.'

A Night to Remember

Arriving by bus from Belfast city centre, my first impression of the Titanic Museum was that it reminded me of an ultra-modern art gallery, similar to the Guggenheim in Bilbao, Spain. It is in itself a work of art, a modern silver sculpture with dramatic angles, and yet, as we entered, we were transported back to a time of sepia photographs and flickering black-and-white films.

Has there ever been a more famous ship than the Titanic? There are a few candidates: Victory, Endeavour, Bounty, Mayflower or the Marie Celeste. Let's not forget Captain Pugwash's Black Pig.

The exhibition centre is on the Harland and Wolff shipyard site where the Titanic was built. Adjacent are the original administration buildings and drawing offices, which have been preserved and converted into function rooms, an elegant Edwardian bar and a hotel.

We were transported through the exhibition in a six-seater car, which took us through several levels of a scale replica with subtle lighting, sound effects and film of tradesmen welding and riveting. And yes, we found it riveting also. The exhibitions display a multitude of artefacts recovered and even staterooms recreated. The shipbuilders hired a full-time photographer to record every construction stage, which is prominent in the displays. We watched a film of the launch, a tremendous occasion witnessed by a 100,000 crowd. Anyone who was anyone seemed to be on the passenger list, including John Astor, the richest man in the world and owner of New York's Astoria Hotel. Another of the world's richest businessmen was the financier J P Morgan, who should have sailed but was delayed by a business meeting. His guardian angel must have been at that meeting.

One of the major criticisms of the ship was that there were insufficient lifeboats. This was due to a variety of circumstances: everyone was convinced that the Titanic was unsinkable due to revolutionary water-tight bulkheads. The owners, White Star, were more interested in elegance and image. The engineer responsible for safety resigned in protest. This belief was reinforced, ironically, by an accident to Titanic's sister ship Olympic. It was holed in a collision with HMS Hawk but stayed afloat due to the bulkhead doors. It was argued that this *proved* that Titanic really was unsinkable. Ominously, the Captain of the Olympic was none other than Edward Smith, who was soon to Captain the Titanic.

There was huge rivalry between White Star Line and Cunard, and great prestige was placed on speed, luxury and size. Titanic even had a false funnel to match the four on Cunard's Lusitania and Mauritania. A true story is that the band played on as the ship went down. There was a quintet and a trio who combined and played together on deck, oblivious to their own survival, in an attempt to keep everyone calm; brave men indeed. A lesser-known story is that one of the entertainers on board was a conjurer and illusionist. He would do card tricks, make bunches of flowers disappear and all the standard music hall illusions of the Victorian and Edwardian eras. His gimmick was that he had a parrot as his comedy stooge. The parrot would give the game away by shouting to the audience, 'It's up his sleeve, it's in his pocket, it's down his trousers.' After the Titanic sank, the magician survived by floating on a makeshift raft of wooden deck chairs. The parrot had been flying around and perched on anything available. Eventually, it found the conjurer and landed on his shoulder. Nothing was said between them for a few minutes as they looked around forlornly towards the empty horizon, illuminated by the moonlight reflecting off the glistening iceberg. Eventually, the parrot looked at the illusionist and said, 'Alright, I give up. What have you done with the ship?'

Fake news seems to be a modern media phenomenon, but on April 16, 1912, the Daily Mail in Britain and some American newspapers carried front page headlines proclaiming that the Titanic had capsized, but *every* passenger had survived (plus, presumably, one parrot). In actual fact, 1535 passengers had been lost, but the newspapers were in cut-throat competition to get the first editions out.

The Carpathian rescued survivors and recovered bodies; even in death, the corpses were laid out according to first, second or third class. Such was the Edwardian class system. After the sinking in 1912, it took 73 years to find the wreck.

Amazingly, it cost more money to make the 1997 movie Titanic than it did to build the actual ship! It was a blockbuster box-office success which gained a record-equalling eleven Oscars.

Trivia Alert... equal with Ben-Hur in case you are wondering.

I remember when it was in the cinemas and l was teaching my A-level art class at college. As the students were painting, the conversation came round to the movie.

"I went to see Titanic last night," announced David to no one in particular. Most of the others had seen it and nodded approval.

"The special effects were unbelievable," he continued, "Especially at the end when it sank."

"Are you going to see it, Mr Meadows?" asked Diane as l was helping her with her work.

"Well, l was going to," l replied, "But there isn't much point now."

"Why?"

"David has told me how the film ends. I hate people who do that."

"B..b..but l thought you would have known that," stuttered David.

"David, l think Mr Meadows is having you on."

My wry smile was a giveaway.

Amongst countless books on the subject, one which I think is worthy of a special mention is the 'Wreck of the Titan', by author Morgan Robertson. It tells the story of an ocean liner which hits an iceberg in the North Atlantic and sinks with a huge loss of life. A central point of the story is that the Titan had insufficient lifeboats on board. So why should this book be singled out above all others? Only because the Titanic sank in 1912, but this book was published in 1898, 14 years earlier! I found that more chilling than any iceberg.

After a fabulous time in Belfast, we travelled south to the beautiful seaside town of Newcastle in County Down and followed the scenic coastal route through Kilkeel and Warrenpoint.

We left Northern Ireland and took the M1 motorway to Dublin to close the circle, not only of Ireland but also the entire journey around the UK and Ireland. As we drove, we reminisced about an unbelievable trip.

You might wonder, whatever happened to winter? We followed the migrating birds south for the winter months. We toured Spain several times before returning to pick up where we had left off.

On a worldwide scale, there are higher mountains, mightier rivers, far bigger lakes, forests, cliffs and glacial valleys, but here is my point. In the small islands of Britain and Ireland, everything is in harmony and proportion, shaped by nature to create one of the most beautiful places on earth. To do full justice to our travels in mere words, I would need to have the vocabulary of Shakespeare, the romantic poetry of Wordsworth and the atmospheric, descriptive prose of Thomas Hardy. 'A picture paints a thousand words' sounds like a phrase Shakespeare would have come up with, but actually, it was coined in 1911 by newspaper editor Arthur Brisbane, advocating the use of pictures. Everywhere we have visited is famous, and photographs are readily accessible.

Furthermore, the contribution to culture, music, art, literature, science, engineering, sport, theatre and film is astounding from such a small place. It punches above its weight. If countries were boxing weight divisions, we would be a welterweight... But it would be Sugar Ray Robinson.

It feels like end-of-term prize-giving. Let's start with the most important...: fish and chips, which has got to be the national dish. Whitby must be the capital, but the most memorable was in Stonehaven, the origin of the deep-fried, battered Mars Bar, Scotland's gift to the world of fine cuisine.

Our gastronomically themed tour, which threads its way through the book, began as a novelty but gathered momentum and added flavour to our travels. We sampled famous names such as Kendal Mint Cake, Melton Mowbray Pork Pie, Cornish Pasty and Devon Cream Tea Cake. We had Yorkshire Pudding in Yorkshire, Lancashire Hotpot in Lancashire and Scouse in Liverpool. From Welsh cakes to Irish Stew and Guinness at the Brewery in Dublin, to Plymouth Gin, Oban Whisky, Bushmills Whiskey, Eden Project Beer and Hawkshead Beer. Let's not forget Cornish Cock and a Galway Hooker. We loved the Bath Bun in Bath, Manx Kippers on the Isle of Man, Blarney Stone

Cake at Blarney, Dundee Cake and Orkney Fudge. The list goes on. When we were in Lancashire, we decided to bypass Ramsbottom.

Also by John Meadows

You Did Say Have Another Sausage?
ISBN 978-1944156152

Ten Camels For My Wife
ISBN 978-1944156367

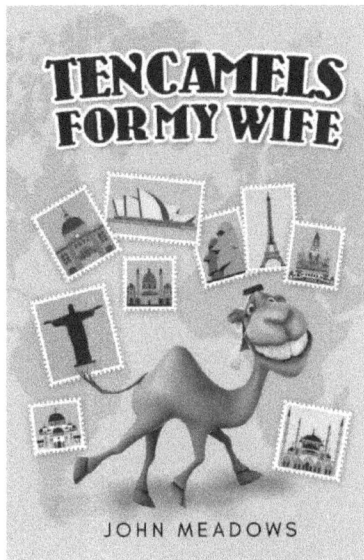

Sir, Where's ' Toilet?
ISBN 978-1944156565

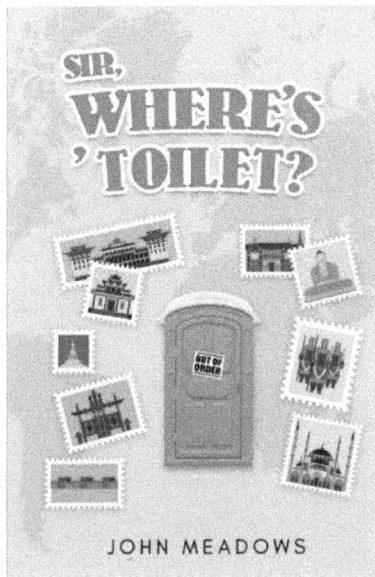

Milton Keynes UK
Ingram Content Group UK Ltd.
UKHW020946191223
434643UK00012B/450